The One Dish

COLLECTION

Canadian Living

The One Dish
COLLECTION

BY THE CANADIAN LIVING TEST KITCHEN

Transcontinental Books

Opposite: Classic Lasagna,
page 226

Most Canadians have fond memories associated with food. In the Test Kitchen, we all have our favourite childhood recipes. Irene Fong's mother used to make a fried rice and pork chop casserole with a ketchup-based sauce – a Hong Kong specialty. Amanda Barnier's mom made an easy chicken à la king for a quick, comforting dinner. Adell Shneer's mother, an accomplished cook, made a savoury beef stroganoff that still brings back tasty memories. Rheanna Kish's mother would often have "the best chili in the universe" waiting for the family after a day of skiing. My mum used to make a delicious ricotta-laden lasagna that – though the recipe probably came from the back of the noodle box – would disappear within minutes of hitting the table.

Noticing a trend? They're all one-dish meals.

Over the years, our tastes as food professionals have grown and evolved. Our mothers' small repertoires of go-to recipes have, for us, turned into a vast array of from-scratch, comfort food recipes, inspired by cuisines from around the world.

In this collection, some of our one-dish meals – such as an easy slow cooker chili or stew – are simple Wednesday night fare. Some – such as braised lamb shanks or pasta with a saucy beef ragout – are worthy of the most special occasions.

That said, for me, there's still nothing that beats a good lasagna.

Eat well,
Annabelle Waugh, food director

Clockwise from bottom right: Roasted Salmon, Bacon and Spinach Salad, page 118; Oxtail Two-Potato Stew, page 74; Sesame Rice Omelette, page 220; Beef and Polenta Bake, page 182; Roasted Squash, Spinach and Three-Cheese Cannelloni, page 262; Vegetarian Chef's Salad, page 124

Curried Mussel Chowder,
page 43

Soups

For a Mexican-style garnish, top this hearty soup with sour cream, shredded cheese and fresh cilantro leaves. If you don't have chorizo, substitute hot Italian sausages and add 1 tsp sweet or smoked paprika.

Slow Cooker Black Bean and Chorizo Soup

In skillet, sauté chorizo over medium-high heat until browned, about 5 minutes.

Drain fat from pan; reduce heat to medium. Fry onion, garlic, carrots, chili powder, fennel seeds and pepper until vegetables are softened, about 5 minutes. Scrape into slow cooker.

Stir in broth, black beans and tomato paste. Cover and cook on low for 6 hours.

Add red pepper and corn; cover and cook on high for 15 minutes. (*Make-ahead: Let cool for 30 minutes. Refrigerate, uncovered, in airtight container until cold. Cover and refrigerate for up to 2 days.*)

Makes 6 servings. PER SERVING: about 468 cal, 27 g pro, 23 g total fat (8 g sat. fat), 41 g carb, 13 g fibre, 51 mg chol, 1,714 mg sodium. % RDI: 7% calcium, 29% iron, 74% vit A, 73% vit C, 46% folate.

VARIATION
Stove-Top Black Bean and Chorizo Soup
Brown chorizo in large heavy saucepan instead of skillet. Add remaining ingredients and bring to boil. Reduce heat, cover and simmer until red pepper is tender, about 20 minutes.

12 oz (340 g) **fresh chorizo sausage** (see Tip, below), sliced

1 **onion,** chopped

4 cloves **garlic,** minced

2 **carrots,** diced

1 tbsp **chili powder**

1 tsp **fennel seeds,** crushed

¼ tsp **pepper**

5 cups **sodium-reduced chicken broth**

2 cans (each 19 oz/540 mL) **black beans,** drained and rinsed

2 tbsp **tomato paste**

1 **sweet red pepper,** diced

1½ cups **frozen corn kernels**

Tip: Fresh, uncooked Mexican or South American chorizo is the choice for this soup. Spanish chorizo is dry-cured and, while tasty, doesn't have the flavour you're looking for in this dish. Look for uncooked chorizo at butcher shops and Latin American grocery stores or substitute fresh Italian sausage.

This low-fat soup dishes up deep flavour and is packed with a healthy dose of fibre and nutrients. It doesn't take long to cook, but it tastes like you've been simmering it all day. Serve with a crusty roll to round out the meal.

Black Bean Soup

1 tbsp **vegetable oil**

Half **onion,** diced

2 **carrots,** diced

2 ribs **celery,** diced

2 cloves **garlic,** minced

½ tsp **dried oregano**

¼ tsp **ground cumin**

Pinch each **salt** and **pepper**

2 cups **sodium-reduced chicken broth** or vegetable broth

2 cans (each 19 oz/540 mL) **black beans,** drained and rinsed

2 tbsp chopped **fresh cilantro** or green onions

In large saucepan, heat oil over medium heat; cook onion, carrots, celery, garlic, oregano, cumin, salt and pepper, stirring occasionally, until softened, about 5 minutes.

Add broth and 4 cups water, scraping up any brown bits from bottom of pan. Add beans and bring to boil; reduce heat, cover and simmer for 20 minutes.

In blender, in batches, purée half of the soup until smooth; return to pot. Ladle into bowls; garnish with cilantro.

Makes 4 to 6 servings. PER EACH OF 6 SERVINGS: about 138 cal, 8 g pro, 3 g total fat (1 g sat. fat), 21 g carb, 8 g fibre, 2 mg chol, 554 mg sodium. % RDI: 5% calcium, 14% iron, 33% vit A, 7% vit C, 28% folate.

You can make this robust soup as spicy as you like depending on the kind of curry paste you use – mild, medium or hot. Thin the soup with a little water, if desired. A dollop of yogurt and a sprinkle of chopped green onion make a nice garnish.

Curried Mushroom Barley Lentil Soup

In large Dutch oven, heat oil over medium heat; fry onions, garlic, mushrooms, ginger, curry paste, salt and pepper, stirring often, until no liquid remains, about 10 minutes.

Add broth, 3 cups water, lentils and barley; bring to boil. Cover, reduce heat and simmer until lentils and barley are tender, about 1 hour. (*Make-ahead: Let cool for 30 minutes. Refrigerate, uncovered, in airtight container until cold. Cover and refrigerate for up to 3 days or freeze for up to 2 weeks.*)

Makes about 10 servings. PER SERVING: about 192 cal, 8 g pro, 4 g total fat (1 g sat. fat), 32 g carb, 6 g fibre, 0 mg chol, 958 mg sodium. % RDI: 4% calcium, 26% iron, 10% vit C, 56% folate.

1 tbsp **vegetable oil**

2 large **onions,** chopped

8 cloves **garlic,** minced

12 cups sliced **mushrooms** (2 lb/900 g)

2 tbsp minced **fresh ginger**

2 tbsp **curry paste**

½ tsp each **salt** and **pepper**

12 cups **vegetable broth** or beef broth

1 cup **dried green lentils**

⅔ cup **pot barley** or pearl barley

The fresh scent and flavour of lemon are lovely complements to the earthy lentils and kale in this light dinner soup. For a simple, tasty side, spread pieces of baguette with garlic butter and top with a sprinkle of cheese and sliced green onions; broil until crisp.

Slow Cooker Lemon Lentil Soup

1 large **onion,** diced

2 **carrots,** thinly sliced

2 ribs **celery,** thinly sliced

¾ cup **dried green lentils**

½ tsp **dried oregano**

1 **bay leaf**

¼ tsp **salt**

3 cups **vegetable broth**

3 cups chopped **kale leaves** or fresh spinach

2 tbsp **lemon juice**

Dash **hot pepper sauce**

Lemon wedges (optional)

In slow cooker, combine onion, carrots, celery, lentils, oregano, bay leaf and salt; pour in broth and 3 cups water. Cover and cook on low until lentils and vegetables are tender, 5 to 7 hours.

Add kale; cover and cook on high until wilted, about 20 minutes. Discard bay leaf. Stir in lemon juice and hot pepper sauce. Serve with lemon wedges (if using).

Makes 4 servings. PER SERVING: about 192 cal, 12 g pro, 2 g total fat (trace sat. fat), 36 g carb, 8 g fibre, 0 mg chol, 627 mg sodium. % RDI: 12% calcium, 35% iron, 138% vit A, 101% vit C, 99% folate.

This is just the recipe for busy nights when you need something hearty, comforting and fast as lightning to put together. This vegan soup brims with flavour – and nutrients. Serve with whole grain bread to sop up the tasty broth.

20-Minute Lentil Soup

1 tbsp **vegetable oil**

4 **green onions,** chopped

3 **carrots,** chopped

1 **potato,** peeled and chopped

1 tbsp **tomato paste**

2 tsp **mild curry paste**

2½ cups **vegetable broth**

1 cup **dried red lentils**

2 cups packed **fresh baby spinach**

In large saucepan, heat oil over medium heat; fry green onions, carrots and potato, stirring occasionally, until onions are softened, about 4 minutes. Stir in tomato paste and curry paste.

Add vegetable broth, 2½ cups water and lentils; bring to boil. Reduce heat, cover and simmer until lentils are tender, about 12 minutes. Stir in spinach.

Makes 4 servings. PER SERVING: about 283 cal, 15 g pro, 5 g total fat (trace sat. fat), 46 g carb, 9 g fibre, 0 mg chol, 750 mg sodium. % RDI: 9% calcium, 46% iron, 164% vit A, 20% vit C, 140% folate.

Like pea soup, lentil soup is enhanced by the addition of smoked meat. The hock's natural gelatin helps thicken the soup, giving the broth a velvety texture. If you can't find a ham hock, replace it with 8 oz (225 g) lean smoked slab bacon (dice to serve).

Lentil Soup With Ham Hock

In Dutch oven, heat oil over medium heat; cook onions, stirring often, until lightly browned, about 15 minutes. Add garlic, minced cilantro, bay leaf, pepper, cloves and nutmeg; cook, stirring constantly, until fragrant, about 2 minutes.

Add 8 cups water, ham hock and lentils; bring to boil. Reduce heat and skim off foam; cover and simmer for 1 hour. Add carrots, celery and turnip; cook until ham hock is tender, about 30 minutes. Skim off fat.

Remove ham hock; discarding skin, fat and bone, cut meat into bite-size pieces. Return meat to pan; stir in lemon juice and salt. Cook until heated through, adding more water if soup is too thick. Remove bay leaf. *(Make-ahead: Let cool for 30 minutes. Refrigerate, uncovered, in airtight container until cold. Cover and refrigerate for up to 3 days.)*

Garnish with cilantro sprigs.

Makes 6 to 8 servings. PER EACH OF 8 SERVINGS: about 234 cal, 19 g pro, 5 g total fat (1 g sat. fat), 30 g carb, 6 g fibre, 22 mg chol, 285 mg sodium. % RDI: 6% calcium, 31% iron, 69% vit A, 20% vit C, 93% folate.

1 tbsp **vegetable oil**

2 **onions,** chopped

2 cloves **garlic,** minced

⅓ cup minced **fresh cilantro** or parsley

1 **bay leaf**

½ tsp **pepper**

¼ tsp **ground cloves**

¼ tsp **nutmeg**

1 **smoked ham hock** (about 2 lb/900 g)

1½ cups **dried green lentils** or dried brown lentils

3 **carrots,** diced

2 ribs **celery,** diced

2 cups diced **turnip** or rutabaga

2 tbsp **lemon juice**

¾ tsp **salt**

Cilantro sprigs or chopped fresh parsley

Hummus lovers will really appreciate this mildly spiced soup. Sesame oil gives the dish a rich, toasted flavour that complements the earthy cumin. Serve with toasted pita triangles or bread for a complete meal.

Cumin Chickpea Soup

2 tsp **extra-virgin olive oil**

2 **onions,** chopped

4 **carrots,** diced

2 **sweet green peppers,** diced

1 tbsp **ground cumin**

½ tsp each **salt** and **pepper**

2 cans (each 19 oz/540 mL) **chickpeas,** drained and rinsed

12 cups **vegetable broth** or chicken broth

6 cloves **garlic,** minced

2 tbsp **lemon juice**

4 tsp **sesame oil**

GARNISH:
Chopped **fresh mint** and/or **parsley**

Lemon wedges

In large Dutch oven, heat olive oil over medium heat; fry onions, carrots, peppers, cumin, salt and pepper until softened, 5 minutes.

In blender, purée 1 cup of the chickpeas. Add puréed and whole chickpeas, broth and 3 cups water to onion mixture; bring to boil. Cover, reduce heat and simmer for 5 minutes.

Add garlic, lemon juice and sesame oil. (*Make-ahead: Let cool for 30 minutes. Refrigerate, uncovered, in airtight container until cold. Cover and refrigerate for up to 3 days or freeze for up to 2 weeks. Reheat before garnishing.*)

GARNISH: Top each bowl with mint and/or parsley; serve with lemon wedge.

Makes about 10 servings. PER SERVING: about 180 cal, 6 g pro, 4 g total fat (1 g sat. fat), 30 g carb, 6 g fibre, 0 mg chol, 1,166 mg sodium. % RDI: 4% calcium, 12% iron, 74% vit A, 36% vit C, 28% folate.

A filling, hot soup that's ready in less than 25 minutes is welcome any time of year, but it's especially great on busy school nights when the autumn chill has set in. A simple salad is particularly nice on the side.

Red Bean and Bacon Soup

In large saucepan, sauté bacon over medium-high heat until crisp, about 5 minutes.

Drain fat from pan; add onion, garlic, carrots, celery, thyme and pepper. Fry over medium heat until softened, about 5 minutes.

Add broth, tomatoes, beans, rice and tomato paste; bring to boil. Reduce heat, cover and simmer until rice is tender, about 25 minutes. (*Make-ahead: Let cool for 30 minutes. Refrigerate, uncovered, in airtight container until cold. Cover and refrigerate for up to 2 days.*)

Makes 6 servings. PER SERVING: about 241 cal, 12 g pro, 5 g total fat (2 g sat. fat), 38 g carb, 8 g fibre, 8 mg chol, 966 mg sodium. % RDI: 9% calcium, 19% iron, 71% vit A, 45% vit C, 25% folate.

6 slices **bacon,** chopped

1 **onion,** chopped

4 cloves **garlic,** minced

2 **carrots,** diced

2 ribs **celery,** diced

1½ tsp **dried thyme**

¼ tsp **pepper**

4 cups **sodium-reduced chicken broth**

1 can (28 oz/796 mL) **diced tomatoes**

1 can (19 oz/540 mL) **red kidney beans,** drained and rinsed

½ cup **parboiled long-grain rice**

¼ cup **tomato paste**

Ham hocks come in different sizes; for this recipe, the weight doesn't need to be exact. You can substitute Great Northern beans for the navy beans if you like. The croutons are delicious on salads, so make extra if you have enough ingredients.

Bean and Ham Hock Soup With Kale and Croutons

BROTH: In stockpot or slow cooker, combine ham hock, onion, celery, thyme, bay leaves, peppercorns and 12 cups cold water. Cover and cook on low heat, skimming off foam as necessary, for 4 hours on stove top or 8 to 10 hours in slow cooker. Remove hock and let cool enough to handle. Discarding skin, fat and bone, shred meat. *(Make-ahead: Cover and refrigerate for up to 2 days.)*

Strain broth through fine sieve into large bowl, pressing vegetables to extract liquid. Skim off fat. *(Make-ahead: Let cool for 30 minutes; cover and refrigerate for up to 2 days.)*

CROUTONS: Toss together bread, oil, salt and pepper; spread on rimmed baking sheet. Bake in 400°F (200°C) oven, tossing once, until golden and crisp, 6 to 8 minutes. Let cool on pan on rack.

In Dutch oven, heat oil over medium heat; fry onion, celery, carrots and garlic until softened, about 8 minutes. Add tomato paste and pepper; cook, stirring, for 2 minutes. Add broth, beans and shredded meat; bring to boil. Reduce heat and simmer, uncovered, for 20 minutes. Add kale; simmer until tender, about 7 minutes. Serve topped with croutons.

Makes 12 servings. PER SERVING: about 251 cal, 16 g pro, 10 g total fat (2 g sat. fat), 25 g carb, 6 g fibre, 25 mg chol, 669 mg sodium. % RDI: 10% calcium, 22% iron, 81% vit A, 65% vit C, 41% folate.

2 tbsp **extra-virgin olive oil**

1 large **onion,** chopped

3 each ribs **celery** and **carrots,** thinly sliced

3 cloves **garlic,** minced

1 can (5½ oz/156 mL) **tomato paste**

½ tsp **pepper**

3 cups **cooked navy beans** (see Tip, below)

6 cups chopped **kale leaves**

BROTH:

1 **smoked ham hock** (about 3 lb/1.35 kg)

1 each **onion** and rib **celery,** quartered

4 sprigs **fresh thyme**

2 **bay leaves**

½ tsp **black peppercorns**

CROUTONS:

3 cups cubed trimmed **Italian bread**

3 tbsp **extra-virgin olive oil**

Pinch each **salt** and **pepper**

Tip: To quickly make the amount of cooked beans you need for this recipe, follow this method: First, rinse 1½ cups dried navy beans. Then, in saucepan, cover with 4½ cups water; bring to boil and boil gently for 2 minutes. Remove from heat, cover and let stand for 1 hour. Drain. In saucepan, cover beans again with fresh water, using three times the new volume of the beans. Bring to boil. Reduce heat, cover and simmer until tender, 30 to 35 minutes. Drain.

Simmer a tasty pot of this soup while you're relaxing around the house. If you cook a bone-in ham for a party, save the bone and use it instead of the ham hock. For a pretty presentation, sprinkle ham over each bowlful instead of stirring it back into the soup.

Classic Pea Soup With Ham

1 **smoked ham hock** (about 1 lb/450 g)

1 tbsp **vegetable oil**

1 large **onion,** finely chopped

2 **carrots,** finely chopped

2 ribs **celery,** finely chopped

2 cloves **garlic,** minced

2 **bay leaves**

½ tsp each **salt** and **pepper**

4 cups **sodium-reduced chicken broth**

2 cups **dried yellow split peas** or green split peas

3 **green onions,** sliced

Using paring knife, peel off and discard skin from ham hock. Trim off and discard fat. Set hock aside.

In Dutch oven, heat oil over medium-low heat; fry onion, carrots, celery, garlic, bay leaves, salt, pepper and ham hock until vegetables are softened, about 5 minutes.

Add broth, split peas and 2 cups water; bring to boil over medium-high heat, skimming off any foam. Cover and simmer over medium-low heat until peas break down and meat is tender enough to fall off bone, about 1¾ hours.

Remove ham hock; discarding bone, shred meat and set aside. Discard bay leaves. In blender, purée half of the soup; return to pot along with meat. (*Make-ahead: Let cool for 30 minutes. Refrigerate, uncovered, in airtight container until cold. Cover and refrigerate for up to 2 days. Reheat before garnishing.*)

Ladle into bowls; garnish with green onions.

Makes 8 servings. PER SERVING: about 232 cal, 16 g pro, 3 g total fat (trace sat. fat), 36 g carb, 5 g fibre, 6 mg chol, 594 mg sodium. % RDI: 4% calcium, 17% iron, 46% vit A, 8% vit C, 49% folate.

Tip: After removing the ham hock, you can use an immersion blender in the pot to blend the soup to a semi-chunky consistency.

An Italian classic, pasta fagioli is good old-fashioned comfort food. This version uses canned beans instead of dried beans, reducing the amount of cooking time. Serve the soup with crusty Italian bread.

Simple Pasta Fagioli Soup

5 slices **bacon,** diced

1 tbsp **extra-virgin olive oil**

½ cup diced **onion**

½ cup diced **celery**

1 **carrot,** diced

1 small **potato,** peeled and diced

2 cloves **garlic,** minced

¼ cup **white wine** or sodium-reduced chicken broth

3 **plum tomatoes,** diced

Pinch each **salt** and **pepper**

2½ cups **sodium-reduced chicken broth**

2 cans (each 19 oz/540 mL) **romano beans,** drained and rinsed

1½ cups **tubetti** or other small pasta

½ cup grated **Parmesan cheese**

In Dutch oven, fry bacon over medium heat, stirring often, until crisp, about 8 minutes. Using slotted spoon, transfer to paper towel–lined plate.

Drain fat from pan; add oil and heat over medium heat. Fry onion, celery, carrot, potato and garlic, stirring often, until golden and softened, about 10 minutes.

Stir in wine, tomatoes, salt and pepper; bring to boil. Reduce heat and simmer, stirring often, until thickened and tomatoes release juices, about 10 minutes.

Stir in broth, 1½ cups water, beans and bacon. *(Make-ahead: Let cool for 30 minutes. Refrigerate, uncovered, in airtight container until cold. Cover and refrigerate for up to 2 days.)*

Bring soup to boil. Add pasta; reduce heat and simmer until pasta is tender but firm, about 8 minutes. Sprinkle with Parmesan cheese.

Makes 8 servings. PER SERVING: about 327 cal, 16 g pro, 8 g total fat (3 g sat. fat), 49 g carb, 8 g fibre, 11 mg chol, 699 mg sodium. % RDI: 12% calcium, 16% iron, 19% vit A, 10% vit C, 42% folate.

Tip: For a touch of green, toss 1 cup slivered green beans, chopped spinach or chopped Swiss chard into the pot during the final 2 minutes of pasta cooking time. Or combine the Parmesan cheese with 2 tbsp chopped fresh parsley and sprinkle over top.

Peppery arugula adds a spicy lift to this velvety soup. If you're in the mood to bake, the rustic flavours of the soup go well with corn bread or corn muffins. Make double batches of both to enjoy as a casual dinner with friends.

Potato and Arugula Soup With Chorizo

In large saucepan, heat oil over medium heat; fry onion, garlic, salt and pepper, stirring often, until onion is softened, about 4 minutes.

Add broth, 3 cups water and potato; bring to boil. Reduce heat, cover and simmer until potatoes are tender, about 15 minutes. In batches, transfer to blender or food processor and purée until smooth. Return to pan. *(Make-ahead: Let cool for 30 minutes. Refrigerate, uncovered, in airtight container until cold. Cover and refrigerate for up to 3 days.)*

GARNISH: Meanwhile, in small skillet, heat oil over medium-high heat; sauté sausage until browned, about 3 minutes.

Meanwhile, slice arugula into thin strips. Bring soup to boil and remove from heat; add arugula and lemon juice. Serve sprinkled with sausage.

Makes 6 servings. PER SERVING: about 181 cal, 8 g pro, 11 g total fat (3 g sat. fat), 13 g carb, 1 g fibre, 11 mg chol, 367 mg sodium. % RDI: 5% calcium, 9% iron, 5% vit A, 13% vit C, 12% folate.

VARIATION

Potato and Arugula Soup With Blue Cheese
Replace chicken broth with vegetable broth. Omit garnish. Sprinkle each serving with 1 tbsp crumbled blue cheese.

2 tbsp **extra-virgin olive oil**

1 **onion,** chopped

4 cloves **garlic,** minced

½ tsp each **salt** and **pepper**

4 cups **sodium-reduced chicken broth** (or Homemade Chicken Stock, recipe, page 32)

2 cups cubed peeled **potato**

1 bunch **arugula,** stemmed (about 3 cups)

1 tbsp **lemon juice**

GARNISH:

1 tsp **vegetable oil**

½ cup chopped **dry-cured chorizo sausage** (see Tip, page 11)

You can spice up this soup as much as you like by choosing hot Italian sausages and increasing the amount of hot pepper. If desired, garnish with shavings of Parmesan cheese or drizzle with a touch of extra-virgin olive oil.

Hearty Tomato, Sausage and Bean Soup

In Dutch oven, heat oil over medium heat; fry onion, carrot, celery, garlic, hot pepper (if using), salt and pepper, stirring occasionally, until softened, about 6 minutes.

Increase heat to medium-high; add sausages and sauté for 5 minutes, breaking up with spoon.

Stir in tomatoes, breaking up with spoon. Add beans, broth, 1 cup water, oregano and sugar; bring to boil. Reduce heat and simmer until slightly thickened, 15 to 20 minutes. Discard hot pepper.

Makes 8 to 10 servings. PER EACH OF 10 SERVINGS: about 171 cal, 9 g pro, 8 g total fat (2 g sat. fat), 19 g carb, 3 g fibre, 12 mg chol, 647 mg sodium, 526 mg potassium. % RDI: 8% calcium, 21% iron, 15% vit A, 38% vit C, 17% folate.

4 tsp **vegetable oil**

1 **onion,** finely chopped

1 **carrot,** finely chopped

1 rib **celery,** finely chopped

2 cloves **garlic,** minced

1 **green hot pepper** (optional)

¼ tsp each **salt** and **pepper**

2 **Italian sausages** (8 oz/225 g total), casings removed

2 cans (each 28 oz/796 mL) **whole tomatoes**

1 can (19 oz/540 mL) **navy beans,** drained and rinsed

1 cup **sodium-reduced chicken broth**

⅓ cup chopped **fresh oregano**

1 tsp **granulated sugar**

Chicken noodle soup is like a warm hug – always welcome. This version features a tasty homemade stock as the base. It's more work than using prepared broth, but the flavour is worth it. The stock freezes beautifully, so you might want to make a double batch.

Homestyle Chicken Noodle Soup

1 tbsp **vegetable oil**

1 **onion,** chopped

2 small **carrots,** sliced

2 ribs **celery,** sliced

¾ cup sliced **mushrooms**

1 clove **garlic,** chopped

½ tsp each **salt** and **pepper**

¼ tsp **dried thyme**

1 **bay leaf**

Homemade Chicken Stock (recipe, page 32)

2 **chicken breasts**

¾ cup **green beans,** chopped

1 cup **egg noodles**

2 tbsp chopped **fresh parsley**

In Dutch oven, heat oil over medium-high heat; cook onion, carrots, celery, mushrooms, garlic, salt, pepper, thyme and bay leaf, stirring often, until softened, about 10 minutes.

Add stock; bring to boil. Add chicken breasts and return to boil; reduce heat and simmer until no longer pink inside, about 20 minutes. Remove chicken; let cool enough to handle. Discarding skin and bones, dice meat and return to soup.

Add green beans; cook until tender, about 7 minutes. Discard bay leaf. *(Make-ahead: Let cool for 30 minutes. Refrigerate, uncovered, in airtight container until cold. Cover and refrigerate for up to 3 days or freeze for up to 4 months.)*

Meanwhile, in saucepan of boiling water, cook noodles until tender but firm. Drain and add to soup along with parsley.

Makes 6 to 8 servings. PER EACH OF 8 SERVINGS: about 147 cal, 13 g pro, 6 g total fat (1 g sat. fat), 8 g carb, 1 g fibre, 29 mg chol, 352 mg sodium. % RDI: 3% calcium, 8% iron, 27% vit A, 5% vit C, 8% folate.

Homemade wontons add an element of surprise to this soup. You'll need about 1 cup raw fresh spinach to make the 2 tbsp cooked that's called for. You can also use frozen spinach, squeezing out the excess liquid before using.

Chicken Vegetable Soup With Wontons

In stockpot, bring chicken and 12 cups water to boil; skim off foam. Add carrots, celery, garlic, onion, bay leaves, thyme, salt and pepper; simmer, uncovered, over medium-low heat until chicken is tender enough to easily come off bones, about 1 hour.

Remove chicken; refrigerate until cold, about 30 minutes. Discarding bones, chop meat. Meanwhile, strain stock through cheesecloth-lined sieve into large bowl. Remove carrots; dice and set aside. Press remaining vegetables to extract liquid; discard solids.

In clean saucepan, combine stock, chopped chicken, diced carrots and parsley; heat through. *(Make-ahead: Refrigerate in alrtight container for up to 2 days. Reheat.)*

WONTONS: Meanwhile, finely chop shrimp; place in bowl. Add spinach, garlic, cornstarch, ginger and sesame oil; stir to combine. Working with 4 wonton wrappers at a time, place about 1 tsp shrimp mixture onto centre of each; brush edge with some of the egg yolk. Pull edge up over filling to form purse, pinching around filling to seal. *(Make-ahead: Place on baking sheet; cover and refrigerate for up to 1 day.)*

Add wontons to soup; simmer until shrimp mixture is pink through dough, about 5 minutes. Divide wontons among bowls; ladle soup over top. Sprinkle with chives.

Makes 4 servings. PER SERVING: about 312 cal, 35 g pro, 7 g total fat (2 g sat. fat), 27 g carb, 2 g fibre, 163 mg chol, 644 mg sodium. % RDI: 9% calcium, 26% iron, 148% vit A, 12% vit C, 28% folate.

2 lb (900 g) **chicken pieces,** skinned

3 **carrots**

2 ribs **celery,** halved

2 cloves **garlic**

1 **onion,** halved

2 **bay leaves**

½ tsp **dried thyme**

½ tsp each **salt** and **pepper**

2 tbsp chopped **fresh parsley**

2 tbsp chopped **fresh chives**

WONTONS:

2 oz (55 g) **raw shrimp,** peeled and deveined

2 tbsp **cooked spinach,** finely chopped

1 small clove **garlic,** minced

1 tsp **cornstarch**

1 tsp minced **fresh ginger**

½ tsp **sesame oil**

16 **wonton wrappers**

1 **egg yolk,** lightly beaten

When cold winds howl at the door, put on a pot of this simple, satisfying soup. Using prepared broth saves time, but if you have some Homemade Chicken Stock (recipe, page 32) tucked away in the freezer, feel free to substitute it.

Cosy Chicken and Rice Soup

1 tbsp **olive oil**

12 oz (340 g) **boneless skinless chicken thighs**

1 **leek** (white and light green parts only), diced

2 ribs **celery,** diced

2 **carrots,** diced

1 **Yukon Gold potato,** peeled and diced

Half **sweet potato,** peeled and diced

3 sprigs each **fresh thyme** and **parsley**

¼ tsp each **salt** and **pepper**

4 cups **sodium-reduced chicken broth**

½ cup **basmati rice,** rinsed

1 cup **frozen peas**

In large Dutch oven, heat oil over medium-high heat; brown chicken. Remove and cut into chunks; set aside.

Add leek and celery to pan; cook over medium heat until softened, about 2 minutes. Add carrots, potato, sweet potato, thyme, parsley, salt and pepper; cook, stirring often, for 3 minutes.

Return chicken to pan along with any accumulated juices. Stir in broth and 4 cups water; bring to boil. Reduce heat and simmer for 5 minutes.

Stir in rice; cook until vegetables and rice are tender, about 13 minutes. Add peas. Discard thyme and parsley.

Makes 4 servings. PER SERVING: about 345 cal, 25 g pro, 8 g total fat (2 g sat. fat), 43 g carb, 5 g fibre, 71 mg chol, 887 mg sodium, 625 mg potassium. % RDI: 7% calcium, 17% iron, 117% vit A, 27% vit C, 21% folate.

To freeze some of this hearty soup for up to one month, omit the spinach and pasta, then add them when reheating. If you don't have Homemade Chicken Stock (recipe, below), use 6 cups sodium-reduced chicken broth plus 2 cups water.

Lemon Chicken and Spinach Noodle Soup

2 tbsp **extra-virgin olive oil**

1 **onion,** diced

2 cloves **garlic,** minced

1 **carrot,** diced

1 rib **celery,** diced

1 **sweet red pepper,** diced

1 tsp **ground cumin**

¼ tsp **pepper**

Homemade Chicken Stock (recipe, right)

4 cups packed **fresh spinach,** trimmed and chopped

2 cups cooked **small pasta,** such as stars or small shells (1 cup uncooked)

2 cups diced **cooked chicken**

2 tsp grated **lemon zest**

⅓ cup **lemon juice**

In large saucepan, heat oil over medium heat; fry onion, garlic, carrot, celery, red pepper, cumin and pepper, stirring often, until softened, about 8 minutes.

Pour in stock and bring to boil; reduce heat, cover and simmer until vegetables are tender, about 15 minutes. Stir in spinach, pasta, chicken, and lemon zest and juice; simmer for 5 minutes.

Makes 8 servings. PER SERVING: about 196 cal, 17 g pro, 8 g total fat (2 g sat. fat), 14 g carb, 2 g fibre, 32 mg chol, 110 mg sodium. % RDI: 5% calcium, 16% iron, 37% vit A, 53% vit C, 26% folate.

Homemade Chicken Stock

In stockpot or slow cooker, combine 1 stewing hen (or 3 lb/1.35 kg chicken); 3 each small carrots (unpeeled), onions (unpeeled) and ribs celery, coarsely chopped; 1 cup sliced mushrooms; 3 cloves garlic, smashed; 10 sprigs fresh parsley; ½ tsp each dried thyme, salt and black peppercorns; and 2 bay leaves. Pour in 8 cups cold water. Cover and cook over low heat on stove top for 4 hours or on low in slow cooker for 8 to 10 hours. Discard hen. Strain broth through cheesecloth-lined sieve into large bowl, pressing vegetables to extract liquid. Skim off fat. (*Make-ahead: Let cool for 30 minutes. Refrigerate, uncovered, in airtight container until cold. Cover and refrigerate for up to 3 days or freeze for up to 4 months.*)

Makes 8 cups.

Tip: If you don't have leftover cooked chicken, heat 1 tsp oil in nonstick skillet over medium heat; cook 2 small boneless skinless chicken breasts, turning once, until golden and no longer pink inside, 10 to 12 minutes. Let cool enough to handle; dice.

Who doesn't like meatballs? These turkey meatballs are especially nice, with their delicate flavour and texture. The peas and red pepper add a tasty vegetable element to the soup and a bright pop of colour to each bowl.

Turkey Meatball Soup

TURKEY MEATBALLS: In bowl, combine egg, onion, Parmesan cheese, parsley, salt and pepper; mix in turkey. Shape mixture by 1 tbsp into balls. Bake on greased baking sheet in 400°F (200°C) oven until digital thermometer inserted into centre of several registers 165°F (74°C), about 15 minutes.

Meanwhile, in large saucepan, bring broth and 3 cups water to boil. Add green onions, carrot, celery, pepper and thyme; reduce heat, cover and simmer for 10 minutes.

Add red pepper, egg noodles and meatballs; simmer, covered, until pasta is tender but firm, about 5 minutes. Add peas; heat through.

Makes 4 to 6 servings. PER EACH OF 6 SERVINGS: about 198 cal, 19 g pro, 9 g total fat (3 g sat. fat), 10 g carb, 2 g fibre, 100 mg chol, 560 mg sodium. % RDI: 8% calcium, 13% iron, 34% vit A, 62% vit C, 12% folate.

3 cups **sodium-reduced chicken broth**

2 **green onions,** sliced

1 **carrot,** sliced

1 rib **celery,** sliced

¼ tsp **pepper**

¼ tsp **dried thyme**

1 **sweet red pepper,** chopped

1 cup **vermicelli egg noodles**

½ cup **frozen peas**

TURKEY MEATBALLS:

1 **egg**

¼ cup grated **onion**

¼ cup grated **Parmesan cheese**

2 tbsp minced **fresh parsley**

¼ tsp each **salt** and **pepper**

1 lb (450 g) **lean ground turkey** or veal

This simple soup takes some of its inspiration from Vietnam's famous rare beef soup, called *pho.* This version skips the hours of boiling to make a homemade stock and uses prepared beef broth to create a dish that's easy enough to make on a weeknight.

Beef Noodle Soup

Combine steak, half each of the cornstarch, soy sauce, and sherry (if using), the sesame oil, five-spice powder and sugar. Let marinate for 15 minutes.

Meanwhile, cook noodles according to package directions; drain and divide among 4 bowls. Cut carrots into thin 2-inch (5 cm) long strips. Separate bok choy into leaves. Set aside.

In large Dutch oven, bring broth, 2 cups water, and remaining soy sauce and sherry to boil. Stir in steak mixture, separating with spoon; reduce heat and simmer for 3 minutes. Add carrots and bok choy; cook until wilted, about 2 minutes.

Whisk remaining cornstarch with 1 tbsp water; stir into soup and simmer until glossy and slightly thickened, about 2 minutes. Return soup to boil. With fork, stir in egg in slow thin stream, pulling into strands. Pour over noodles; sprinkle with green onions.

Makes 4 servings. PER SERVING: about 315 cal, 20 g pro, 5 g total fat (1 g sat. fat), 47 g carb, 4 g fibre, 76 mg chol, 1,067 mg sodium. % RDI: 11% calcium, 22% iron, 100% vit A, 40% vit C, 26% folate.

8 oz (225 g) **top sirloin grilling steak,** thinly sliced across the grain

2 tbsp **cornstarch**

2 tbsp **sodium-reduced soy sauce**

2 tbsp **dry sherry** (optional)

1 tsp **sesame oil**

¾ tsp **five-spice powder**

¾ tsp **granulated sugar**

6 oz (170 g) **wide rice sticks** (½ inch/1 cm)

2 **carrots**

4 heads **baby bok choy**

4 cups **sodium-reduced beef broth**

1 **egg,** beaten

2 **green onions,** thinly sliced

Cabbage adds a sweet note to this nicely spiced beef soup. When you need a warm, comforting dish that's ready in a flash, this is the one: It only takes half an hour to cook and is a great way to use up leftover cooked rice. Serve with multigrain rolls.

Beef and Cabbage Soup

12 oz (340 g) **lean ground beef**

1 tbsp **vegetable oil**

1 **onion,** diced

1 clove **garlic,** minced

2 **bay leaves**

½ tsp each **dried thyme** and **marjoram**

½ tsp **salt**

¼ tsp **pepper**

Pinch **ground cloves**

3 cups chopped **cabbage**

2 **carrots,** halved lengthwise and sliced

2 ribs **celery,** sliced

3 cups **sodium-reduced beef broth**

¼ cup **tomato paste**

1 cup **cooked rice**

Lemon wedges

In large saucepan, brown beef over medium-high heat, breaking up with spoon. With slotted spoon, transfer to bowl. Drain fat from pan; wipe out pan.

In same pan, heat oil over medium heat; cook onion, garlic, bay leaves, thyme, marjoram, salt, pepper and cloves, stirring often, until onion is softened, about 5 minutes. Stir in cabbage, carrots and celery; cook, stirring, for 3 minutes.

Add broth, 3 cups water and tomato paste. Return beef to pan and bring to boil; reduce heat, cover and simmer until cabbage is tender, about 15 minutes.

Stir in rice and heat through, about 2 minutes. Discard bay leaves. Serve with lemon wedges.

Makes 4 to 6 servings. PER EACH OF 6 SERVINGS: about 204 cal, 14 g pro, 8 g total fat (2 g sat. fat), 18 g carb, 3 g fibre, 31 mg chol, 588 mg sodium. % RDI: 4% calcium, 14% iron, 45% vit A, 18% vit C, 8% folate.

This meal-in-a-bowl will disappear quickly. If you do have leftovers, add a bit of water when you reheat, as the soup will thicken as it stands. If you don't feel like making the Parmesan Crisps and Crostini, ready-made breads are delicious dipped into the soup.

Hearty Minestrone

Pesto (recipe, opposite)

Parmesan Crisps
  (recipe, opposite)

MINESTRONE:

1 tbsp **extra-virgin olive oil**

1 large **onion,** chopped

3 ribs **celery,** sliced

3 **carrots,** sliced

3 cloves **garlic,** minced

2 **bay leaves**

½ tsp each **salt** and **pepper**

1 can (5½ oz/156 mL) **tomato paste**

1 **smoked ham hock** (about 1 lb/450 g)

1 large **potato,** peeled and cubed

1 **sweet red pepper,** diced

1 small **zucchini**

1 cup **dried pasta** (such as garganelli, radiatore or macaroni)

1 cup each rinsed drained **canned red** and **white kidney beans**

CROSTINI:

2½ cups cubed trimmed **Italian bread**

3 tbsp **extra-virgin olive oil**

½ tsp coarsely cracked **pepper**

CROSTINI: Toss together bread, oil and pepper; spread on rimmed baking sheet. Bake in 400°F (200°C) oven, tossing once, until golden and crisp, 6 to 8 minutes. (*Make-ahead: Let cool. Store in airtight container for up to 24 hours.*)

MINESTRONE: In Dutch oven, heat oil over medium heat; fry onion, celery, carrots, garlic, bay leaves, salt and pepper until softened, about 4 minutes.

Add tomato paste; cook, stirring, for 2 minutes. Add ham hock and 8 cups water; bring to boil. Reduce heat to low; cover and simmer for 30 minutes. Skim off foam. Add potato and red pepper; simmer, covered, for 1 hour.

Remove ham hock and let cool enough to handle. Discarding skin, fat and bone, shred ham and return to soup. Discard bay leaves. (*Make-ahead: Let cool for 30 minutes. Refrigerate, uncovered, until cold. Cover and refrigerate in airtight container for up to 2 days.*)

Cut zucchini in half lengthwise; slice crosswise. Add pasta, red and white kidney beans and zucchini to soup; bring to boil. Reduce heat and simmer until pasta is tender but firm, about 12 minutes.

Ladle soup into bowls; garnish with pesto and crostini. Serve with Parmesan crisps.

Makes 8 servings. PER SERVING: about 361 cal, 12 g pro, 18 g total fat (4 g sat. fat), 40 g carb, 7 g fibre, 10 mg chol, 715 mg sodium. % RDI: 13% calcium, 20% iron, 81% vit A, 68% vit C, 34% folate.

Pesto

In food processor, purée together ½ cup fresh basil leaves; ¼ cup extra-virgin olive oil; 1 tbsp toasted pine nuts; and ¼ tsp each salt and pepper until smooth, 1 minute. Add 1 clove garlic, minced. (*Make-ahead: Refrigerate in airtight container for up to 2 days.*)

Makes ⅓ cup.

Parmesan Crisps

Line rimless baking sheet with nonstick baking mat or parchment paper. Divide ¾ cup grated Parmesan cheese into 16 mounds on pan; spread each to 2-inch (5 cm) circle. Bake In 400°F (200°C) oven until bottoms are light golden, about 5 minutes. Immediately drape on rolling pin to create curve; let cool. (*Make-ahead: Store in airtight container for up to 2 days.*)

Makes 16 crisps.

Tip: For large Parmesan Crisps, on 2 prepared baking sheets, divide 2¼ cups cheese into 8 mounds; spread into 4-inch (10 cm) circles. Bake as directed.

This simple chowder combines everyday cold-weather ingredients to make a satisfying supper. You can use about 8 cups torn Swiss chard leaves instead of the spinach if you like. Serve with crusty country-style bread.

Chalet Supper Soup

3 **carrots**

3 **leeks** (white and light green parts only)

1 thick slice **ham** (6 oz/170 g)

2 lb small **red-skinned potatoes,** scrubbed

2 tbsp **butter**

1 **onion,** chopped

1 tsp **salt**

3 cups **milk**

1½ cups **wide egg noodles**

1 pkg (10 oz/284 g) **fresh spinach**

1 cup finely shredded **Gruyère cheese** or extra-old Cheddar cheese

½ tsp **pepper**

Cut carrots into 1½-inch (4 cm) lengths. Cut leeks lengthwise almost but not all the way to root end; spreading leaves, flush out grit under running water. Cut crosswise into 1½-inch (4 cm) lengths. Cut ham into ¾-inch (2 cm) chunks. Halve or quarter potatoes; set aside.

In large Dutch oven, melt butter over medium-high heat; sauté carrots, leeks, ham and onion until leeks and onion are softened, about 8 minutes.

Add potatoes, 4 cups water and salt; bring to boil. Reduce heat, cover and simmer, stirring occasionally, until potatoes are just tender, about 20 minutes.

Add milk; bring to simmer. Stir in noodles and spinach; simmer, uncovered, until noodles are tender, about 10 minutes. Stir in cheese and pepper.

Makes 6 to 8 servings. PER EACH OF 8 SERVINGS: about 303 cal, 16 g pro, 11 g total fat (6 g sat. fat), 37 g carb, 5 g fibre, 48 mg chol, 736 mg sodium. % RDI: 31% calcium, 23% iron, 108% vit A, 32% vit C, 38% folate.

Loaded with chunks of potato, sweet corn, broccoli and smoky bacon, this creamy chowder is surprisingly easy – and quick – to cook. If you can find them, tiny oyster crackers are delicious sprinkled over top.

Corn and Bacon Chowder

3 slices **bacon,** chopped

2 **onions,** chopped

1 clove **garlic,** minced

2 **potatoes**

3 cups **chicken broth**

2 cups **frozen corn kernels**

2 cups **broccoli florets**

1 cup **milk**

½ tsp each **salt** and **pepper**

½ cup shredded **light Cheddar-style cheese**

In saucepan, cook bacon over medium heat until crisp, about 5 minutes. Drain fat from pan; add onions and garlic. Fry, stirring occasionally, until softened, about 5 minutes.

Meanwhile, peel and cube potatoes. Add to pan along with half of the broth; bring to boil. Reduce heat to medium-low; cover and simmer until potatoes are tender, about 10 minutes. Using potato masher or immersion blender, mash several times to break up about half of the potatoes.

Add remaining broth, corn and broccoli; simmer until broccoli is tender, about 6 minutes.

Reduce heat to low. Stir in milk, salt and pepper; heat through but do not boil. Sprinkle each serving with cheese.

Makes 4 servings. PER SERVING: about 294 cal, 16 g pro, 8 g total fat (4 g sat. fat), 43 g carb, 4 g fibre, 18 mg chol, 1,367 mg sodium. % RDI: 20% calcium, 11% iron, 9% vit A, 50% vit C, 36% folate.

The beautiful saffron colour of this creamy seafood soup comes from the addition of curry paste. We call for mild curry paste, but use whatever level of heat you prefer. Experiment with different brands to find a spice mix you love.

Curried Mussel Chowder

Scrub mussels and remove any beards. Discard any that do not close when tapped.

In Dutch oven, cover and steam mussels with ¾ cup water over medium-high heat, stirring once, until mussels open, about 8 minutes. Strain, reserving liquid and discarding any mussels that do not open. Let cool. Remove mussels from shells; place in bowl. Set aside.

In Dutch oven, melt butter over medium heat; cook potato, leeks, onion and celery, stirring often, until softened, about 5 minutes. Stir in curry paste; cook for 2 minutes. Stir in flour and salt; cook, stirring, for 1 minute.

Whisk in milk; reduce heat and simmer, stirring occasionally, until thickened and potatoes are tender, about 20 minutes.

Add reserved mussel cooking liquid and corn; simmer until corn is tender-crisp, about 5 minutes. Stir in mussels just before serving; sprinkle with cilantro.

Makes 4 servings. PER SERVING: about 312 cal, 15 g pro, 14 g total fat (7 g sat. fat), 33 g carb, 2 g fibre, 51 mg chol, 458 mg sodium, 688 mg potassium. % RDI: 17% calcium, 27% iron, 18% vit A, 17% vit C, 31% folate.

2 lb (900 g) **fresh mussels**

3 tbsp **butter**

1 cup diced peeled **potato**

1 cup chopped **leeks** (white and light green parts only)

¾ cup finely chopped **onion**

¾ cup finely chopped **celery**

2 tsp **mild Indian curry paste**

¼ cup **all-purpose flour**

¼ tsp **salt**

2 cups **milk**

1 cup **frozen corn kernels**

2 tbsp chopped **fresh cilantro**

This recipe makes great use of leftover roast turkey or cooked chicken. If you have it, use Homemade Turkey Stock (recipe, page 165) to add exceptional flavour to this hearty, satisfying dish. It takes a little time to cook, but it's very low-maintenance.

Creamy Turkey Chowder

In large Dutch oven, heat butter over medium heat; cook carrots, celery, onion, potato, thyme, salt, sage and pepper, stirring occasionally, until onion is softened, about 6 minutes.

Stir in flour; cook, stirring, for 2 minutes. Whisk in broth and 2 cups water; bring to boil. Reduce heat, cover and simmer until potatoes are tender, about 15 minutes.

Stir in turkey and milk and bring just to simmer (do not boil); simmer gently until heated through, about 5 minutes.

Makes 4 servings. PER SERVING: about 318 cal, 28 g pro, 11 g total fat (6 g sat. fat), 26 g carb, 3 g fibre, 76 mg chol, 751 mg sodium, 686 mg potassium. % RDI: 15% calcium, 16% iron, 74% vit A, 12% vit C, 19% folate.

2 tbsp **butter**

2 **carrots,** diced

2 ribs **celery,** diced

1 **onion,** diced

8 oz (225 g) **Yukon Gold potato** (1 large), peeled and diced

½ tsp **dried thyme**

½ tsp **salt**

¼ tsp crumbled **dried sage**

¼ tsp **pepper**

¼ cup **all-purpose flour**

2 cups **sodium-reduced chicken broth**

2 cups diced **cooked turkey**

1½ cups **milk**

You can have this tomato-based chowder on the table in less than 30 minutes, especially if you keep the pantry-friendly clams, broth and tomatoes on hand for busy nights. If you prefer a corn-free version, simply skip that addition.

Halibut and Clam Chowder

1 tbsp **vegetable oil**

1 **onion,** chopped

1 clove **garlic,** minced

2 ribs **celery,** diced

1 cup diced peeled **potato**

1 tsp **dried thyme**

¼ tsp **salt**

1 can (19 oz/540 mL) **stewed tomatoes**

1⅓ cups **sodium-reduced chicken broth**

¼ cup **tomato paste**

12 oz (340 g) **halibut fillets** or tilapia fillets

1 can (5 oz/150 mL) **whole baby clams**

1 **sweet green pepper,** diced

1 cup **frozen corn kernels**

In large saucepan, heat oil over medium heat; fry onion, garlic, celery, potato, thyme and salt, stirring often, until softened and light golden, about 10 minutes.

Add tomatoes, broth and tomato paste; bring to boil. Reduce heat, cover and simmer until potato is tender, about 12 minutes.

Cut fish into 1-inch (2.5 cm) pieces; add to pan along with clams, green pepper and corn. Simmer, covered, over medium-low heat until fish flakes easily when tested, about 5 minutes.

Makes 4 servings. PER SERVING: about 271 cal, 26 g pro, 6 g total fat (1 g sat. fat), 30 g carb, 4 g fibre, 37 mg chol, 617 mg sodium. % RDI: 12% calcium, 52% iron, 13% vit A, 87% vit C, 24% folate.

Chock-full of a variety of seafood, fish and vegetables, this rich soup is inspired by a similar chowder served at the Masstown Market, near Truro, N.S. Enjoy a hearty bowlful with your favourite biscuits or rolls.

Nova Scotia Seafood Chowder

Scrub mussels; remove any beards. Discard any mussels that do not close when tapped.

In saucepan, bring mussels and wine to boil over high heat. Reduce heat and simmer, covered, until mussels open, about 5 minutes. Reserving broth, strain; discard any mussels that do not open. Let cool enough to handle. Remove and discard shells; set mussels aside.

In Dutch oven, melt butter over medium heat; fry celery, onions, salt, paprika and cayenne pepper, stirring occasionally, until softened, about 6 minutes. Stir in flour; cook, stirring constantly, for 1 minute.

Stir in reserved broth, 1½ cups water and clam juice, scraping up any brown bits from bottom of pan. Add potatoes; bring to boil. Reduce heat and simmer, covered and stirring occasionally, until potatoes are tender, about 15 minutes.

Stir in haddock, scallops and lobster; bring to boil. Reduce heat and simmer for 5 minutes. Stir in cream, mussels and parsley. Stir until heated through, about 2 minutes. *(Make-ahead: Let cool. Refrigerate, uncovered, in airtight container until cold. Cover and refrigerate for up to 2 days.)*

Makes 12 servings. PER SERVING: about 236 cal, 21 g pro, 10 g total fat (6 g sat. fat), 14 g carb, 1 g fibre, 78 mg chol, 405 mg sodium, 582 mg potassium. % RDI: 11% calcium, 13% iron, 12% vit A, 12% vit C, 14% folate.

2 lb (900 g) **fresh mussels**

⅔ cup **dry white wine**

3 tbsp **butter**

3 ribs **celery,** thinly sliced

2 **onions,** chopped

½ tsp **salt**

½ tsp **sweet paprika**

¼ tsp **cayenne pepper**

3 tbsp **all-purpose flour**

1 bottle (240 mL) **clam juice**

2 **yellow-fleshed potatoes,** peeled and cubed

12 oz (340 g) **haddock fillets** or other firm-fleshed fish fillets, cut in 2-inch (5 cm) chunks

12 oz (340 g) **sea scallops,** halved horizontally

1 can (11.3 oz/320 g) **frozen lobster meat,** thawed and drained

3 cups **10% cream**

¼ cup chopped **fresh parsley**

Canned broth and sliced bamboo shoots, water chestnuts and mushrooms speed the preparation of this traditional restaurant-style soup. For a substantially spicier bowlful, replace the sesame oil with chili oil.

Mushroom Hot-and-Sour Soup

2 cans (each 10 oz/284 mL) **chicken broth**

1 pkg (454 g) **medium tofu**

1 can (8 oz/227 mL) **sliced bamboo shoots,** drained and rinsed

1 can (8 oz/227 mL) **sliced water chestnuts,** drained and rinsed

1 pkg (8 oz/228 g) **sliced fresh mushrooms**

3 oz (85 g) **egg noodles**

1 clove **garlic,** minced

3 tbsp **cornstarch**

3 tbsp **white vinegar**

2 tbsp **sodium-reduced soy sauce**

½ tsp **white pepper** or black pepper

1 **egg**

1 tsp **sesame oil**

1 cup **bean sprouts**

1 **green onion,** thinly sliced

Half **sweet red pepper,** thinly sliced

Dilute broth according to package directions; add to large saucepan. Add 1 cup water; bring to boil. Meanwhile, cut tofu and bamboo shoots into ¼-inch (5 mm) thick strips. Add to saucepan along with water chestnuts, mushrooms and noodles; return to boil.

Whisk together garlic, cornstarch, vinegar, soy sauce and white pepper; whisk into pan. Reduce heat to medium-low; simmer, stirring, until thickened and noodles are tender, about 5 minutes.

Whisk egg; stirring constantly, slowly pour into soup until egg floats to surface, about 2 minutes. Drizzle in sesame oil. Top each serving with bean sprouts, green onion and red pepper.

Makes 4 servings. PER SERVING: about 242 cal, 19 g pro, 9 g total fat (2 g sat. fat), 25 g carb, 4 g fibre, 49 mg chol, 1,303 mg sodium. % RDI: 15% calcium, 29% iron, 3% vit A, 28% vit C, 41% folate.

Packed with protein, peanuts give this colourful soup a velvety texture and rich, creamy taste. If you have the time to make it, Roasted Vegetable Stock (recipe, below) makes the tastiest base for this soup, and it's terrific in other vegetarian dishes.

Tomato Peanut Soup

In large Dutch oven or saucepan, heat oil over medium heat; fry onion, celery, garlic, ginger, salt, coriander and cayenne, stirring occasionally, until softened, about 3 minutes.

Add tomatoes, sweet potatoes and broth; bring to boil. Whisk in peanut butter; reduce heat and simmer until potatoes are tender, about 20 minutes.

Stir in kale and lemon juice; simmer until kale is wilted, about 3 minutes. *(Make-ahead: Let cool for 30 minutes. Refrigerate, uncovered, in airtight container until cold. Cover and refrigerate for up to 2 days.)*

Makes 8 servings. PER SERVING: about 201 cal, 6 g pro, 10 g total fat (1 g sat. fat), 25 g carb, 3 g fibre, 0 mg chol, 922 mg sodium. % RDI: 8% calcium, 12% iron, 108% vit A, 68% vit C, 10% folate.

Roasted Vegetable Stock
In roasting pan, combine 3 each carrots, onions and ribs celery, coarsely chopped; 1 cup sliced mushroom stems or caps; 3 cloves garlic; and 2 tsp vegetable oil until coated. Roast in 450°F (230°C) oven, stirring halfway through, until softened and browned, about 40 minutes. Transfer to stockpot. Add 10 sprigs fresh parsley; 10 black peppercorns, cracked; 2 bay leaves; and 7 cups water. Pour 1 cup water into roasting pan, scraping up brown bits, over heat if necessary. Scrape into pot and bring to boil; skim off any foam. Reduce heat to medium; simmer for 40 minutes. Strain through fine sieve, gently pressing vegetables. Stir in ½ tsp salt. *(Make-ahead: Let cool for 30 minutes. Refrigerate, uncovered, in airtight container until cold. Cover; refrigerate for up to 3 days or freeze for up to 4 months.)*

Makes about 5 cups.

1 tbsp **vegetable oil**

1 **onion,** diced

1 rib **celery,** diced

1 clove **garlic,** minced

1 tsp grated **fresh ginger** (or ¼ tsp ground ginger)

½ tsp **salt**

½ tsp **ground coriander**

Pinch **cayenne pepper**

1 can (28 oz/796 mL) **diced tomatoes**

2 **sweet potatoes,** peeled and diced

5 cups **vegetable broth** or Roasted Vegetable Stock (recipe, left)

½ cup **smooth natural peanut butter**

2 cups chopped **kale leaves** or collard greens

1 tbsp **lemon juice**

A smoked turkey leg or drumstick adds richness to the simple broth that forms the base of this hearty root vegetable soup. Leftovers make a great lunch the following day or can be refrigerated for later.

Chunky Vegetable Barley Soup

2 tbsp **vegetable oil**

1 **onion,** diced

2 **carrots,** diced

2 ribs **celery,** diced

1 lb (450 g) **mini red potatoes,** scrubbed and diced

12 oz (340 g) **white turnips,** peeled and diced

2 **parsnips,** peeled and diced

1 tsp **dried thyme**

½ tsp **salt**

¼ tsp **pepper**

¾ cup **pot barley** or pearl barley

¼ cup chopped **fresh parsley**

SMOKED TURKEY BROTH:

1 lb (450 g) **smoked turkey leg** or smoked turkey drumstick

1 each **onion, carrot** and rib **celery,** quartered

8 oz (225 g) **mushrooms,** halved

8 **black peppercorns**

3 sprigs **fresh parsley**

1 **bay leaf**

SMOKED TURKEY BROTH: Remove skin and meat from smoked turkey leg. Reserve bone; discard skin. Cut meat into bite-size pieces; set aside. In Dutch oven, combine turkey bone, onion, carrot, celery, mushrooms, peppercorns, parsley, bay leaf and 12 cups water; bring to boil. Reduce heat, cover and simmer until flavourful, about 4 hours. Strain broth to make about 8 cups; set aside. (*Make-ahead: Let cool for 30 minutes. Refrigerate, uncovered, in airtight container until cold. Cover and refrigerate for up to 3 days.*)

In clean Dutch oven, heat oil over medium heat; cook onion, carrots and celery, stirring occasionally, until softened, about 5 minutes. Add potatoes, turnips, parsnips, thyme, salt and pepper; cook, stirring occasionally, for 5 minutes. Add barley; cook, stirring, for 1 minute.

Add reserved broth and 2 cups water; bring to boil. Reduce heat, cover and simmer until barley is tender, about 40 minutes.

Stir in reserved turkey meat and parsley; cook for 5 minutes. (*Make-ahead: Let cool for 30 minutes. Refrigerate, uncovered, in airtight container until cold. Cover and refrigerate for up to 3 days.*)

Makes 12 servings. PER SERVING: about 209 cal, 13 g pro, 7 g total fat (1 g sat. fat), 25 g carb, 4 g fibre, 24 mg chol, 424 mg sodium, 607 mg potassium. % RDI: 5% calcium, 16% iron, 23% vit A, 23% vit C, 19% folate.

Tip: To clean and chop leeks, trim off and discard dark green parts, saving white and light green parts. Cut off root ends and split leeks lengthwise. Fanning apart layers, rinse thoroughly under running water to remove grit; chop finely.

The creaminess of this lovely old-fashioned soup comes not from milk or cream but from puréed cooked potatoes. If you have the time and inclination, serve it alongside a simple tossed salad for a light bistro-style meal.

Leek and Potato Soup

3 tbsp **vegetable oil**

2 **leeks** (white and light green parts only), thinly sliced

1 rib **celery,** diced

1 **carrot,** diced

½ tsp **salt**

¼ tsp **dried thyme**

¼ tsp **white pepper** or pepper

2 large **Yukon Gold potatoes,** peeled and chopped

3 cups **sodium-reduced chicken broth**

2 slices **thick-cut bacon**

¼ cup shredded **Cheddar cheese**

2 tbsp minced **fresh parsley**

In Dutch oven, heat oil over medium-high heat; sauté leeks, celery, carrot, salt, thyme and pepper until softened, about 8 minutes.

Add potatoes, broth and 3 cups water; bring to boil. Reduce heat, cover and simmer until potatoes are tender, about 20 minutes. Let cool slightly.

Meanwhile, in skillet, fry bacon until crisp; drain on paper towel–lined plate. Crumble bacon and set aside.

In batches in blender, purée soup until smooth; strain into clean pot and reheat gently. Sprinkle each serving with bacon, cheese and parsley.

Makes 4 to 6 servings. PER EACH OF 6 SERVINGS: about 206 cal, 6 g pro, 10 g total fat (2 g sat. fat), 25 g carb, 2 g fibre, 8 mg chol, 589 mg sodium. % RDI: 6% calcium, 8% iron, 24% vit A, 20% vit C, 11% folate.

Delicate yet rich-tasting dumplings simmer away in this easy-to-prepare soup. If you're in a rush, you can skip the dumplings and serve the soup with grated Parmesan cheese instead.

Leek Soup With Cheese Dumplings

In large saucepan, melt butter over medium heat; cook leeks and onion, stirring often, until softened, about 10 minutes. Stir in flour and pepper; cook for 1 minute.

Stir in wine; increase heat to medium-high. Boil until reduced by half, about 3 minutes. Stir in broth and salt; bring to boil. Reduce heat; cover and simmer for 20 minutes. (*Make-ahead: Let cool for 30 minutes. Refrigerate, uncovered, in airtight container until cold. Cover and refrigerate for up to 2 days or freeze for up to 2 weeks. Thaw in refrigerator for 24 hours. Reheat.*)

CHEESE DUMPLINGS: Meanwhile, using fork, mash together cheese, flour, butter, egg, parsley, salt and pepper to make firm dough. With lightly dampened hands, roll dough by 1 tbsp into balls; place on plate. Drop all at once into simmering soup. Simmer until dumplings float to surface, about 10 minutes.

Makes 4 servings. PER SERVING: about 338 cal, 20 g pro, 19 g total fat (11 g sat. fat), 17 g carb, 2 g fibre, 103 mg chol, 1,830 mg sodium. % RDI: 27% calcium, 16% iron, 14% vit A, 5% vit C, 21% folate.

1 tbsp **butter**

3 **leeks** (white and light green parts only), chopped

1 **onion,** finely chopped

1 tbsp **all-purpose flour**

¼ tsp **pepper**

1 cup **dry white wine**

6 cups **chicken broth**

¼ tsp **salt**

CHEESE DUMPLINGS:

1¼ cups shredded **aged Gouda cheese** or Gruyère cheese

⅓ cup **all-purpose flour**

1 tbsp **butter,** softened

1 **egg**

1 tbsp minced **fresh parsley**

¼ tsp each **salt** and **pepper**

Chicken Tagine With Olives and
Preserved Lemons, page 83

Stews

This rich, dark beef stew, brimming with root vegetables and peas, is comfort food at its finest and perfect for a blustery night. Serve with crusty rolls for dipping in the delicious beer-laced sauce.

Slow Cooker Beef and Stout Stew

1½ lb (675 g) **Yukon Gold potatoes,** peeled and cubed

1 lb (450 g) each **carrots** and **parsnips,** coarsely chopped

2 ribs **celery,** chopped

1 **onion,** chopped

2 **bay leaves**

1 tsp **dried thyme**

¾ tsp **salt**

½ tsp **pepper**

3 lb (1.35 kg) **stewing beef cubes**

4 slices **thick-cut bacon,** chopped

1½ cups **stout beer**

¾ cup **sodium-reduced beef broth**

2 tsp **Worcestershire sauce**

⅓ cup **all-purpose flour**

1 cup **frozen peas**

In slow cooker, combine potatoes, carrots, parsnips, celery, onion, bay leaves, thyme, salt and pepper. Top with beef and bacon.

Whisk together stout, broth, ½ cup water and Worcestershire sauce; pour over beef. Cover and cook on low until beef and vegetables are tender, 7 to 8 hours. Discard bay leaves.

Whisk flour with 1 cup of the cooking liquid until smooth; whisk into slow cooker. Stir in peas; cook, covered, on high until thickened, about 30 minutes.

Makes 6 to 8 servings. PER EACH OF 8 SERVINGS: about 528 cal, 39 g pro, 25 g total fat (11 g sat. fat), 36 g carb, 5 g fibre, 110 mg chol, 547 mg sodium, 1,119 mg potassium. % RDI: 7% calcium, 35% iron, 78% vit A, 27% vit C, 34% folate.

Tip: This recipe makes a generous amount of stew and is best suited to a slow cooker with at least a 6-quart (5.7 L) capacity.

This traditional French dish is renowned for its luscious flavours and simple cooking method. The pig's foot contains natural gelatin that gives extra body to the sauce, but it's purely optional. Ask your butcher to cut it in half for you for easy prep.

Braised Beef in Wine

3 lb (1.35 kg) **boneless beef blade pot roast**

1 **pig's foot,** halved (optional)

1¼ cups **dry red wine** or dry white wine

2 tsp **dried thyme**

½ tsp each **salt** and **pepper**

8 slices **lean thick-cut bacon,** coarsely chopped

1 can (28 oz/796 mL) **whole tomatoes**

2 cups halved **mushrooms**

2 cups thickly sliced **carrots**

½ cup chopped **fresh parsley**

2 **onions,** chopped

4 cloves **garlic,** minced

2 **bay leaves**

2 strips (3 x 1 inch/8 x 2.5 cm) **orange zest**

¼ cup **tomato paste**

1 cup **all-purpose flour**

Cut beef into 8 chunks; place in nonmetallic bowl. Add pig's foot (if using), wine, thyme, salt and pepper; mix well. Cover and marinate in refrigerator, stirring occasionally, for 24 hours.

Sprinkle half of the bacon in large Dutch oven or tall covered casserole dish. Place remaining bacon in large bowl. Drain tomatoes (reserve juice for another use, such as soup or sauce); halve tomatoes and squeeze out seeds. Add to bowl along with mushrooms, carrots, parsley, onions and garlic; mix well.

With slotted spoon, arrange pig's foot (if using) and half of the beef over bacon in Dutch oven; cover with half of the tomato mixture. Add bay leaves and orange zest. Repeat layers of beef and tomato mixture. Whisk tomato paste into beef marinade; pour into pan.

In bowl, mix flour with ½ cup water to make stiff paste. Cover pan with lid; with floured hands, press paste onto edge of lid and pan to seal. Bake in 400°F (200°C) oven for 20 minutes. Reduce heat to 250°F (120°C); bake for 4 hours. Remove seal. Skim off fat; discard bay leaves and orange zest. *(Make-ahead: Let cool for 30 minutes. Refrigerate, uncovered, in airtight container until cold. Cover and refrigerate for up to 2 days. Reheat, covered, over medium heat, about 30 minutes, or in 375°F/190°C oven, about 45 minutes.)*

Makes 6 to 8 servings. PER EACH OF 8 SERVINGS: about 447 cal, 40 g pro, 20 g total fat (10 g sat. fat), 24 g carb, 3 g fibre, 105 mg chol, 552 mg sodium. % RDI: 7% calcium, 44% iron, 76% vit A, 33% vit C, 21% folate.

Tip: For a dramatic presentation, serve the braised beef directly from the oven and break the seal at the table. Your guests will adore the fantastic scent of the first steam to emerge from the pot.

Tension melts away when you open the door to the welcoming aromas of this hearty stew. Since it has lots of flavourful sauce, you'll want a loaf of crusty bread to mop up every last drop.

Slow Cooker Beef and Mushroom Stew

Trim and cut beef into 1-inch (2.5 cm) cubes; toss with ¼ cup of the flour. Sprinkle with salt and pepper. In large skillet, heat half of the oil over medium-high heat; brown meat, in batches and adding more oil if necessary. Transfer to slow cooker.

Add broth to skillet and bring to boil, scraping up any brown bits; pour into slow cooker. In same skillet, heat remaining oil over medium heat; fry onion, bacon and thyme for 1 minute. Add button mushrooms; cook until softened and almost no liquid remains, about 8 minutes. Add to slow cooker.

Add celery, potatoes, porcini mushrooms, bay leaf and 1 cup water to slow cooker; stir to combine. Cover and cook on low until meat and vegetables are tender, about 6 hours.

Whisk remaining flour with ¼ cup water; whisk into slow cooker. Add peas. Cover and cook on high until thickened, about 15 minutes. Discard bay leaf.

Makes 8 servings. PER SERVING: about 344 cal, 30 g pro, 14 g total fat (5 g sat. fat), 23 g carb, 3 g fibre, 60 mg chol, 503 mg sodium. % RDI: 3% calcium, 28% iron, 4% vit A, 12% vit C, 22% folate.

VARIATION
Stove-Top Beef and Mushroom Stew
Reduce flour to ¼ cup and use only for browning meat. In Dutch oven, brown beef as directed; transfer beef to plate. Deglaze pan with broth as directed and set aside. In same pan, heat remaining oil; fry onion, bacon, thyme and button mushrooms as directed. Stir in celery, potatoes, porcini mushrooms, bay leaf, broth mixture, 1 cup water and beef; bring to boil. Reduce heat, cover and simmer until beef is tender, about 1 hour. Add peas; simmer until heated through. Discard bay leaf.

2 lb (900 g) **stewing beef cubes**

½ cup **all-purpose flour**

¾ tsp **salt**

¼ tsp **pepper**

2 tbsp **vegetable oil**

2 cups **sodium-reduced beef broth**

1 **onion,** sliced

2 slices **bacon,** chopped

1 tsp **dried thyme**

4 cups **button mushrooms** (12 oz/340 g), halved

2 ribs **celery,** chopped

3 cups cubed peeled **potatoes**

1 pkg (14 g) **dried porcini mushrooms**

1 **bay leaf**

1 cup **frozen peas**

Roasted garlic adds a deep caramelized sweetness to this simple, traditional stew. To save some prep time, the garlic is quick-roasted on the stove top instead of in the oven.

Roasted Garlic Beef Stew

12 cloves **garlic**

2 tbsp **vegetable oil**

2 **carrots**

2 **parsnips**

2 **Yukon Gold potatoes**

1½ lb (675 g) **stewing beef cubes**

½ tsp each **salt** and **pepper**

1 **onion,** chopped

1½ tsp each **dried thyme** and **sage**

1½ cups **sodium-reduced beef broth**

1 cup **red wine** or beef broth

¼ cup **tomato paste**

1 cup **frozen peas**

¼ cup chopped **fresh parsley**

In small saucepan, cover and fry garlic with oil over low heat, shaking pan occasionally, until softened and golden, about 30 minutes. Transfer garlic to large plate. Drain and reserve oil.

Meanwhile, peel carrots, parsnips and potatoes; cut into 1-inch (2.5 cm) chunks. Set aside. Season beef with half each of the salt and pepper. In Dutch oven, heat 1 tbsp of the reserved oil over medium-high heat; brown beef, in batches. Transfer to plate.

Drain any fat from pan; add remaining reserved oil. Fry onion, 1 tsp each of the thyme and sage, and remaining salt and pepper over medium heat, stirring occasionally, until light golden, 5 minutes.

Add broth, wine and tomato paste; bring to boil, scraping up brown bits. Return beef and any juices to pan along with garlic. Add carrots, parsnips and potatoes; reduce heat, cover and simmer until beef and vegetables are tender, about 1½ hours. *(Make-ahead: Let cool for 30 minutes. Refrigerate, uncovered, in airtight container until cold. Cover and refrigerate for up to 2 days. Reheat.)*

Add peas and remaining thyme and sage; heat through. Sprinkle with parsley.

Makes 8 servings. PER SERVING: about 275 cal, 22 g pro, 10 g total fat (3 g sat. fat), 24 g carb, 4 g fibre, 42 mg chol, 355 mg sodium. % RDI: 5% calcium, 24% iron, 38% vit A, 27% vit C, 23% folate.

VARIATION
Slow Cooker Roasted Garlic Beef Stew
Follow first 3 paragraphs. Combine garlic, carrots, parsnips and potatoes in slow cooker. Add beef, onion, broth, wine and tomato paste. Cover and cook on low until beef is tender, 8 to 10 hours. Increase heat to high. Add peas and remaining thyme and sage; cover and cook until hot, about 10 minutes. Sprinkle with parsley.

Inspired by Hungarian goulash, this hearty stew is delicious with a loaf of your favourite artisanal bread. If you want a more authentic experience and have time, cook up a pot of egg noodles to serve with the stew.

Slow Cooker Paprika Beef Stew

In slow cooker, combine potatoes, half of the Cubanelle peppers, the carrots, onion and garlic. Top with beef.

Whisk together broth, tomato paste, paprika, marjoram, salt, caraway seeds, pepper and ½ cup water; pour over beef. Cover and cook on low until beef and vegetables are tender, about 8 hours.

Whisk together flour, 1 cup of the cooking liquid and ¼ cup water until smooth; whisk into slow cooker. Stir in beans and remaining Cubanelle peppers; cook, covered, on high until thickened, about 30 minutes. Stir in vinegar.

Makes 8 servings. PER SERVING: about 500 cal, 41 g pro, 19 g total fat (8 g sat. fat), 41 g carb, 8 g fibre, 101 mg chol, 707 mg sodium, 1,236 mg potassium. % RDI: 7% calcium, 40% iron, 58% vit A, 52% vit C, 27% folate.

2 lb (900 g) **potatoes,** peeled, halved and cut in ¼-inch (5 mm) thick slices

8 oz (225 g) **Cubanelle peppers** (3 large), seeded and chopped

3 **carrots,** cut in ¼-inch (5 mm) thick rounds

1 **white onion,** chopped

6 cloves **garlic,** minced

3 lb (1.35 kg) **stewing beef cubes**

1½ cups **sodium-reduced beef broth**

⅓ cup **tomato paste**

2 tbsp **sweet paprika**

1 tsp each **dried marjoram** and **salt**

½ tsp each **caraway seeds** and **pepper**

¼ cup **all-purpose flour**

1 can (19 oz/540 mL) **white kidney beans,** drained and rinsed

1 tbsp **red wine vinegar**

A quintessential Sunday roast, this all-in-one-pot dinner contains meat, potatoes and vegetables cooked in a tangy beer-based sauce. Any leftover corned beef is terrific the next day in sandwiches.

Beer-Braised Corned Beef and Cabbage

Rinse brisket and pat dry; place in slow cooker. Spread mustard over brisket; sprinkle with pickling spices.

Cut leeks, carrots and parsnips in half lengthwise; cut into about 4-inch (10 cm) lengths.

In large skillet, heat oil over medium-high heat; cook leeks, carrots, parsnips, garlic and pinch each of the salt and pepper, stirring occasionally, until softened and caramelized, about 6 minutes. Arrange over brisket.

Add broth, beer, remaining salt and pepper, and enough water to cover brisket by 1 inch (2.5 cm). Cover and cook on low for 5 hours.

Add cabbage; cook until brisket is tender, about 3 hours.

Transfer vegetables to serving platter and keep warm. Place brisket on cutting board and tent with foil; let stand for 3 to 5 minutes before thinly slicing across the grain. Arrange with vegetables on serving platter. Strain cooking liquid; drizzle 2½ cups over brisket and vegetables.

Makes 10 to 12 servings. PER EACH OF 12 SERVINGS: about 264 cal, 22 g pro, 16 g total fat (4 g sat. fat), 10 g carb, 2 g fibre, 80 mg chol, 2,080 mg sodium, 449 mg potassium. % RDI: 5% calcium, 23% iron, 22% vit A, 21% vit C, 16% folate.

4 lb (1.8 kg) **corned beef brisket**

2 tbsp **grainy mustard**

2 tbsp **mixed pickling spices**

2 each **leeks, carrots** and **parsnips**

1 tbsp **vegetable oil**

2 cloves **garlic,** smashed

¼ tsp each **salt** and **pepper**

4 cups **sodium-reduced beef broth**

1 bottle (12 oz/355 mL) **dark beer**

Half **cabbage,** thinly sliced

Tip: Corned beef is very high in sodium. If you want to indulge in high-sodium foods, do so only occasionally and be mindful of your other food choices that day.

Minute steaks cooked in a flavourful mixture of broth and beer make an economical meal, and the meat comes out tender enough to cut with a fork. Healthy, earthy root vegetables are also cooked right in the sauce for a balanced meal.

Beer-Simmered Steaks

2 lb (900 g) **inside round fast-fry steaks**

1 tsp **salt**

½ tsp **pepper**

2 tbsp **vegetable oil**

2 large **onions,** sliced

3 cloves **garlic,** minced

¾ tsp **dried thyme**

3 cups **beef broth**

1 bottle (341 mL) **beer**

2 **bay leaves**

Quarter **rutabaga**

4 **potatoes,** peeled and thickly sliced

2 **carrots,** sliced

2 ribs **celery,** sliced

⅓ cup **all-purpose flour**

2 tbsp chopped **fresh parsley**

1 tsp **cider vinegar**

If steaks are large, cut into serving-size pieces. Sprinkle steaks with half each of the salt and pepper. In Dutch oven, heat half of the oil over medium-high heat; brown steaks, in batches and adding remaining oil as necessary. Transfer to plate. Drain any fat from pan; fry onions, garlic, thyme and remaining salt and pepper until dark golden, 15 minutes.

Return steaks and any accumulated juices to pan; add broth, beer and bay leaves. Bring to boil; reduce heat, cover and simmer until steaks are tender, about 1½ hours.

Peel and cut rutabaga in half lengthwise; cut crosswise into slices.

Add rutabaga to pan along with potatoes, carrots and celery; cook, covered, until potatoes are tender, 40 minutes. Whisk flour with ⅓ cup cold water. Stir into pan; cook, stirring, over medium heat until thickened, about 7 minutes. Discard bay leaves. *(Make-ahead: Let cool for 30 minutes. Refrigerate, uncovered, in airtight container until cold. Cover and refrigerate for up to 2 days. Reheat.)*

Stir parsley and vinegar into sauce.

Makes 6 servings. PER SERVING: about 384 cal, 40 g pro, 8 g total fat (2 g sat. fat), 35 g carb, 4 g fibre, 65 mg chol, 899 mg sodium. % RDI: 6% calcium, 32% iron, 61% vit A, 30% vit C, 22% folate.

Beef pot roast is such a versatile dish: So many different flavours and cuts of meat lend themselves to this method. Both boneless and bone-in roasts are tender and delicious in this recipe, but meat on the bone is more flavourful than boneless.

Red Wine and Rosemary Pot Roast

1 **boneless beef pot roast** (such as top blade), about 3 lb (1.35 kg)

¾ tsp each **salt** and **pepper**

2 tbsp **vegetable oil**

3 cloves **garlic,** minced

4 **onions,** quartered

1 cup **beef broth**

1 cup **tomato juice**

1 cup **dry red wine** or beef broth

2 tsp crumbled **dried rosemary**

8 small **red potatoes**

8 **carrots**

2 large **parsnips,** cut in chunks

1 **acorn squash,** cut in wedges (or 2 cups whole pattypan squash)

3 tbsp **all-purpose flour**

2 tbsp chopped **fresh parsley**

Sprinkle beef with salt and pepper. In large Dutch oven, heat oil over medium-high heat; brown beef all over. Transfer to plate.

Reduce heat to medium and drain off fat; cook garlic and onions, stirring occasionally, until softened, about 4 minutes. Add broth, tomato juice, wine and rosemary, scraping up brown bits from bottom of pan.

Return beef and any accumulated juices to pan; bring to simmer. Cover and braise in 300°F (150°C) oven, basting every 30 minutes and turning once, until beef is tender, about 3 hours. Add potatoes, carrots, parsnips and squash to pan; cover and braise until vegetables are tender and beef is very tender, about 1 hour. With slotted spoon, transfer vegetables to platter; cover and keep warm.

Transfer beef to cutting board and tent with foil; let stand for 10 minutes. Cut string; slice thinly across the grain and add to platter.

Meanwhile, whisk flour with ¼ cup cold water to make thin, smooth paste; whisk into pan juices. Place pan over high heat; boil, whisking, until gravy is thick enough to coat back of spoon, about 4 minutes. Stir in parsley. Serve sauce and vegetables with sliced beef.

Makes 8 servings. PER SERVING: about 533 cal, 37 g pro, 20 g total fat (7 g sat. fat), 52 g carb, 8 g fibre, 90 mg chol, 540 mg sodium. % RDI: 10% calcium, 44% iron, 186% vit A, 50% vit C, 35% folate.

VARIATION
Pressure Cooker Red Wine and Rosemary Pot Roast
Using pressure cooker instead of Dutch oven, follow first
2 paragraphs as directed, increasing broth to 1½ cups.

Secure lid; bring to high pressure over high heat. Reduce heat to
just maintain high pressure; cook for 40 minutes. Remove from
heat. Let pressure release completely, about 10 minutes. Continue
as directed in paragraph 4.

Add potatoes, carrots, parsnips and squash to pressure cooker;
cover but do not seal. Simmer over medium heat until vegetables
are tender, about 30 minutes. Arrange on platter with beef.

Continue as directed in paragraph 5, whisking flour mixture into
pressure cooker and cooking over medium heat until thick
enough to coat back of spoon, about 15 minutes. Stir in parsley.
Serve as directed.

Rustic lamb shanks become melt-in-your-mouth tender when braised in the slow cooker. This French-inspired combination of lamb, beans and fennel is tasty enough to serve as a casual meal with friends.

Slow Cooker Lamb Shanks With Fennel and White Beans

6 **lamb shanks** (about 4 lb/1.8 kg)

½ tsp each **salt** and **pepper**

2 tbsp **vegetable oil**

1 **onion,** finely diced

1½ cups each diced **carrot** and **fennel bulb**

2 cloves **garlic,** minced

1 tsp each **dried thyme** and **fennel seeds**

1 cup **dry white wine** or sodium-reduced chicken broth

1 cup **sodium-reduced chicken broth**

2 cans (each 19 oz/540 mL) **navy beans,** drained and rinsed

½ cup chopped drained **oil-packed sun-dried tomatoes**

¼ cup chopped **fresh parsley**

Sprinkle lamb with salt and pepper. In skillet, heat half of the oil over medium-high heat; brown lamb, in batches. Transfer to plate.

Drain fat from pan; add remaining oil and heat over medium heat. Fry onion, carrot, diced fennel, garlic, thyme and fennel seeds, stirring occasionally, until softened, about 5 minutes.

Add wine and broth; bring to boil, stirring and scraping up brown bits from bottom of pan. Pour into slow cooker.

Add navy beans and tomatoes to slow cooker. Add lamb, pushing into liquid. Cover and cook on low until meat is tender and separates easily from bone, about 6 hours. Transfer lamb to plate.

Skim off fat in slow cooker. Stir in parsley. Spoon bean mixture into shallow bowls; top with lamb.

Makes 6 servings. PER SERVING: about 649 cal, 58 g pro, 28 g total fat (9 g sat. fat), 40 g carb, 5 g fibre, 150 mg chol, 1,030 mg sodium. % RDI: 11% calcium, 53% iron, 52% vit A, 28% vit C, 55% folate.

Serve this colourful one-pot meal with plenty of bread to mop up the delicious juices. Or spoon it into large hollowed-out rolls as we did for our photo. You can also make the stew with lean pork instead of veal.

Lemon Thyme Veal Stew With Potatoes

Sprinkle veal with salt and pepper. In large shallow Dutch oven, heat 1 tbsp of the oil over medium-high heat; brown veal, in batches. Transfer to plate. Drain any fat from pan; add remaining oil. Cook onions, garlic, thyme and oregano over medium heat, stirring occasionally, until softened, about 3 minutes.

Sprinkle with 2 tbsp of the flour; stir to coat. Add wine and broth; bring to boil, scraping up any brown bits.

Return veal and any accumulated juices to pan. Reduce heat to medium-low; cover and simmer for 45 minutes.

Whisk remaining flour with 2 tbsp cold water; stir into stew. Add potatoes and squash; cover and cook for 10 minutes. Add green beans; simmer, covered, until thickened and potatoes are tender, about 10 minutes. Stir in lemon juice. Serve sprinkled with parsley.

Makes 6 to 8 servings. PER EACH OF 8 SERVINGS: about 248 cal, 26 g pro, 7 g total fat (1 g sat. fat), 20 g carb, 2 g fibre, 95 mg chol, 486 mg sodium. % RDI: 5% calcium, 15% iron, 29% vit A, 23% vit C, 17% folate.

VARIATIONS
Lemon Thyme Veal Stew With Sweet Potatoes
Substitute 2 sweet potatoes for the white potatoes.

Slow Cooker Lemon Thyme Veal Stew With Potatoes
Increase broth to 2 cups. Follow first 2 paragraphs. Transfer veal and broth mixture to 16-cup (4 L) slow cooker. Add potatoes and squash. Cover and cook on low until veal is tender, about 8 hours. Add 2 tbsp all-purpose flour to the remaining flour to make ¼ cup; mix with ⅓ cup cold water to form paste and stir into slow cooker. Add beans; cook on high until thickened and beans are tender, 15 to 20 minutes. Stir in lemon juice; sprinkle with parsley.

2 lb (900 g) **stewing veal,** cut in 1-inch (2.5 cm) pieces

1 tsp **salt**

½ tsp **pepper**

2 tbsp **vegetable oil**

2 **onions,** chopped

2 cloves **garlic,** minced

½ tsp each **dried thyme and oregano**

¼ cup **all-purpose flour**

1 cup **white wine** or chicken broth

1 cup **chicken broth**

2 **potatoes** (1 lb/450 g total), peeled and cut in 1-inch (2.5 cm) cubes

2 cups cubed (1 inch/2.5 cm) peeled **butternut squash**

1 cup fresh or frozen **cut green beans** (1-inch/2.5 cm pieces)

3 tbsp **lemon juice**

2 tbsp chopped **fresh parsley**

Meat on the bone is always tasty, and oxtail has the most flavour of all beef cuts. It requires long, slow cooking to become tender, but the pressure cooker method trims the time by about two-thirds.

Oxtail Two-Potato Stew

4 lb (1.8 kg) **oxtail pieces**

1 tbsp **vegetable oil**

1 **onion,** chopped

2 ribs **celery,** chopped

1 **jalapeño pepper,**
   seeded and minced

4 cloves **garlic,** minced

¾ tsp each **pepper,**
   ground allspice and
   dried thyme

½ tsp **salt**

½ cup **tomato paste**

⅓ cup **all-purpose flour**

5 cups **beef broth**

4 **potatoes** (1½ lb/675 g),
   peeled and cubed

1 **sweet potato** (1 lb/450 g),
   peeled and cubed

4 tsp **lemon juice**

2 **green onions,** chopped

Trim outside fat off oxtails. In Dutch oven, heat oil over medium-high heat; brown oxtails. Transfer to plate. Drain fat from pan; fry onion, celery, jalapeño pepper, garlic, pepper, allspice, thyme and salt over medium heat, stirring, until softened, about 5 minutes.

Add tomato paste and flour; cook, stirring, for 2 minutes. Whisk in broth. Return oxtails and any juices to pan; bring to boil. Reduce heat, cover and simmer until oxtails are tender, 3 hours. Skim off fat.

Add potatoes and sweet potato; simmer, covered, until potatoes are tender, 35 minutes. *(Make-ahead: Let cool for 30 minutes. Refrigerate, uncovered, until cold. Cover and refrigerate for up to 2 days. Reheat.)* Stir in lemon juice; sprinkle with green onions.

Makes 8 servings. PER SERVING: about 387 cal, 31 g pro, 14 g total fat (trace sat. fat), 36 g carb, 4 g fibre, 92 mg chol, 821 mg sodium. % RDI: 5% calcium, 36% iron, 102% vit A, 45% vit C, 17% folate.

VARIATION

Pressure Cooker Oxtail Two-Potato Stew

Using pressure cooker instead of Dutch oven, follow first paragraph. Set flour aside. Add tomato paste; cook, stirring, for 2 minutes. Whisk in broth; return oxtails to pan. Secure lid; bring to high pressure over high heat. Reduce heat to maintain high pressure; cook for 27 minutes. Remove from heat; let pressure release completely, 10 minutes. Add potatoes and sweet potato; simmer, covered, over medium heat until tender, 35 minutes. Whisk reserved flour with ⅓ cup cold water; whisk into stew. Simmer, uncovered, until thickened, 5 minutes. Stir in lemon juice; sprinkle with green onions.

Tip: To freeze stew, omit white and sweet potatoes and freeze for up to 2 weeks. Thaw and reheat while cooking potatoes in boiling salted water until tender, 25 minutes; drain and add to stew.

This spin on the French classic *blanquette de veau* is a tad more rustic than the original. If you don't want to use wine, use 1 cup sodium-reduced chicken broth and 2 tsp lemon juice.

Braised Pork, Potatoes and Beans in White Wine Sauce

In Dutch oven, heat oil over high heat; brown pork, in batches. With slotted spoon, transfer to bowl. Add butter to pan; fry onions and celery over medium heat until softened, about 6 minutes.

Return pork and accumulated juices to pan. Add flour, salt, pepper and nutmeg; cook, stirring often, for 2 minutes.

Stir in broth and wine; bring to boil, scraping up brown bits from bottom of pan. Reduce heat, cover and simmer for 45 minutes.

Add potatoes; cover and simmer until potatoes and pork are tender, about 40 minutes.

Stir in lima beans, cream and dill; simmer until beans are tender, about 7 minutes.

Makes about 8 servings. PER SERVING: about 399 cal, 36 g pro, 15 g total fat (6 g sat. fat), 28 g carb, 4 g fibre, 112 mg chol, 364 mg sodium. % RDI: 5% calcium, 27% iron, 6% vit A, 20% vit C, 16% folate.

2 tbsp **vegetable oil**

3 lb (1.35 kg) **boneless pork shoulder butt,** trimmed and cut in 1½-inch (4 cm) cubes

1 tbsp **butter** or vegetable oil

2 **onions,** chopped

2 ribs **celery,** chopped

¼ cup **all-purpose flour**

½ tsp each **salt** and **white pepper**

¼ tsp **nutmeg**

1 cup **sodium-reduced chicken broth**

1 cup **dry white wine**

1¼ lb (565 g) **baby potatoes,** halved (about 5 cups)

2 cups **frozen lima beans** or peas

⅓ cup **whipping cream**

1 tbsp chopped **fresh dill**

Tip: If baby potatoes are unavailable, use new or waxy potatoes cut into 2-inch (5 cm) cubes. Peel potatoes, if you prefer.

This quicker version of the traditional braised French country classic contains several no-salt-added ingredients to bring the usually high sodium level down. If you can't find a smoked ham hock in the deli section, substitute a smoked turkey leg of equal weight.

Slow Cooker Cassoulet

4 cans (each 14 oz/398 mL) **no-salt-added navy beans,** drained and rinsed (or 6 cups cooked dried beans; see Tip, page 21)

1 can (28 oz/796 mL) **no-salt-added whole tomatoes,** drained

2 **onions,** diced

1 **carrot,** diced

1 rib **celery,** diced

4 cloves **garlic,** minced

2 **bay leaves**

2 sprigs each **fresh thyme** and **parsley**

¼ tsp **pepper**

1 **smoked ham hock** (12 oz/340 g)

1 pkg (375 g) **fully cooked smoked Polish sausages,** cut diagonally in 1½-inch (4 cm) thick slices

3 slices **sodium-reduced bacon,** sliced

¾ cup **sodium-reduced chicken broth**

¾ cup **white wine**

In slow cooker, combine beans, tomatoes, onions, carrot, celery, garlic, bay leaves, thyme, parsley and pepper.

Top with ham hock, sausages and bacon. Stir in broth and wine. Cover and cook on low for 6 to 8 hours.

Discard bay leaves, thyme and parsley. With slotted spoon, remove ham hock; discarding bones, skin and fat, shred meat into large chunks. Stir back into bean mixture.

Makes 6 to 8 servings. PER EACH OF 8 SERVINGS: about 431 cal, 24 g pro, 18 g total fat (6 g sat. fat), 42 g carb, 13 g fibre, 53 mg chol, 693 mg sodium, 920 mg potassium. % RDI: 19% calcium, 40% iron, 19% vit A, 10% vit C, 30% folate.

Bone-in skin-on chicken thighs are the best bet in the slow cooker. They stay moister than chicken breasts and give the dish a meatier flavour. The skin can get a little flabby when cooked this way, so you might want to remove it before serving.

Slow Cooker Braised Chicken and Potatoes

Mix together marjoram, salt, rosemary and pepper; sprinkle 1½ tsp over chicken. In large skillet, heat oil over medium-high heat; brown chicken, in batches if necessary. Transfer to slow cooker.

Drain fat from pan; cook onion, garlic, carrots, celery and remaining spice mixture over medium heat, stirring occasionally, until onion is softened, about 5 minutes. Add to slow cooker along with potatoes and bay leaf.

Add broth to skillet, stirring and scraping up brown bits; pour into slow cooker and stir to combine.

Cover and cook on low until juices run clear when chicken is pierced, about 4 hours. Skim off fat. Move chicken mixture to 1 side of slow cooker.

Whisk flour with ⅓ cup water; stir into liquid in slow cooker, gently redistributing ingredients. Cover and cook on high until thickened, about 15 minutes. Discard bay leaf. Sprinkle with parsley.

Makes 4 servings. PER SERVING: about 404 cal, 30 g pro, 17 g total fat (4 g sat. fat), 32 g carb, 4 g fibre, 116 mg chol, 817 mg sodium, 972 mg potassium. % RDI: 6% calcium, 24% iron, 72% vit A, 42% vit C, 25% folate.

1 tsp **dried marjoram**

¾ tsp **salt**

½ tsp **dried rosemary**

½ tsp **pepper**

8 **bone-in skin-on chicken thighs**

1 tbsp **vegetable oil**

1 **onion,** chopped

2 cloves **garlic,** minced

2 **carrots,** diagonally sliced

2 ribs **celery,** diagonally sliced

3 **red potatoes,** cut in eighths (about 1 lb/450 g)

1 **bay leaf**

1½ cups **sodium-reduced chicken broth**

¼ cup **all-purpose flour**

2 tbsp **fresh parsley**

Curly egg noodles are an excellent base for this chicken stew, because they readily soak up the savoury sauce. This recipe calls for only ½ cup chicken broth, so it's great for using up small containers of leftover broth in your freezer.

Chicken and Green Bean Stew

8 **boneless skinless chicken thighs** (1 lb/450 g)

2 tbsp **all-purpose flour**

2 tbsp **vegetable oil**

1 **onion,** chopped

3 cloves **garlic,** minced

1 tsp **dried oregano**

½ tsp each **salt** and **pepper**

1 can (28 oz/796 mL) **stewed tomatoes**

½ cup **sodium-reduced chicken broth**

2 cups **green beans,** trimmed and halved

12 oz (340 g) **medium curly egg noodles**

2 tbsp minced **fresh parsley**

1 tbsp **balsamic vinegar**

Dredge chicken in flour, shaking off excess. In large shallow Dutch oven, heat half of the oil over medium-high heat; brown chicken, about 5 minutes. Transfer to plate; set aside.

Add remaining oil to pan; sauté onion, garlic, oregano, salt and pepper over medium-high heat until onion is softened, about 4 minutes. Add tomatoes and broth; bring to boil, stirring and scraping up any brown bits from bottom of pan.

Return chicken to pan. Reduce heat, cover and simmer until juices run clear when chicken is pierced, about 12 minutes.

Add green beans; cook, uncovered, over medium-high heat until tender-crisp and sauce is thickened, about 10 minutes.

Meanwhile, in saucepan of boiling water, cook egg noodles according to package directions. Drain.

Stir parsley and vinegar into sauce. Serve stew over noodles.

Makes 4 servings. PER SERVING: about 618 cal, 37 g pro, 17 g total fat (3 g sat. fat), 80 g carb, 9 g fibre, 176 mg chol, 740 mg sodium. % RDI: 13% calcium, 40% iron, 11% vit A, 63% vit C, 30% folate.

Dried mushrooms develop rich, earthy flavours in the slow cooker. Dried chanterelles are light coloured and have a lovely taste, but feel free to substitute other dried mushrooms if you prefer.

Slow Cooker Creamy Mushroom Chicken Stew

12 oz (340 g) **button mushrooms,** halved

1 **onion,** finely chopped

2 cloves **garlic,** minced

1 pkg (14 g) **dried chanterelle mushrooms**

½ tsp **dried tarragon** or thyme

¼ tsp each **salt** and **pepper**

12 **boneless skinless chicken thighs,** quartered

1 cup **sodium-reduced chicken broth**

½ cup **white wine**

1 tbsp **Dijon mustard**

¼ cup **all-purpose flour**

¼ cup chopped **fresh parsley**

¼ cup **10% cream**

2 tsp **white wine vinegar**

In slow cooker, combine button mushrooms, onion, garlic, chanterelles, tarragon, salt and pepper. Top with chicken.

Whisk together broth, wine and Dijon mustard; pour over chicken. Cover and cook on low until juices run clear when chicken is pierced, 6 to 8 hours.

Whisk flour with 1 cup of the cooking liquid until smooth; whisk into slow cooker. Cook, covered, on high until thickened, about 15 minutes. Stir in parsley, cream and vinegar.

Makes 6 servings. PER SERVING: about 204 cal, 25 g pro, 7 g total fat (2 g sat. fat), 9 g carb, 2 g fibre, 98 mg chol, 335 mg sodium, 492 mg potassium. % RDI: 4% calcium, 18% iron, 5% vit A, 13% vit C, 14% folate.

Preserved lemons give this dish a unique, mellow flavour that you can't get from fresh lemons. Look for preserved lemons in Middle Eastern stores or make our quick version (recipe, below). If you like, leave the olives whole as we did in our photo (page 57).

Chicken Tagine With Olives and Preserved Lemons

In Dutch oven, heat 1 tbsp of the oil over medium-high heat; brown chicken, in batches, adding remaining oil as necessary. Transfer chicken to plate. Drain fat from pan; cook onion and garlic over medium heat, stirring occasionally, until softened, 5 minutes. Add tomato, all but 2 tbsp of the cilantro, ginger, paprika, saffron, cumin, pepper, cinnamon and 2 cups water. Return chicken and accumulated juices to pan; bring to boil. Reduce heat, cover and simmer until juices run clear when chicken is pierced, 45 minutes.

Meanwhile, in bowl, stir couscous with 3 cups boiling water; cover and let stand for 5 minutes. Fluff with fork.

Meanwhile, in small saucepan of boiling water, blanch olives for 5 minutes; drain. With slotted spoon, transfer chicken to platter; cover and keep warm. Add olives and lemons to sauce; boil, uncovered, over medium-high heat until thickened and reduced by one-third, 12 minutes. Pour over chicken. (*Make-ahead: Let cool for 30 minutes; refrigerate until cold. Cover; refrigerate for up to 2 days.*) Serve chicken over couscous; sprinkle with remaining cilantro.

Makes 8 servings. PER SERVING: about 525 cal, 36 g pro, 23 g total fat (5 g sat. fat), 47 g carb, 9 g fibre, 107 mg chol, 639 mg sodium, 580 mg potassium. % RDI: 6% calcium, 22% iron, 7% vit A, 42% vit C, 11% folate.

Preserved Lemons

Scrub 4 lemons (preferably organic) in warm soapy water. Rinse well; pat dry. Make eight 2-inch (5 cm) vertical cuts around lemons, cutting just to but not through membrane. In saucepan, cover and bring 4 cups water, lemons and ¼ cup coarse sea salt to boil. Reduce heat; simmer until skins soften, 15 minutes. Remove from heat; let cool. Place lemons in 4-cup (1 L) canning jar; add cooking liquid. Seal; shake gently. Let stand for 5 days at room temperature. Rinse before using. (*Make-ahead: After opening, refrigerate lemons for up to 1 week.*)

Makes 4 lemons.

2 tbsp **vegetable oil**

2 **whole chickens** (3 lb/1.35 kg each), cut in pieces, or 6 lb (2.7 kg) chicken drumsticks and thighs

1 **Spanish onion,** thinly sliced

3 cloves **garlic**

1 **tomato,** peeled, seeded and chopped

⅔ cup chopped **fresh cilantro** or parsley

1 tsp each **ground ginger** and **sweet paprika**

½ tsp **saffron**

¼ tsp each **ground cumin** and **pepper**

1 **cinnamon stick,** broken

2 cups **whole wheat couscous**

¾ cup **green** and/or **black olives,** pitted if desired

2 **preserved lemons,** rinsed and chopped

This is a slow cooker version of one of The Canadian Living Test Kitchen's favourite braised chicken dishes. Rice is nice with this stew, but couscous, which only needs to be mixed with hot water, is the simplest side dish you can serve.

Slow Cooker Lemon and Olive Chicken

In slow cooker, combine carrots, celery, fennel, onion, olives, garlic, bay leaves, oregano, salt and pepper.

Top vegetables with chicken. Add broth and ¾ cup water. Cover and cook on low until juices run clear when chicken is pierced, 5½ to 6 hours. Discard bay leaves.

Whisk flour with 1 cup of the cooking liquid until smooth; whisk in lemon juice. Whisk into slow cooker; cook, covered, on high until thickened, about 15 minutes.

GREMOLATA GARNISH: Mix parsley with lemon zest; serve sprinkled over chicken mixture.

Makes 6 to 8 servings. PER EACH OF 8 SERVINGS: about 176 cal, 18 g pro, 7 g total fat (2 g sat. fat), 10 g carb, 3 g fibre, 71 mg chol, 481 mg sodium, 455 mg potassium. % RDI: 5% calcium, 13% iron, 38% vit A, 23% vit C, 15% folate.

2 **carrots,** chopped

2 ribs **celery,** chopped

1 **fennel bulb,** cored and chopped

1 **onion,** chopped

16 large **stuffed green olives**

4 cloves **garlic,** crushed

2 **bay leaves**

½ tsp **dried oregano**

¼ tsp each **salt** and **pepper**

12 **boneless skinless chicken thighs**

¾ cup **sodium-reduced chicken broth**

¼ cup **all-purpose flour**

2 tbsp **lemon juice**

GREMOLATA GARNISH:
½ cup chopped **fresh parsley**

Grated zest of 1 **lemon**

This homey, old-fashioned fish stew has a light, lemony flavour and, because fish cooks quickly, takes much less time to make than a meat stew. If you have a favourite scone or biscuit recipe, serve it alongside to dip into the savoury sauce.

Seafood Simmer

3 **red-skinned potatoes**
(1½ lb/675 g)

1 large **carrot**

2 **leeks** (white and light green
parts only), chopped

1 rib **celery,** chopped

2 cups **vegetable broth**

½ cup **white wine**

1 tsp **salt**

¼ tsp **pepper**

1 lb (450 g) **cod fillets,** each cut
in 6 pieces

8 oz (225 g) **raw large shrimp,**
peeled and deveined

¼ cup **all-purpose flour**

2 tbsp **butter,** softened

1 tbsp chopped **fresh dill**

1 tbsp **lemon juice**

1 **green onion,** chopped

Scrub potatoes and peel carrot; cut into 1-inch (2.5 cm) chunks. In large saucepan, combine potatoes, carrot, leeks, celery, 2 cups water, broth, wine, salt and pepper; bring to boil. Reduce heat, cover and simmer just until potatoes are tender, about 15 minutes.

Add fish; simmer, covered, for 5 minutes. Add shrimp; simmer, covered, until shrimp are pink and fish flakes easily when tested, 3 to 5 minutes. With slotted spoon, transfer fish, shrimp and vegetables to large bowl, being careful not to break up fish.

In small bowl, mix flour with butter; whisk in ½ cup hot cooking liquid until blended. Whisk back into pan; cook, whisking, over medium-high heat until thick enough to coat back of spoon, about 5 minutes.

Stir in dill and lemon juice. Return fish mixture to pan; heat through, about 2 minutes. Sprinkle with green onion.

Makes 4 servings. PER SERVING: about 389 cal, 34 g pro, 8 g total fat (4 g sat. fat), 44 g carb, 5 g fibre, 129 mg chol, 1,109 mg sodium. % RDI: 7% calcium, 27% iron, 66% vit A, 40% vit C, 26% folate.

Fennel, tomatoes and olives add their sun-drenched Mediterranean flavours to a simple chickpea stew. If you prefer, you can also serve this dish with whole wheat pita instead of the couscous.

Mediterranean Stewed Chickpeas

2 tbsp **extra-virgin olive oil**

1 **onion,** chopped

1 **sweet green pepper,** chopped

2 cloves **garlic,** minced

½ tsp crushed **fennel seeds**

¼ tsp **pepper**

¼ tsp **hot pepper flakes**

1 can (28 oz/796 mL) **no-salt-added diced tomatoes**

1 can (19 oz/540 mL) **chickpeas,** drained and rinsed

½ cup sliced large **stuffed green olives**

½ cup chopped **fresh parsley**

¼ tsp **dried mint**

1 cup **whole wheat couscous**

In shallow Dutch oven, heat oil over medium heat; cook onion, green pepper, garlic, fennel seeds, pepper and hot pepper flakes, stirring occasionally, until tender, about 5 minutes.

Stir in tomatoes, chickpeas, olives, half of the parsley, and the dried mint; bring to boil. Reduce heat and simmer, stirring occasionally, until slightly thickened, about 15 minutes. Stir in remaining parsley; cook for 5 minutes.

Meanwhile, in bowl, stir couscous with 1½ cups boiling water; cover and let stand for 5 minutes. Fluff with fork. Serve with stew.

Makes 4 servings. PER SERVING: about 462 cal, 15 g pro, 12 g total fat (2 g sat. fat), 78 g carb, 14 g fibre, 0 mg chol, 617 mg sodium, 317 mg potassium. % RDI: 18% calcium, 52% iron, 18% vit A, 83% vit C, 38% folate.

When you're adding the thickener at the end of cooking, push the pork and sweet potatoes gently to one side of the slow cooker, then whisk the flour mixture into the liquid on the other side. This helps keep the tender sweet potatoes from falling apart.

Slow Cooker Barbecue Pork Stew

In slow cooker, combine pork, onions, garlic, bay leaves, chili powder, cumin, coriander, oregano, mustard, salt and pepper; top with sweet potatoes.

Whisk together strained tomatoes, broth, molasses and vinegar; pour over pork mixture. Cover and cook on low until pork is tender, 6 to 8 hours. Discard bay leaves.

Whisk flour with 1 cup of the cooking liquid until smooth; whisk into slow cooker. Add kale; cook, covered, on high until thickened and kale is wilted, about 30 minutes.

Makes 6 to 8 servings. PER EACH OF 8 SERVINGS: about 572 cal, 33 g pro, 33 g total fat (12 g sat. fat), 35 g carb, 4 g fibre, 119 mg chol, 386 mg sodium, 1,106 mg potassium. % RDI: 11% calcium, 33% iron, 206% vit A, 83% vit C, 16% folate.

3 lb (1.35 kg) **boneless pork shoulder blade roast,** cubed

2 **onions,** chopped

6 cloves **garlic,** minced

2 **bay leaves**

2 tsp **chili powder**

1 tsp each **ground cumin** and **coriander**

1 tsp **dried oregano**

½ tsp **dry mustard**

½ tsp each **salt** and **pepper**

2 lb (900 g) **sweet potatoes,** peeled, halved and cut in 1½-inch (4 cm) thick slices

1 cup **bottled strained tomatoes** (passata)

1 cup **sodium-reduced chicken broth**

3 tbsp **cooking molasses**

3 tbsp **cider vinegar**

3 tbsp **all-purpose flour**

4 cups packed chopped **kale leaves**

Serve this flavourful curry with warmed naan or Greek pita for a simple option. Or serve with rice if you feel like cooking a simple side dish. Yogurt makes a cool accompaniment.

Lamb Curry With Peas

In large skillet, heat oil over medium-high heat; cook lamb, breaking up with spoon, until no longer pink, about 3 minutes.

Add onions, garlic, ginger, coriander, cumin, cinnamon and cayenne pepper; cook, stirring occasionally, until onions are softened, 6 to 8 minutes. Add tomatoes; cook, stirring often, until almost dry, about 10 minutes.

Stir in peas; heat through. Remove from heat. Stir in 2 tbsp of the mint. Transfer to serving dish; sprinkle with remaining mint.

Makes 4 servings. PER SERVING: about 334 cal, 24 g pro, 18 g total fat (8 g sat. fat), 20 g carb, 5 g fibre, 74 mg chol, 363 mg sodium, 853 mg potassium. % RDI: 11% calcium, 33% iron, 11% vit A, 53% vit C, 30% folate.

1 tsp **canola oil**

1 lb (450 g) **ground lamb**

2 **onions,** finely chopped

2 cloves **garlic,** minced

1 tbsp grated **fresh ginger**

1 tsp each **ground coriander** and **cumin**

½ tsp **cinnamon**

¼ tsp **cayenne pepper**

1 can (28 oz/796 mL) **diced tomatoes**

1 cup **frozen peas**

3 tbsp chopped **fresh mint**

Chickpeas and earthy Swiss chard are a healthy, tasty combination. If you like a little heat, increase the number of hot peppers. Even if you're not usually a spice fan, try the peppers in this dish to balance the flavours of all the seasonings.

Chickpea and Swiss Chard Curry

2 tbsp **vegetable oil**

1 tsp **cumin seeds**

1 **onion,** finely chopped

2 **green hot peppers** (or 1 jalapeño pepper), seeded and chopped

2 tsp each finely minced **fresh ginger** and **garlic**

¾ tsp each **ground cumin** and **coriander**

½ tsp **garam masala** (optional)

2 tsp **tomato paste**

¼ tsp each **cayenne pepper** and **turmeric**

1 cup chopped **canned whole tomatoes**

½ tsp **salt**

1 can (19 oz/540 mL) **chickpeas,** drained and rinsed

4 cups chopped **Swiss chard leaves**

In saucepan, heat oil over medium heat; cook cumin seeds until beginning to pop, about 1 minute. Add onion and hot peppers; cook until onion is translucent, about 10 minutes.

Add ginger and garlic; cook for 1 minute. Add ground cumin and coriander; cook until fragrant, about 2 minutes. Add garam masala (if using); cook for 1 minute. Add tomato paste, cayenne pepper and turmeric; cook for 1 minute.

Add tomatoes and salt; cook, stirring, until softened. Stir in 1¼ cups water; bring to boil. Add chickpeas; reduce heat and simmer for 10 minutes. Stir in Swiss chard; simmer until tender, 3 to 4 minutes.

Makes 4 servings. PER SERVING: about 260 cal, 10 g pro, 9 g total fat (1 g sat. fat), 39 g carb, 10 g fibre, 0 mg chol, 946 mg sodium, 1,269 mg potassium. % RDI: 15% calcium, 46% iron, 52% vit A, 72% vit C, 40% folate.

Fish curries are a bit lighter and more refreshing than meat-based ones. This curry has the zing of fresh ginger and hot peppers to dress up the mild halibut and spinach. Serve with flatbread or rolls on busy nights, or make a pot of rice to serve alongside.

Halibut and Spinach Curry

Remove skin (if any) from halibut; cut fish into 1½-inch (4 cm) pieces. Set aside.

In large skillet, heat oil over medium heat; cook onion, garlic, curry paste, ginger, jalapeño (if using), coriander, salt and turmeric, stirring occasionally, until onion is softened, about 6 minutes.

Add spinach; cook, stirring, until wilted, about 2 minutes.

Stir in tomatoes and 1 cup water; bring to boil. Add fish; reduce heat and simmer, stirring occasionally, until fish flakes easily when tested, about 8 minutes. Stir in lemon juice.

Makes 4 servings. PER SERVING: about 310 cal, 35 g pro, 15 g total fat (1 g sat. fat), 9 g carb, 3 g fibre, 50 mg chol, 625 mg sodium. % RDI: 14% calcium, 26% iron, 52% vit A, 15% vit C, 38% folate.

1½ lb (675 g) **halibut** (or other firm-fleshed white fish)

2 tbsp **vegetable oil**

1 small **onion,** diced

2 cloves **garlic,** minced

2 tbsp **mild curry paste**

1 tbsp minced **fresh ginger**

Half **jalapeño pepper** (optional), minced

1 tsp **ground coriander**

½ tsp **salt**

¼ tsp **turmeric**

4 cups **fresh baby spinach** (about one 6-oz/170 g bag)

¾ cup **canned crushed tomatoes**

1 tbsp **lemon juice**

Ground beef is a budget-friendly ingredient, but sometimes you get tired of meat loaf and burgers. To the rescue: this gently spiced Indian-style curry. For dinner in a hurry, pair it with store-bought naan or another flatbread.

Ground Beef Curry

1 lb (450 g) **lean ground beef**

1 tbsp **vegetable oil**

1 **onion,** chopped

1 **jalapeño pepper** (optional), seeded and minced

¼ cup **mild Indian curry paste**

1 can (28 oz/796 mL) **diced tomatoes**

2 **potatoes,** diced

½ tsp **salt**

1 cup **frozen peas**

¼ cup chopped **fresh cilantro**

1 tbsp chopped **fresh mint** (or 2 tsp dried)

In nonstick skillet, sauté beef over medium-high heat, breaking up with spoon, until no longer pink, about 5 minutes. Using slotted spoon, transfer beef to bowl.

Drain fat from pan; add oil. Fry onion, and jalapeño (if using), until golden, about 4 minutes. Add curry paste; cook, stirring, until fragrant, about 1 minute.

Stir in beef, tomatoes, potatoes and salt; cover and simmer until potatoes are tender, about 15 minutes. Add peas, half of the cilantro and the mint; heat through. Sprinkle with remaining cilantro.

Makes 4 servings. PER SERVING: about 436 cal, 28 g pro, 23 g total fat (5 g sat. fat), 31 g carb, 5 g fibre, 60 mg chol, 1,104 mg sodium. % RDI: 8% calcium, 30% iron, 14% vit A, 62% vit C, 18% folate.

Hearty, warm and comforting, this stew turns ground beef into a feast. If you have any leftovers, the chili is delicious tucked into taco shells with lettuce, tomatoes and salsa for a supereasy dinner the next night.

Ground Beef Chili

In Dutch oven or large saucepan, heat oil over medium heat; cook onions and garlic, stirring occasionally, until golden, 8 to 10 minutes.

Add beef; cook, breaking up with spoon, until browned. Stir in chili powder, cumin, coriander, oregano, salt, pepper, and cayenne pepper (if using); cook for 1 minute.

Crush plum tomatoes with potato masher; add to pot along with strained tomatoes, ½ cup water and beans. Bring to boil; reduce heat, cover and simmer for 20 minutes. Uncover and cook for 10 minutes.

Makes 6 to 8 servings. PER EACH OF 8 SERVINGS: about 373 cal, 26 g pro, 21 g total fat (8 g sat. fat), 20 g carb, 6 g fibre, 68 mg chol, 696 mg sodium, 747 mg potassium. % RDI: 8% calcium, 34% iron, 10% vit A, 28% vit C, 18% folate.

1 tbsp **vegetable oil**

3 **onions,** chopped

4 cloves **garlic,** minced

2 lb (900 g) **medium ground beef** or lean ground beef

3 tbsp **chili powder**

1¼ tsp **ground cumin**

1 tsp **ground coriander**

1 tsp **dried oregano**

1 tsp **salt**

¼ tsp **pepper**

¼ tsp **cayenne pepper** (optional)

1 can (28 oz/796 mL) **plum tomatoes**

½ cup **bottled strained tomatoes** (passata)

1 can (19 oz/540 mL) **red kidney beans,** drained and rinsed

Black beans are packed with nutrients and fibre. They make a hearty addition to chili, especially when combined with sweet corn. Chili is always good with bread or tortilla chips for dipping, but it's excellent with corn bread or rice if you like a separate side.

Beef and Black Bean Chili

1 lb (450 g) **lean ground beef**

1 **onion,** diced

1 **sweet red pepper,** diced

1 **carrot,** diced

1 rib **celery,** diced

2 cloves **garlic,** minced

2 tbsp **chili powder**

1 tsp each **ground cumin** and **dried oregano**

½ tsp each **salt** and **pepper**

1 can (28 oz/796 mL) **diced tomatoes**

1 can (19 oz/540 mL) **black beans,** drained and rinsed

½ cup fresh or frozen **corn kernels**

2 tbsp **tomato paste**

2 tbsp chopped **fresh cilantro**

2 tbsp **lime juice**

½ cup shredded **Cheddar cheese**

In Dutch oven, sauté beef over medium-high heat, breaking up with spoon, until no longer pink, about 5 minutes.

Drain fat from pan; add onion, red pepper, carrot, celery, garlic, chili powder, cumin, oregano, salt and pepper. Fry over medium heat, stirring, until vegetables are softened, about 5 minutes.

Stir in tomatoes; bring to boil. Reduce heat and simmer until thick enough to mound on spoon, about 20 minutes.

Stir in beans, corn and tomato paste; simmer until bubbling, about 5 minutes. Sir in cilantro and lime juice.

Ladle into bowls; sprinkle with cheese.

Makes 4 to 6 servings. PER EACH OF 6 SERVINGS: about 320 cal, 24 g pro, 13 g total fat (6 g sat. fat), 28 g carb, 8 g fibre, 51 mg chol, 780 mg sodium. % RDI: 15% calcium, 33% iron, 58% vit A, 98% vit C, 30% folate.

Leftovers of this vegetarian chili make a great lunch for kids, especially when packed with a whole wheat tortilla, shredded cheese and lettuce (wrapped separately) to create a lunchtime burrito.

Black Bean Chili With Corn

1 tbsp **extra-virgin olive oil**

1 **onion,** chopped

2 cloves **garlic,** minced

½ cup chopped **celery**

½ tsp **ground cumin**

¼ tsp each **salt** and **pepper**

Pinch **cayenne pepper**

1 tbsp **tomato paste**

1 can (28 oz/796 mL) **diced tomatoes**

1 can (19 oz/540 mL) **black beans,** drained and rinsed

1½ cups fresh or frozen **corn kernels**

2 tbsp minced **fresh cilantro**

In saucepan, heat oil over medium heat; fry onion, garlic, celery, cumin, salt, pepper and cayenne, stirring often, until softened, about 5 minutes. Add tomato paste; cook, stirring, for 1 minute.

Add tomatoes and black beans; bring to boil. Reduce heat and simmer, stirring often, until thick enough to mound on spoon, about 30 minutes.

Stir in corn; cook until heated through, about 4 minutes. *(Make-ahead: Let cool for 30 minutes. Refrigerate, uncovered, in airtight container until cold. Cover and refrigerate for up to 2 days.)*

Stir in cilantro before serving.

Makes 4 servings. PER SERVING: about 239 cal, 11 g pro, 5 g total fat (1 g sat. fat), 43 g carb, 12 g fibre, 0 mg chol, 822 mg sodium. % RDI: 10% calcium, 26% iron, 14% vit A, 63% vit C, 45% folate.

So many chilis are based on beef and tomatoes, but this one avoids both and gets its light, fresh flavour from the combination of chicken, spices, fresh herbs and lime juice. Serve with corn tortillas or tortilla chips for a fun dinner.

Slow Cooker Chicken Chili

In large skillet, heat half of the oil over medium-high heat; brown chicken all over. Transfer to slow cooker.

Drain any fat from pan; add remaining oil. Fry onion, garlic, coriander, cumin, chili powder, salt and pepper, stirring occasionally, until softened, about 6 minutes. Scrape into slow cooker. Stir in beans and green chilies; cover and cook on low for 5 hours.

Remove chicken from sauce; cube and set aside.

Whisk flour with 3 tbsp water; whisk into slow cooker. Cover and cook on high until thickened, about 15 minutes.

Stir in chicken, cilantro and lime juice; heat through.

Makes 4 servings. PER SERVING: about 352 cal, 30 g pro, 14 g total fat (2 g sat. fat), 28 g carb, 9 g fibre, 95 mg chol, 708 mg sodium. % RDI: 8% calcium, 29% iron, 5% vit A, 32% vit C, 35% folate.

2 tbsp **vegetable oil**

8 **boneless skinless chicken thighs**

1 **onion,** chopped

3 cloves **garlic,** minced

2 tsp **ground coriander**

1½ tsp **ground cumin**

1 tsp **chipotle chili powder**

¼ tsp each **salt** and **pepper**

1 can (19 oz/540 mL) **white kidney beans,** drained and rinsed

2 cans (each 4½ oz/127 mL) **chopped green chilies**

2 tbsp **all-purpose flour**

⅓ cup chopped **fresh cilantro**

2 tbsp **lime juice**

Salads

**Roasted Salmon,
Bacon and Spinach Salad,
page 118**

Fresh baby spinach is a nutrient-packed partner to buttery slices of grilled steak and golden mushrooms. A strip loin is flavourful, but you could use any other beef grilling steak for this dish.

Spinach, Steak and Mushroom Salad

1 lb (450 g) **strip loin grilling steak,** 1 inch (2.5 cm) thick

½ tsp each **salt** and **pepper**

2 tbsp **vegetable oil**

2 cups **mushrooms,** halved

1 clove **garlic,** minced

1 tsp **dried thyme**

1 bag (6 oz/170 g) **fresh baby spinach**

½ cup thinly sliced **red onion**

CREAMY HORSERADISH DRESSING:
¼ cup **light mayonnaise**

2 tbsp **milk**

2 tbsp **prepared horseradish**

¼ tsp each **salt** and **pepper**

CREAMY HORSERADISH DRESSING: Whisk together mayonnaise, milk, horseradish, salt and pepper. Set aside.

Season steak with half each of the salt and pepper. Place on greased grill or in grill pan over medium-high heat; close lid and grill, turning once, until medium-rare, about 8 minutes. Transfer to cutting board and tent with foil; let stand for 10 minutes. Thinly slice across the grain.

Meanwhile, in large skillet, heat oil over medium-high heat; sauté mushrooms, garlic, thyme and remaining salt and pepper until no liquid remains and mushrooms are golden, about 5 minutes.

Divide spinach among 4 plates. Divide mushrooms, steak and onion over top; drizzle with dressing.

Makes 4 servings. PER SERVING: about 306 cal, 26 g pro, 20 g total fat (4 g sat. fat), 7 g carb, 2 g fibre, 55 mg chol, 623 mg sodium. % RDI: 7% calcium, 29% iron, 41% vit A, 23% vit C, 46% folate.

Flank steak absorbs intense flavours from this tenderizing marinade. But even with marinating, flank steak can get tough if you cook it to more than medium-rare. When cutting hot peppers, wear rubber gloves to keep the irritating chili oil off your skin.

Thai Beef Noodle Salad

1 piece (8 inches/20 cm) **English cucumber**

1 large **carrot**

6 oz (170 g) **wide rice sticks**

Quarter **red onion,** thinly sliced

3 tbsp each chopped **fresh cilantro** and **mint**

3 tbsp **Thai basil leaves** or other basil leaves

¼ cup chopped **unsalted peanuts**

MARINATED STEAK:

2 tbsp **soy sauce**

1 tbsp each **sesame oil** and **vegetable oil**

2 cloves **garlic,** minced

2 tbsp grated **fresh ginger**

1 tbsp **granulated sugar**

1 **flank marinating steak** (about 1 lb/450 g)

DRESSING:

½ cup **hot water**

¼ cup **granulated sugar**

2 tbsp **lime juice**

2 tbsp **fish sauce**

2 **Thai bird's-eye peppers** or serrano peppers, seeded and thinly sliced

MARINATED STEAK: In glass or ceramic dish large enough to hold steak, combine soy sauce, sesame oil, vegetable oil, garlic, ginger and sugar; add steak, turning to coat. Cover and refrigerate for 4 hours, turning occasionally. *(Make-ahead: Refrigerate for up to 12 hours.)*

DRESSING: In jar with tight-fitting lid, shake water with sugar until dissolved. Add lime juice, fish sauce and hot peppers; shake to combine. *(Make-ahead: Refrigerate for up to 5 days.)*

Using vegetable peeler, slice cucumber lengthwise into thin strips, slicing around and discarding centre seeds. Slice carrot lengthwise into thin strips; set aside.

In large pot of boiling salted water, cook rice sticks until tender, 6 to 7 minutes. Drain and chill under cold water; drain and transfer to large bowl. Toss with dressing. Set aside.

Discarding marinade, place steak on greased grill over medium-high heat; close lid and grill, turning once, until desired doneness, about 8 minutes for medium-rare. Transfer to cutting board and tent with foil; let stand for 5 minutes. Thinly slice across the grain.

Add cucumber, carrot, onion, cilantro, mint and basil to noodle mixture; toss to coat. Divide among bowls or plates; top with steak and sprinkle with peanuts.

Makes 4 to 6 servings. PER EACH OF 6 SERVINGS: about 363 cal, 21 g pro, 13 g total fat (3 g sat. fat), 41 g carb, 3 g fibre, 31 mg chol, 873 mg sodium. % RDI: 4% calcium, 15% iron, 26% vit A, 20% vit C, 14% folate.

This summery Middle Eastern–inspired grilled salad gets delicious nuttiness from tahini and pistachios. Experiment with different types of greens, depending on what's in season at your local farmer's market.

Dilled Chicken Salad With Tahini Dressing

In glass or ceramic dish, stir together dill, oil, shallot, lemon zest, salt and pepper. Add chicken, turning to coat. Cover and refrigerate for 4 hours, turning occasionally. *(Make-ahead: Refrigerate for up to 12 hours.)*

DRESSING: Whisk together yogurt, tahini, lemon juice, water, cumin, salt and pepper until smooth. *(Make-ahead: Cover and refrigerate for up to 2 days.)*

Discarding marinade, place chicken on greased grill over medium-high heat. Close lid and grill, turning once, until no longer pink inside, about 10 minutes. Transfer to cutting board and tent with foil; let stand for 5 minutes. Thinly slice chicken crosswise.

SALAD: Meanwhile, in large bowl, toss together endive, watercress, radicchio, celery, green onion, tomatoes, half of the pistachios, and the mint; toss with all but 2 tbsp of the dressing.

Divide salad among plates; top with chicken. Drizzle with remaining dressing; sprinkle with remaining pistachios.

Makes 4 to 6 servings. PER EACH OF 6 SERVINGS: about 225 cal, 24 g pro, 12 g total fat (2 g sat. fat), 7 g carb, 3 g fibre, 54 mg chol, 270 mg sodium. % RDI: 10% calcium, 14% iron, 13% vit A, 30% vit C, 19% folate.

¼ cup chopped **fresh dill**

2 tbsp **extra-virgin olive oil**

1 **shallot** (or half small onion), minced

1 tbsp grated **lemon zest**

¼ tsp each **salt** and **pepper**

4 **boneless skinless chicken breasts**

DRESSING:

¼ cup **Balkan-style plain yogurt**

¼ cup **tahini**

3 tbsp **lemon juice**

2 tbsp **warm water**

½ tsp **ground cumin**

¼ tsp each **salt** and **pepper**

SALAD:

2 heads **Belgian endive,** chopped

1 bunch **watercress** (tough stems removed), coarsely chopped

Half head **radicchio,** chopped

1 each rib **celery** and **green onion,** thinly sliced

1 cup halved **grape tomatoes** or cherry tomatoes

¼ cup hulled **pistachios** or slivered almonds

2 tbsp chopped **fresh mint** or parsley

This grilled salad is a great excuse to eat – and cook – alfresco. The smoked paprika adds to the smoky grilled flavour, but you can use regular sweet or hot paprika in its place if you prefer.

Grilled Chicken and Charred Corn Salad

Sprinkle chicken with half each of the salt and pepper. Brush corn and asparagus with 1 tbsp of the oil.

Place chicken and corn on greased grill over medium-high heat; close lid and grill, turning chicken once and corn as needed, until chicken is no longer pink inside and corn is tender and slightly charred, about 10 minutes for chicken, 15 minutes for corn. Transfer to plate; keep warm.

Add asparagus to grill; close lid and grill, turning often, until tender-crisp, 6 to 8 minutes. Add to plate.

Diagonally slice chicken. Cut corn kernels from cobs. Cut asparagus into 1-inch (2.5 cm) pieces. Whisk together vinegar, mustard, garlic, paprika and remaining oil, salt and pepper.

In large bowl, toss together corn, asparagus, lettuce, tomatoes, green onion and dressing; top with chicken.

Makes 4 servings. PER SERVING: about 364 cal, 32 g pro, 17 g total fat (3 g sat. fat), 26 g carb, 7 g fibre, 67 mg chol, 384 mg sodium, 1,113 mg potassium. % RDI: 6% calcium, 21% iron, 101% vit A, 75% vit C, 133% folate.

2 **boneless skinless chicken breasts**

½ tsp each **salt** and **pepper**

2 **corn cobs,** husked

1 bunch **asparagus,** trimmed

¼ cup **olive oil**

4 tsp **white wine vinegar**

¼ tsp **Dijon mustard**

1 clove **garlic,** minced

¼ tsp **smoked paprika**

8 cups torn **romaine lettuce**

2 large **tomatoes,** chopped

1 **green onion,** sliced

Barley is an interesting and nutritious alternative to other grains in salads. Here, it provides a chewy backdrop for simple grilled chicken and fresh vegetables. The vinaigrette doubles as the dressing and marinade, making the prep very simple.

Grilled Chicken Barley Salad

2 **boneless skinless chicken breasts**

⅔ cup **pearl barley**

1½ cups chopped trimmed **green beans**

1 cup **grape tomatoes,** halved

¼ cup finely minced **red onion**

2 tbsp chopped **fresh basil**

VINAIGRETTE:
¼ cup **extra-virgin olive oil**

2 tbsp **wine vinegar**

1 tbsp **Dijon mustard**

½ tsp **dried Italian herb seasoning**

¼ tsp each **salt** and **pepper**

VINAIGRETTE: In large bowl, whisk together oil, vinegar, mustard, Italian herb seasoning, salt and pepper. Transfer 2 tbsp to large shallow dish; add chicken, turning to coat. Cover and refrigerate for 10 minutes. *(Make-ahead: Refrigerate for up to 8 hours.)*

Meanwhile, in saucepan of boiling water, cover and cook barley for 10 minutes. Add green beans; cook until beans are tender-crisp and barley is tender, about 10 minutes. Drain and toss with remaining vinaigrette.

Place chicken on greased grill over medium-high heat; close lid and cook, turning once, until no longer pink inside, about 10 minutes. Cut into cubes.

Add chicken to barley mixture. Add tomatoes, onion and basil; toss to combine.

Makes 4 servings. PER SERVING: about 340 cal, 19 g pro, 15 g total fat (2 g sat. fat), 33 g carb, 4 g fibre, 39 mg chol, 236 mg sodium. % RDI: 4% calcium, 1% iron, 7% vit A, 13% vit C, 16% folate.

The combination of savoury sausage, sweet apple, crisp vegetables and tangy vinaigrette makes for a refreshing dinner. Grill pita wedges alongside the sausages and serve with the salad.

Turkey Sausage and Apple Salad

Broil or grill sausages over medium-high heat, turning occasionally, until browned and no longer pink in centre, 18 to 20 minutes. Slice thickly.

Meanwhile, in large bowl, whisk together oil, vinegar, mustard, honey, salt, pepper and thyme.

Add escarole, endive, carrot, apple, cucumber, walnuts and onion to bowl. Add sausage and toss to coat.

Makes 4 to 6 servings. PER EACH OF 6 SERVINGS: about 278 cal, 16 g pro, 20 g total fat (3 g sat. fat), 10 g carb, 3 g fibre, 55 mg chol, 524 mg sodium, 521 mg potassium. % RDI: 6% calcium, 14% iron, 28% vit A, 12% vit C, 44% folate.

1 lb (450 g) **mild Italian turkey sausages**

¼ cup **extra-virgin olive oil**

2 tbsp **cider vinegar**

1 tsp **Dijon mustard**

1 tsp **liquid honey**

¼ tsp each **salt** and **pepper**

¼ tsp **dried thyme**

6 cups chopped loosely packed **escarole**

2 cups chopped loosely packed **curly endive**

1 **carrot**, grated

1 **Gala apple**, thinly sliced

½ cup sliced **English cucumber**

⅓ cup **walnuts**, toasted and chopped

¼ cup sliced **red onion**

Mango salad is a Thai restaurant staple. Look for mangoes that just yield to the pressure of your fingers – this means they are ripe but not overripe.

Mango Chicken Salad With Thai-Style Vinaigrette

6 cups loosely packed **mixed salad greens**

3 cups shredded **cooked chicken**

1 firm ripe **mango,** peeled, pitted and sliced

1 cup **cherry tomatoes** or grape tomatoes, halved

¼ cup chopped **fresh cilantro**

⅓ cup **unsalted dry-roasted peanuts,** coarsely chopped

THAI-STYLE VINAIGRETTE:
3 tbsp **vegetable oil**

2 tbsp **lime juice**

2 tsp packed **brown sugar**

2 tsp **fish sauce**

½ tsp **Asian chili sauce** (such as sriracha)

THAI-STYLE VINAIGRETTE: Whisk together oil, lime juice, brown sugar, fish sauce and chili sauce.

In large bowl, toss together salad greens, chicken, mango, tomatoes and cilantro. Add vinaigrette; toss gently to coat. Sprinkle with peanuts.

Makes 4 servings. PER SERVING: about 431 cal, 36 g pro, 25 g total fat (4 g sat. fat), 18 g carb, 4 g fibre, 95 mg chol, 355 mg sodium, 777 mg potassium. % RDI: 8% calcium, 17% iron, 27% vit A, 52% vit C, 50% folate.

Having a selection of ingredients on hand can bring flavours from around the world to your table. For example, this salad features a Moroccan-inspired, pantry-friendly combination of dried fruit, nuts, couscous and spices, plus chicken from the freezer.

Apricot Almond Couscous With Chicken

In bowl, combine 2 tbsp of the oil, cumin, coriander, turmeric, ¼ tsp of the salt, the cinnamon and pepper; set aside 1 tbsp for couscous. Add chicken to remainder; toss to coat.

Grill chicken, covered, on greased grill over medium-high heat, turning once, until no longer pink inside, about 12 minutes. *(Make-ahead: Cover and refrigerate for up to 2 days.)*

Meanwhile, in large bowl, combine couscous and apricots; add 1½ cups boiling water. Let stand for 5 minutes; fluff with fork.

Whisk together orange zest and juice, remaining oil and reserved spice mixture. Using fork, mix into couscous along with almonds, parsley and remaining salt. *(Make-ahead: Cover and refrigerate for up to 2 days.)*

Divide salad among plates. Cut chicken crosswise into thick slices; place on salad. Serve with lemon and orange wedges.

Makes 4 servings. PER SERVING: about 669 cal, 44 g pro, 22 g total fat (2 g sat. fat), 73 g carb, 6 g fibre, 84 mg chol, 378 mg sodium. % RDI: 8% calcium, 29% iron, 18% vit A, 37% vit C, 27% folate.

¼ cup **vegetable oil**

2 tsp **ground cumin**

1 tsp **ground coriander**

½ tsp **turmeric**

½ tsp **salt**

¼ tsp each **cinnamon** and **pepper**

4 **boneless skinless chicken breasts**

1½ cups **couscous**

⅔ cup **dried apricots,** cut in strips

1 tsp grated **orange zest**

¼ cup **orange juice**

⅓ cup **slivered almonds,** toasted

¼ cup chopped **fresh parsley**

4 each **lemon** and **orange wedges**

When cutting the feta, don't worry if a few pieces break. If you prefer simple crumbled feta on top, omit the breading and frying and reduce the amount of cheese to ½ cup.

Spinach Salad With Crispy Feta and Frizzled Prosciutto

3 oz (85 g) thinly sliced **prosciutto** (about 5 slices) or ham

2 tbsp **extra-virgin olive oil**

2 tbsp **all-purpose flour**

¼ tsp each **salt** and **pepper**

1 **egg**

⅓ cup **dry bread crumbs**

1 pkg (200 g) **feta cheese**

1 bag (6 oz/170 g) **fresh baby spinach**

VINAIGRETTE:

⅓ cup **extra-virgin olive oil**

2 tbsp **red wine vinegar**

1 tbsp **Dijon mustard**

¼ tsp each **salt** and **pepper**

Cut prosciutto into ¼-inch (5 mm) wide strips. In nonstick skillet, heat 1 tbsp of the oil over medium-high heat; stir-fry prosciutto until crisp, about 7 minutes. Drain on paper towel–lined plate.

In shallow bowl, mix flour, salt and pepper. In another shallow bowl, whisk egg. Place bread crumbs in third shallow bowl.

Pat feta dry. Cut lengthwise into ¼-inch (5 mm) thick slices; press into flour mixture, turning to coat. Dip into egg, then into bread crumbs, turning to coat. In nonstick skillet, heat remaining oil over medium-high heat; fry feta, turning once, until golden, 4 minutes.

VINAIGRETTE: Meanwhile, in large bowl, whisk together oil, vinegar, mustard, salt and pepper; add spinach and toss to coat. Divide among plates. Top each salad with 2 feta slices; sprinkle with prosciutto.

Makes 4 servings. PER SERVING: about 471 cal, 16 g pro, 40 g total fat (12 g sat. fat), 14 g carb, 1 g fibre, 104 mg chol, 1,312 mg sodium. % RDI: 30% calcium, 20% iron, 37% vit A, 20% vit C, 51% folate.

If you want to save a little time, you can use 2 cans (each 19 oz/540 mL) lentils, drained and rinsed, instead of dried lentils. Simply simmer with the carrots, without cooking them first.

Lentil Salad With Asiago Cheese

In saucepan, bring lentils and 3 cups water to boil; reduce heat, cover and simmer for 15 minutes. Add carrot and simmer until lentils are tender, 5 to 10 minutes. Drain and let cool.

DRESSING: Meanwhile, in large bowl, whisk together oil, vinegar, mustard, oregano, salt and pepper.

Add lentil mixture, green onions, red pepper, celery, cheese and parsley; toss to combine. (*Make-ahead: Cover and refrigerate for up to 1 day.*)

Makes 4 servings. PER SERVING: about 441 cal, 23 g pro, 19 g total fat (5 g sat. fat), 49 g carb, 10 g fibre, 12 mg chol, 452 mg sodium. % RDI: 16% calcium, 55% iron, 78% vit A, 108% vit C, 181% folate.

1½ cups **dried green lentils** or dried brown lentils, rinsed

1 large **carrot,** diced

2 **green onions,** sliced

1 **sweet red pepper,** chopped

1 rib **celery,** diced

½ cup shredded **Asiago cheese**

2 tbsp chopped **fresh parsley**

DRESSING:

¼ cup **extra-virgin olive oil**

¼ cup **red wine vinegar**

1 tsp **Dijon mustard**

½ tsp **dried oregano**

½ tsp **salt**

¼ tsp **pepper**

Taco salad lovers, this is your dish. Ground beef, turkey or chicken also work in this salad, so substitute them if you have them on hand. If you like spicy food, serve with your favourite hot sauce or pickled jalapeño slices.

Pork Tostada Salad

2 **green onions**

1 lb (450 g) **lean ground pork**

2 cloves **garlic,** minced

1 tbsp **chili powder**

1 tbsp **wine vinegar**

½ tsp **salt**

½ tsp **ground coriander**

Pinch **granulated sugar**

8 **corn tostadas**

2 cups shredded **lettuce**

1 large **tomato,** chopped

½ cup **salsa**

½ cup shredded **Cheddar cheese**

¼ cup **light sour cream**

Thinly slice white and green parts of onions; set aside separately.

In large skillet, sauté pork over medium-high heat, breaking up with spoon, until no longer pink, about 5 minutes.

Drain fat from pan; add garlic, chili powder, vinegar, salt, coriander, sugar and white parts of onions. Fry over medium heat, stirring often, for 5 minutes.

Place 1 tostada on each of 4 plates. Top with about half each of the lettuce, tomato, pork mixture, salsa and cheese. Repeat layers. Top with sour cream; sprinkle with green parts of onions.

Makes 4 servings. PER SERVING: about 422 cal, 28 g pro, 26 g total fat (10 g sat. fat), 21 g carb, 4 g fibre, 93 mg chol, 748 mg sodium. % RDI: 18% calcium, 16% iron, 16% vit A, 18% vit C, 17% folate.

Tip: Tostadas are flat tacos that do not require heating. Look for Charras brand corn tostadas (plain or flavoured) in the Mexican section of grocery stores. If you can't find them, use tortilla chips instead.

It will take about 4 slices (4 oz/115 g) raw bacon to make ½ cup cooked crumbled bacon. While you're at it, why not make extra to keep on hand in the fridge or freezer? It's a delightfully smoky addition to omelettes, pasta dishes and more.

Roasted Salmon, Bacon and Spinach Salad

4 **skin-on salmon fillets** (about 1½ lb/675 g)

½ tsp **pepper**

½ cup cooked crumbled **bacon**

2 tbsp **extra-virgin olive oil**

1 tbsp **wine vinegar**

2 tsp **grainy mustard**

4 cups **fresh baby spinach**

1 cup halved **cherry tomatoes**

Line rimmed baking sheet with parchment paper or grease. Arrange salmon, skin side down and 2 inches (5 cm) apart, on pan. Sprinkle with half of the pepper, then the bacon. Roast in 400°F (200°C) oven until fish flakes easily when tested, about 10 minutes.

Meanwhile, in large bowl, whisk together oil, vinegar, mustard and remaining pepper. Add spinach and tomatoes; toss to coat. Spoon onto plates; top with salmon.

Makes 4 servings. PER SERVING: about 381 cal, 31 g pro, 27 g total fat (6 g sat. fat), 4 g carb, 2 g fibre, 82 mg chol, 305 mg sodium. % RDI: 9% calcium, 20% iron, 48% vit A, 25% vit C, 56% folate.

Dried lentils are an excellent pantry staple. Unlike dried beans, they don't require long soaking, and it takes just half an hour to simmer them to tenderness. Their slightly peppery flavour is a delicious complement to broiled salmon and fresh green beans.

Salmon With Lentil and Green Bean Salad

In saucepan, heat half of the oil over medium heat; cook carrots, onion, celery, jalapeño pepper and garlic, stirring, until softened, about 4 minutes.

Stir in coriander, cumin, ¾ tsp of the salt and ½ tsp of the pepper; cook, stirring, for 2 minutes.

Add lentils and 3 cups water; bring to boil. Reduce heat and simmer, adding more water if mixture dries out, until lentils are tender, 25 to 30 minutes.

Stir in green beans and tomato; cover and cook until beans are tender, about 5 minutes. Let cool for 15 minutes.

Meanwhile, place salmon on greased baking sheet; brush with remaining oil. Sprinkle with remaining salt and pepper. Broil until fish flakes easily when tested, 4 to 6 minutes.

VINAIGRETTE: Whisk together oil, lemon juice, salt and pepper.

To serve, divide lentil mixture among 4 plates. Break salmon into chunks and scatter over top; drizzle with vinaigrette.

Makes 4 servings. PER SERVING: about 441 cal, 22 g pro, 22 g total fat (3 g sat. fat), 42 g carb, 10 g fibre, 21 mg chol, 633 mg sodium, 992 mg potassium. % RDI: 9% calcium, 46% iron, 71% vit A, 32% vit C, 136% folate.

2 tbsp **olive oil**

2 **carrots,** diced

1 **onion,** diced

1 rib **celery,** diced

1 **jalapeño pepper,** seeded and finely chopped

1 clove **garlic,** minced

1 tbsp **ground coriander**

1½ tsp **ground cumin**

1 tsp **salt**

¾ tsp **pepper**

1 cup **dried green lentils**

2½ cups **green beans,** trimmed and quartered

½ cup chopped **tomato**

2 **salmon fillets** (each 3 oz/85 g)

VINAIGRETTE:

3 tbsp **extra-virgin olive oil**

2 tbsp **lemon juice**

Pinch each **salt** and **pepper**

Shrimp and arugula are a tasty duo. And with a superfast cooking time –
only 8 minutes! – this recipe can be a go-to dish on busy weeknights. Keep a
bag of frozen zipperback shrimp in the freezer to defrost for this recipe.

Arugula Shrimp Salad

ORANGE VINAIGRETTE: Grate enough orange zest to make
1 tsp. Working over large bowl, cut off remaining zest and outer
membranes of oranges. Cut between membranes and pulp to
release fruit into bowl; squeeze membranes to extract juice. Transfer
2 tbsp juice to small bowl; whisk in orange zest, oil, vinegar, salt
and pepper. Set orange segments and vinaigrette aside separately.

Peel and devein shrimp. In large skillet, heat oil over medium-high
heat; sauté shrimp, garlic and hot pepper flakes until shrimp are
pink, about 5 minutes. Add 2 tbsp of the vinaigrette; cook, stirring,
until no liquid remains, about 3 minutes. Stir in cilantro.

Add arugula, croutons, onion and remaining vinaigrette to oranges;
toss to coat. Divide among 4 plates. Top with shrimp and olives.

Makes 4 servings. PER SERVING: about 347 cal, 21 g pro, 22 g total fat
(3 g sat. fat), 18 g carb, 3 g fibre, 129 mg chol, 624 mg sodium. % RDI:
16% calcium, 26% iron, 20% vit A, 77% vit C, 41% folate.

1 lb (450 g) **raw medium shrimp**

1 tbsp **extra-virgin olive oil**

1 clove **garlic,** minced

¼ tsp **hot pepper flakes**

3 tbsp minced **fresh cilantro**
  or parsley

4 cups **arugula**

1 cup **croutons**

¼ cup thinly sliced **sweet onion**

½ cup **green olives,** pitted
  and halved

ORANGE VINAIGRETTE:
2 **oranges**

¼ cup **extra-virgin olive oil**

2 tbsp **sherry vinegar**

¼ tsp each **salt** and **pepper**

The same vinaigrette flavours this tender grilled fish and salad, carrying a summery taste throughout the meal. The vegetables vary in size, so skewering them separately by type ensures that they all cook through in the same amount of time.

Grilled Whitefish and Ratatouille Salad

1 small **eggplant,** peeled

1 **zucchini**

Half each **sweet red** and **green pepper**

1 small **red onion**

1½ cups **cherry tomatoes**

⅓ cup **extra-virgin olive oil**

¼ cup chopped **fresh oregano**

3 tbsp **wine vinegar**

2 tsp **Dijon mustard**

2 cloves **garlic,** minced

1 tsp each **salt** and **pepper**

2 **skin-on whitefish fillets,** about 1½ lb (675 g)

Cut eggplant, zucchini, red and green peppers and red onion into 1-inch (2.5 cm) chunks; place in large bowl along with cherry tomatoes. Drizzle with 2 tbsp of the oil; toss to coat. Thread onto 12 long skewers, grouping same vegetables together.

Place skewers on greased grill over medium-high heat; close lid and grill, turning 3 times, until browned and tender, about 12 minutes. Remove vegetables from skewers and return to bowl; set salad aside.

Meanwhile, whisk together remaining oil, oregano, vinegar, mustard, garlic and half each of the salt and pepper; pour ¼ cup over vegetables. Toss to coat; set aside.

Sprinkle remaining salt and pepper over fish; brush both sides with remaining dressing. Place, skin side down, on greased grill over medium-high heat; close lid and grill until fish flakes easily when tested, 8 to 10 minutes. Cut into serving-size pieces. Serve with salad.

Makes 4 to 6 servings. PER EACH OF 6 SERVINGS: about 296 cal, 21 g pro, 18 g total fat (3 g sat. fat), 12 g carb, 3 g fibre, 62 mg chol, 486 mg sodium. % RDI: 5% calcium, 10% iron, 12% vit A, 53% vit C, 17% folate.

Mixed salad greens and a few ingredients from the deli make fast work of dinner. Substitute whatever deli meat or cheese you have in your fridge for the turkey and Havarti.

Chef's Dinner Salad With French-Style Dressing

FRENCH-STYLE DRESSING: In small bowl, whisk together ketchup, vinegar, paprika, mustard, pepper and salt. Drizzle in oil, whisking until emulsified.

In large bowl, toss together salad greens, celery, carrot and dressing. Arrange turkey, cheese and tomatoes on top.

Makes 4 servings. PER SERVING: about 339 cal, 14 g pro, 27 g total fat (10 g sat. fat), 10 g carb, 2 g fibre, 61 mg chol, 884 mg sodium, 490 mg potassium. % RDI: 24% calcium, 13% iron, 44% vit A, 28% vit C, 23% folate.

1 bag (5 oz/140 g) **mixed salad greens** (about 6 cups)

2 ribs **celery,** thinly sliced

1 **carrot,** shredded

6 oz (170 g) **smoked turkey,** cut in sticks or strips

1 cup cubed **garden vegetable Havarti cheese** or dill Havarti

1 cup halved **grape tomatoes**

FRENCH-STYLE DRESSING:

2 tbsp **ketchup**

2 tbsp **red wine vinegar**

½ tsp **sweet paprika**

¼ tsp **dry mustard**

¼ tsp **pepper**

Pinch **salt**

¼ cup **olive oil**

This classic diner-style salad is right at home in your own kitchen. You'll never miss the meat, thanks to the creamy avocado and protein-packed chickpeas. Experiment with different greens, sprouts and vegetables as the base for the delicious dressing.

Vegetarian Chef's Salad

6 cups torn **iceberg lettuce** (about half head)

2 cups torn **radicchio** (about half head)

½ cup **alfalfa sprouts** (about half 35 g pkg)

4 **radishes,** thinly sliced

¾ cup sliced **cucumber**

⅓ cup thinly sliced **sweet onion**

⅓ cup rinsed drained canned **chickpeas**

3 **hard-cooked eggs,** quartered

1 large **tomato,** cut in 12 wedges

Half **avocado,** pitted, peeled and sliced

2 oz (55 g) each **Swiss** and **Cheddar cheese,** cut in sticks

DRESSING:

¼ cup **light mayonnaise**

1 tbsp minced **dill pickle**

1 tbsp **extra-virgin olive oil**

2 tsp **chili sauce**

1½ tsp **lemon juice**

½ tsp **capers,** drained and minced

½ tsp **Dijon mustard**

Pinch each **salt** and **pepper**

DRESSING: Stir together mayonnaise, dill pickle, oil, chili sauce, lemon juice, capers, mustard, salt and pepper.

In large bowl, toss together lettuce, radicchio, sprouts, radishes, cucumber, onion and half of the dressing; arrange on 4 large plates or in bowls.

Top with chickpeas, eggs, tomato, avocado, and Swiss and Cheddar cheeses; spoon remaining dressing over top.

Makes 4 servings. PER SERVING: about 349 cal, 16 g pro, 25 g total fat (9 g sat. fat), 17 g carb, 5 g fibre, 173 mg chol, 430 mg sodium. % RDI: 25% calcium, 14% iron, 20% vit A, 32% vit C, 60% folate.

At a glance, this dish may look like an everything-but-the-kitchen-sink salad, but its autumn-themed ingredients meld beautifully. Soaking the shallots in vinegar pickles them slightly and adds a tang to the dressing.

Harvest Salad

On baking sheet, bake bread cubes in 350°F (180°C) oven until crisp, about 10 minutes. Transfer to large bowl.

DRESSING: Meanwhile, in small skillet, toast caraway seeds over medium-low heat until fragrant, about 2 minutes; let cool slightly. With mortar and pestle or bottom of heavy pot, crush seeds. In small bowl, combine shallots, vinegar and salt; let stand for 5 minutes. Stir in mustard, garlic, pepper and caraway seeds; whisk in oil.

Add mâche, endive, blue cheese, eggs, apple and walnuts to croutons. Pour dressing over top; toss to coat.

Makes 8 servings. PER SERVING: about 246 cal, 8 g pro, 19 g total fat (5 g sat. fat), 13 g carb, 3 g fibre, 57 mg chol, 399 mg sodium, 268 mg potassium. % RDI: 11% calcium, 10% iron, 16% vit A, 13% vit C, 17% folate.

3 cups cubed **pumpernickel bread** or rye bread

1 pkg (4 oz/115 g) **mâche** (lamb's lettuce) or mixed baby greens

3 heads **Belgian endive,** separated into leaves

4 oz (115 g) **blue cheese,** crumbled

2 **hard-cooked eggs,** chopped

1 **apple,** cut in chunks

½ cup **walnut halves**

DRESSING:

2 tsp **caraway seeds**

⅓ cup finely chopped **shallots** or onion

3 tbsp **white wine vinegar**

¼ tsp **salt**

1 tbsp **Dijon mustard**

1 clove **garlic,** minced

¼ tsp **white pepper**

⅓ cup **extra-virgin olive oil**

The original recipe for this salad contained a variety of exotic meats as well as potatoes and vegetables in a mayonnaise-based sauce. Today, there are as many varieties of Russian salad as there are countries that enjoy it.

Russian Salad

4 **large beets** (optional)

3 **potatoes,** peeled

2 **white turnips,** peeled

3 **carrots**

2 cups bite-size **cauliflower florets**

1 **cucumber**

6 oz (170 g) sliced **ham** (optional)

1 head **Bibb lettuce** or romaine lettuce

4 **hard-cooked eggs,** quartered

2 tbsp chopped **fresh dill**

DRESSING:

¾ cup **light mayonnaise**

¾ cup **light sour cream**

⅓ cup chopped **fresh chives** or green onions

¼ cup **prepared horseradish**

½ tsp each **salt** and **pepper**

In large pot of boiling water, cook beets (if using) until fork-tender, about 20 minutes. Drain and let cool; slip off skins. Cut into cubes.

Meanwhile, in large pot of boiling salted water, cover and cook potatoes and turnips for 10 minutes.

Add carrots; cook, covered, until vegetables are just tender, about 15 minutes. With slotted spoon, transfer to ice water and chill; drain well.

Add cauliflower to pot; cook until tender-crisp, 2 to 5 minutes. Drain and chill in ice water; drain well.

Cube potatoes and turnips. Halve carrots lengthwise. Peel cucumber; cut lengthwise into quarters and remove seeds. Cut carrots and cucumber crosswise on diagonal into ½-inch (1 cm) thick slices. Cut ham (if using) into thin strips.

DRESSING: In large bowl, combine mayonnaise, sour cream, 3 tbsp of the chives, the horseradish, salt and pepper. Add potatoes, turnips, carrots, cauliflower and cucumber; stir to coat well.

Trim and separate lettuce into leaves; line shallow serving bowl. Top with vegetable mixture. Arrange eggs, beets and ham over top; sprinkle with dill and remaining chives.

Makes 6 servings. PER SERVING: about 300 cal, 10 g pro, 15 g total fat (4 g sat. fat), 33 g carb, 5 g fibre, 139 mg chol, 1,038 mg sodium, 794 mg potassium. % RDI: 13% calcium, 11% iron, 75% vit A, 58% vit C, 37% folate.

Cobb salads, with their tasty assortment of toppings, make hearty entrées. This one substitutes turkey for the usual chicken, making it a perfect fit for nights when you want to use up leftovers from a holiday bird.

Cobb-Style Turkey Salad

3 cups shredded **romaine lettuce**

1 cup torn **watercress leaves** or arugula (optional)

1 large **tomato,** cubed

1 small **sweet red pepper,** thinly sliced

2 cups cubed **cooked turkey**

1 **avocado,** peeled, pitted and cubed

¼ cup crumbled **blue cheese**

2 **hard-cooked eggs,** sliced

2 tbsp chopped **fresh chives** or green onions

DRESSING:
2 tbsp **red wine vinegar**

½ tsp **Dijon mustard**

1 clove **garlic,** minced

Pinch each **salt** and **pepper**

Pinch **granulated sugar**

3 tbsp **extra-virgin olive oil**

DRESSING: In small bowl, whisk together vinegar, mustard, garlic, salt, pepper and sugar; whisk in oil in thin steady stream.

Arrange romaine on large platter; top with watercress (if using). Arrange tomato, red pepper, turkey, avocado, cheese and eggs in piles on top. Sprinkle with chives.

To serve, drizzle with dressing and toss to coat.

Makes 4 servings. PER SERVING: about 377 cal, 28 g pro, 26 g total fat (6 g sat. fat), 9 g carb, 5 g fibre, 153 mg chol, 215 mg sodium, 750 mg potassium. % RDI: 9% calcium, 18% iron, 37% vit A, 93% vit C, 55% folate.

Quinoa is packed with protein, fibre and nutrients, making it a healthy choice. It has a delicate nutty flavour that's enhanced in this salad by briny feta and a sassy tomato vinaigrette.

Quinoa and Chickpea Salad With Tomato Vinaigrette

In saucepan, bring quinoa and 2 cups water to boil; reduce heat, cover and simmer for 12 minutes. Fluff with fork; let cool.

Meanwhile, in saucepan of boiling salted water, blanch green beans until tender-crisp, about 3 minutes. Drain; refresh in bowl of ice water. Drain; transfer to large bowl.

Stir in cooled quinoa, chickpeas, red pepper and feta cheese.

TOMATO VINAIGRETTE: Whisk together tomatoes, vinegar, oil, honey, Italian herb seasoning, salt, pepper and cayenne pepper; pour over quinoa mixture and stir to coat.

Makes 4 servings. PER SERVING: about 556 cal, 18 g pro, 22 g total fat (8 g sat. fat), 75 g carb, 9 g fibre, 35 mg chol, 1,155 mg sodium, 649 mg potassium. % RDI: 25% calcium, 46% iron, 18% vit A, 108% vit C, 53% folate.

1 cup **quinoa,** rinsed and drained

2 cups **green beans,** trimmed and chopped

1 can (19 oz/540 mL) **chickpeas,** drained and rinsed

1 **sweet red pepper,** diced

1 cup crumbled **feta cheese**

TOMATO VINAIGRETTE:

⅓ cup **bottled strained tomatoes** (passata)

3 tbsp **red wine vinegar**

3 tbsp **olive oil**

3 tbsp **liquid honey**

½ tsp **dried Italian herb seasoning**

½ tsp **salt**

¼ tsp **pepper**

Pinch **cayenne pepper**

Quinoa is naturally gluten-free, as are the other ingredients in this salad. The amount of water you need to cook quinoa varies, so check package directions for best results.

Gluten-Free Quinoa Salad With Creamy Tahini Dressing

In saucepan, bring quinoa, half of the salt and 2 cups water to boil over high heat; reduce heat, cover and simmer until no liquid remains and quinoa is tender, about 15 minutes. Let cool.

In large bowl, whisk together lemon juice, oil, tahini, warm water, garlic, cumin, pepper and remaining salt.

Add quinoa, tomatoes, cucumber, lentils, parsley, mint and onions; toss to coat. (*Make-ahead: Cover and refrigerate for up to 3 days.*)

Makes 4 to 6 servings. PER EACH OF 6 SERVINGS: about 300 cal, 9 g pro, 16 g total fat (2 g sat. fat), 32 g carb, 6 g fibre, 0 mg chol, 291 mg sodium, 581 mg potassium. % RDI: 9% calcium, 43% iron, 12% vit A, 33% vit C, 48% folate.

1 cup **quinoa,** rinsed and drained

½ tsp **salt**

¼ cup **lemon juice**

¼ cup **extra-virgin olive oil**

¼ cup **tahini**

¼ cup **warm water**

1 small clove **garlic,** minced

½ tsp **ground cumin**

¼ tsp **pepper**

2 cups **grape tomatoes** or cherry tomatoes, halved

1 cup diced **English cucumber**

1 cup drained rinsed **canned lentils**

⅔ cup chopped **fresh parsley**

⅓ cup chopped **fresh mint**

3 **green onions,** thinly sliced

Toasting corn and beans brings out their nuttiness and transforms this dish into an exotic South American–style salad. This vegetarian main is practically bursting with fibre, vitamins and flavour.

Brown Rice and Toasted Bean Salad

1 cup **brown rice,** rinsed

1 cup **frozen corn kernels,** thawed, drained and patted dry

3 large **plum tomatoes,** halved lengthwise

6 **green onions**

1 can (19 oz/540 mL) **black beans,** drained and rinsed

¾ tsp **dried oregano**

¾ tsp **ground cumin**

3 cups **baby arugula**

⅔ cup **roasted pumpkin seeds** or sliced almonds

⅔ cup crumbled **feta cheese**

½ cup chopped **fresh cilantro**

DRESSING:

⅓ cup **extra-virgin olive oil**

3 tbsp **lime juice**

1 clove **garlic,** minced

½ tsp each **salt** and **pepper**

DRESSING: Whisk together oil, lime juice, garlic, salt and pepper; set aside.

In saucepan, bring rice and 2 cups water to boil; reduce heat, cover and simmer until no liquid remains, 30 to 35 minutes. Let cool for 10 minutes. Fluff with fork.

Meanwhile, in cast-iron or other heavy skillet, toast corn over high heat, shaking pan, until fragrant and charred, 1 to 2 minutes. Transfer to large bowl.

In same skillet, cook tomatoes and onions, turning once, until softened and charred, about 3 minutes. Let cool on cutting board; cut into small chunks and add to bowl.

Add black beans, oregano and cumin to skillet; cook until beans are dry and fragrant, about 2 minutes. Add to bowl. Stir in rice, arugula and pumpkin seeds.

Add dressing, feta cheese and cilantro; toss to coat.

Makes 4 servings. PER SERVING: about 758 cal, 30 g pro, 42 g total fat (10 g sat. fat), 74 g carb, 18 g fibre, 23 mg chol, 959 mg sodium, 1,154 mg potassium. % RDI: 26% calcium, 73% iron, 23% vit A, 37% vit C, 75% folate.

Instead of a mayonnaise-based dressing, this potluck classic is updated with a simple garlic-and-herb vinaigrette. The best part? You can whip this salad together in just the time it takes to cook the pasta.

Tuna Fusilli Salad

In large pot of boiling salted water, cook fusilli for 5 minutes. Add green beans; cook until pasta is tender but firm, about 3 minutes. Drain well.

DRESSING: Meanwhile, in large bowl, whisk together oil, vinegar, garlic, herbes de Provence, salt and pepper.

Add pasta mixture, tomatoes and olives. Drain tuna and break into chunks; add to bowl and toss lightly.

Makes 4 servings. PER SERVING: about 361 cal, 15 g pro, 17 g total fat (2 g sat. fat), 38 g carb, 4 g fibre, 10 mg chol, 468 mg sodium. % RDI: 4% calcium, 18% iron, 5% vit A, 28% vit C, 32% folate.

2 cups **fusilli pasta**

1 cup chopped **green beans** or peas

½ cup sliced drained **oil-packed sun-dried tomatoes**

¼ cup slivered **black olives**

1 can (170 g) **water-packed tuna**

DRESSING:

¼ cup **extra-virgin olive oil**

3 tbsp **red wine vinegar**

1 clove **garlic,** minced

½ tsp **dried herbes de Provence** (or ¼ tsp each dried basil and thyme)

¼ tsp each **salt** and **pepper**

Fresh, light and lively flavours mingle in this summery salad. Any short, thick pasta can work if you don't have penne on hand. To get the proper texture, cook the pasta according to package directions.

Grilled Sausage, Pepper and Bocconcini Pasta Salad

In saucepan of boiling salted water, cook pasta according to package directions; drain and set aside.

Meanwhile, mince garlic with salt. In large bowl, whisk together garlic mixture, oil, vinegar and pepper. Set aside.

Place sausages and red, yellow and green peppers on greased grill over medium heat; close lid and grill, turning often, until juices run clear when sausages are pierced and peppers are charred all over, 10 to 15 minutes.

Cut sausages into bite-size pieces; set aside. Peel, quarter and seed peppers; slice and add to dressing. Toss to coat.

Cut radicchio in half lengthwise; remove core. Grill, turning often, until leaves are tender and slightly charred, about 5 minutes.

Transfer radicchio to cutting board; slice. Add to pepper mixture along with pasta, sausage, cheese and basil; toss to combine.

Makes 4 servings. PER SERVING: about 726 cal, 35 g pro, 40 g total fat (14 g sat. fat), 57 g carb, 5 g fibre, 81 mg chol, 1,166 mg sodium, 508 mg potassium. % RDI: 32% calcium, 31% iron, 23% vit A, 197% vit C, 76% folate.

3 cups **penne pasta**
1 large clove **garlic**
¼ tsp **salt**
¼ cup **extra-virgin olive oil**
3 tbsp **red wine vinegar**
¼ tsp **pepper**
4 hot or mild **Italian sausages**
1 each **sweet red, yellow** and **green pepper**
1 head **radicchio**
1 tub (200 g) **small bocconcini cheese**
¼ cup loosely packed **fresh basil,** thinly sliced

A little sweet, a little sour and a lot delicious, this filling main-dish salad is a creative mix of flavours and textures. Sour gherkins, also known as cornichons, can be harder to find than sweet gherkins, but they add a delightful tang and are worth searching for.

Cauliflower and Spiced Gouda Salad

1 head **cauliflower** (about 2 lb/900 g)

1½ cups diced **spiced Gouda cheese** (cumin, coriander or fenugreek)

1 thick slice (½ inch/1 cm) **Black Forest ham** (about 8 oz/225 g), diced

1 cup diced **sweet onion**

⅓ cup diced **sour gherkin pickles** or sweet gherkin pickles

1 **apple,** diced

¼ cup **mayonnaise**

3 tbsp each finely chopped **fresh parsley** and **chives**

3 tbsp **sour cream**

4 tsp **cider vinegar**

1 tbsp **gherkin juice** from jar

1½ tsp **curry powder**

½ tsp **granulated sugar**

Dash **hot pepper sauce**

Pinch each **salt** and **pepper**

1 head **Boston lettuce,** separated into leaves

Remove any leaves from cauliflower. In large pot of boiling salted water, blanch cauliflower until tender-crisp, about 3 minutes. Drain and chill under cold water; drain well. Cut into florets.

In large bowl, combine cauliflower, cheese, ham, onion, gherkins and apple.

Whisk together mayonnaise, parsley, chives, sour cream, vinegar, gherkin juice, curry powder, sugar, hot pepper sauce, salt and pepper. Scrape over cauliflower mixture; toss to coat.

Line bowls with lettuce leaves; top with salad.

Makes 4 to 6 servings. PER EACH OF 6 SERVINGS: about 290 cal, 18 g pro, 19 g total fat (8 g sat. fat), 14 g carb, 4 g fibre, 63 mg chol, 1,507 mg sodium, 480 mg potassium. % RDI: 26% calcium, 11% iron, 13% vit A, 83% vit C, 38% folate.

For this spicy salad, you'll need to buy the kimchi and gochujang at an Asian market, but their authentic flavours are worth searching out. To make kimchi juice, gently squeeze kimchi or pour out the excess from the jar.

Korean Cold Somen Noodle Salad

9 oz (255 g) **somen noodles**

Half **cucumber,** cored and julienned

4 oz (115 g) **deli ham,** julienned (optional)

1½ cups sliced **Asian pear**

1 cup **kimchi,** chopped

½ cup finely chopped **green onion**

¼ cup **kimchi juice**

4 cups shredded **curly endive** or red leaf lettuce

1 sheet **nori,** cut in strips

SAUCE:

3 tbsp **gochujang** (Korean hot pepper paste)

3 tbsp **unseasoned rice vinegar**

2 tbsp toasted **sesame seeds**

2 tbsp **sesame oil**

4 tsp **granulated sugar**

1 tbsp **sodium-reduced soy sauce**

PICKLED DAIKON:

½ cup thinly sliced peeled **daikon radish**

1 tbsp **unseasoned rice vinegar**

½ tsp **granulated sugar**

PICKLED DAIKON: Combine daikon, vinegar and sugar; refrigerate for 15 minutes.

Meanwhile, in large pot of boiling water, cook noodles according to package directions, about 2 minutes. Drain and rinse under cold running water until no longer starchy. Drain well; shake. Set aside to air-dry for 10 minutes.

SAUCE: Meanwhile, stir together gochujang, vinegar, sesame seeds, sesame oil, sugar and soy sauce.

In bowl, combine noodles, cucumber, ham (if using), Asian pear, kimchi, green onion and kimchi juice; add half of the sauce and toss to coat.

Add endive and nori, tossing gently. Divide among bowls; top with pickled daikon. Add remaining sauce to taste at table.

Makes 4 to 6 servings. PER EACH OF 6 SERVINGS: about 257 cal, 6 g pro, 7 g total fat (1 g sat. fat), 43 g carb, 6 g fibre, 0 mg chol, 908 mg sodium, 269 mg potassium. % RDI: 4% calcium, 12% iron, 22% vit A, 23% vit C, 30% folate.

You can top the noodles in this wholesome lunch or supper dish with other kinds of seafood or even chicken. Natural peanut butter contains only peanuts (no salt, sugar or other additives) and is available in supermarkets and bulk food stores.

Chinese Garlic and Peanut Noodles With Shrimp

PEANUT SAUCE: In small saucepan, heat sesame oil with hot pepper flakes over medium-low heat just until pepper begins to darken; pour into bowl. Add peanut butter, rice vinegar, soy sauce, fish sauce, five-spice powder, salt, garlic and ⅓ cup water; mix well. *(Make-ahead: Cover and refrigerate for up to 3 days. Bring to room temperature.)*

Pinch off root ends of bean sprouts; place sprouts in colander. Immerse colander in large pot of boiling salted water for 5 seconds. Remove colander and immediately chill under cold water; drain sprouts and set aside.

Add noodles to boiling salted water in pot; cook until tender but firm, about 5 minutes. Drain and chill under cold water; drain well.

In shallow serving bowl, mix noodles with sesame oil. Top with mounds of bean sprouts, cucumber, shrimp and cilantro. *(Make-ahead: Cover and refrigerate for up to 2 hours.)*

Pour peanut sauce over salad; toss to coat.

Makes 4 servings. PER SERVING: about 818 cal, 40 g pro, 44 g total fat (11 g sat. fat), 71 g carb, 8 g fibre, 166 mg chol, 1,184 mg sodium. % RDI: 10% calcium, 41% iron, 8% vit A, 25% vit C, 51% folate.

4 cups **bean sprouts** (about 8 oz/225 g)

12 oz (340 g) **Chinese wheat noodles**

1 tbsp **sesame oil**

2 cups julienned **English cucumber**

12 oz (340 g) **cooked shrimp**

¼ cup **fresh cilantro leaves**

PEANUT SAUCE:
2 tbsp **sesame oil**

½ tsp **hot pepper flakes**

½ cup **natural peanut butter**

2 tbsp **unseasoned rice vinegar** or cider vinegar

1 tbsp **soy sauce**

1 tbsp **fish sauce**

½ tsp **five-spice powder**

¼ tsp **salt**

4 cloves **garlic,** minced

Enjoy this cool salad as a light supper or pack it to take for lunch. Unseasoned rice vinegar provides a subtle tang to the sauce. Don't substitute seasoned rice vinegar, which contains sugar and salt; save that for making sushi rice.

Chilled Asian Noodle Salad

Soak mushrooms in ½ cup boiling water for 15 minutes. Reserving liquid, squeeze mushrooms dry; chop and place in large bowl.

Whisk together ¼ cup of the reserved soaking liquid, tahini, soy sauce, sesame oil, vegetable oil, vinegar, ginger, sugar and hot sauce.

Meanwhile, in large saucepan of boiling salted water, cook spaghetti until tender but firm, about 8 minutes. Drain and rinse under cold water; drain well and add to mushrooms.

Add soy sauce mixture, cabbage, carrot, snow peas, green onion, cilantro and peanuts; toss to combine. (*Make-ahead: Cover and refrigerate for up to 4 hours.*)

Makes 4 servings. PER SERVING: about 670 cal, 15 g pro, 37 g total fat (4 g sat. fat), 76 g carb, 9 g fibre, 0 mg chol, 847 mg sodium. % RDI: 8% calcium, 32% iron, 83% vit A, 45% vit C, 96% folate.

6 **dried shiitake mushrooms**

¼ cup **tahini**

¼ cup **sodium-reduced soy sauce**

¼ cup **sesame oil**

¼ cup **vegetable oil**

3 tbsp **unseasoned rice vinegar**

2 tsp grated **fresh ginger**

1 tsp **granulated sugar**

Dash **Asian chili sauce** (such as sriracha) or hot pepper sauce

8 oz (225 g) **spaghetti**

2 cups shredded **napa cabbage**

1 cup grated **carrot**

1 cup **snow peas,** thinly sliced lengthwise on diagonal

1 **green onion,** thinly sliced

¼ cup chopped **fresh cilantro** or parsley

¼ cup **roasted peanuts,** chopped

Potato-Topped
Chicken Pot Pies,
page 159

Casseroles & Bakes

Cooking the shallots until they're caramelized creates the flavour base, and their subtle sweetness naturally balances with the sharp blue cheese. If you're not a fan of blue, try the same amount of shredded extra-old Cheddar instead.

Beef Stew With Blue Cheese Biscuits

2 lb (900 g) **stewing beef cubes,** trimmed

½ tsp each **salt** and **pepper**

2 tbsp **olive oil**

1 bag (8 oz/225 g) **shallots,** peeled and quartered

3 cups **cremini mushrooms,** quartered

2 **carrots,** chopped

1 **turnip,** cubed

3 cloves **garlic,** thinly sliced

6 sprigs **fresh thyme**

2 **bay leaves**

3 tbsp **all-purpose flour**

½ cup **red wine** or white wine

¾ cup **sodium-reduced beef broth**

1 can (28 oz/796 mL) **whole tomatoes,** drained and coarsely chopped

CHEESE BISCUITS:

2¼ cups **all-purpose flour**

4 tsp **baking powder**

¼ tsp **salt**

½ cup cold **unsalted butter,** cubed

1 cup crumbled **blue cheese** (about 4 oz/115 g)

1 cup **buttermilk** (approx)

Sprinkle beef with salt and pepper. In Dutch oven, heat 2 tsp of the oil over medium-high heat; brown beef, in batches. Transfer to bowl. Add remaining oil to pan; cook shallots over medium heat, stirring, until caramelized, 8 minutes. Stir in mushrooms, carrots, turnip, garlic, thyme and bay leaves; cook for 2 minutes. Sprinkle with flour; cook, stirring, for 1 minute. Add wine, scraping up brown bits. Add broth and tomatoes. Return beef to pan; bring to boil. Reduce heat to low; cover and simmer, stirring occasionally, for 1¼ hours.

Uncover and cook until thickened and beef is tender, about 20 minutes. Discard thyme and bay leaves. Scrape into 13- x 9-inch (3 L) baking dish.

CHEESE BISCUITS: Meanwhile, in bowl, whisk together flour, baking powder and salt. Using pastry blender or 2 knives, cut in butter until crumbly; stir in blue cheese. Drizzle with 1 cup buttermilk, stirring, just until soft sticky dough forms. Turn out onto lightly floured surface; knead 6 times or just until smooth. Roll out into 10- x 8-inch (25 x 20 cm) rectangle; cut into 12 biscuits. Arrange over stew; brush biscuits with 1 tbsp more buttermilk. Bake in 375°F (190°C) oven until filling is bubbly and biscuits are golden and no longer doughy underneath, about 35 minutes.

Makes 8 to 10 servings. PER EACH OF 10 SERVINGS: about 487 cal, 27 g pro, 27 g total fat (13 g sat. fat), 35 g carb, 3 g fibre, 90 mg chol, 705 mg sodium, 730 mg potassium. % RDI: 20% calcium, 31% iron, 40% vit A, 18% vit C, 39% folate.

TO FREEZE: Refrigerate thickened stew for 30 minutes; freeze in airtight container for up to 2 months. Freeze unbaked biscuits on lined baking sheet; transfer to airtight container and freeze for up to 2 months. Thaw stew; scrape into baking dish and arrange frozen biscuits over top. Bake as directed, increasing baking time to 45 to 50 minutes and covering with foil if browning too quickly.

Here's an authentic version of the consummate Greek comfort-food casserole.
The cheese of choice is Kefalograviera (or graviera), which is made from a mixture of
cow's, goat's and sheep's milk. If you can't find it, a good substitute is Gruyère.

Moussaka

6 large **Yukon Gold potatoes**
(2½ lb/1.125 kg)

1 large **eggplant** (1¼ lb/565 g)

3 tbsp **extra-virgin olive oil**

½ tsp each **salt** and **pepper**

1½ cups shredded **Kefalograviera
cheese** or Gruyère cheese

BOLOGNESE SAUCE:

2 lb (900 g) **lean ground lamb**
or beef

2 **onions,** chopped

4 cloves **garlic,** minced

4 tsp **dried oregano**

1½ tsp **cinnamon**

½ tsp each **salt** and **pepper**

¼ tsp **ground allspice**

1 can (28 oz/796 mL) **whole
tomatoes**

1 cup **red wine**

1 can (5½ oz/156 mL) **tomato
paste**

BÉCHAMEL SAUCE:

2 tbsp **butter**

⅓ cup **all-purpose flour**

3 cups **milk**

½ tsp **salt**

¼ tsp **pepper**

Pinch **grated nutmeg**

BOLOGNESE SAUCE: In Dutch oven, sauté lamb over medium-high heat, breaking up with spoon, until no longer pink, 10 minutes. Drain fat from pan; add onions, garlic, oregano, cinnamon, salt, pepper and allspice. Fry over medium heat until onion is softened, 5 minutes. Add tomatoes, mashing with spoon. Add wine and tomato paste; bring to boil. Reduce heat; simmer until space does not fill in after spoon is drawn across bottom of pan, 30 minutes.

Meanwhile, peel potatoes and eggplant; cut into ½-inch (1 cm) thick slices. Arrange in single layer on parchment paper–lined rimmed baking sheets. Brush both sides with oil; sprinkle with salt and pepper. Roast in 450°F (230°C) oven, turning once, until tender and golden, about 30 minutes.

BÉCHAMEL SAUCE: Meanwhile, in saucepan, melt butter over medium heat; whisk in flour and cook, whisking, for 1 minute. Gradually whisk in milk; cook, whisking often, until boiling and thickened enough to coat back of spoon, about 12 minutes. Add salt, pepper and nutmeg.

Spread 1 cup of the Bolognese Sauce in 13- x 9-inch (3 L) baking dish. Top with half of the potatoes, 2 cups of the Bolognese Sauce, all of the eggplant, 2 cups of the Bolognese Sauce, remaining potatoes and remaining Bolognese Sauce. Spread Béchamel Sauce over top. (*Make-ahead: Let cool for 30 minutes. Refrigerate, uncovered, until cold. Cover and refrigerate for up to 24 hours. Add 40 minutes to baking time.*)

Sprinkle with cheese. Bake in 350°F (180°C) oven until browned and bubbly, about 1 hour. Let stand for 10 minutes; cut into squares.

Makes 10 to 12 servings. PER EACH OF 12 SERVINGS: about 411 cal, 23 g pro, 21 g total fat (9 g sat. fat), 32 g carb, 4 g fibre, 72 mg chol, 523 mg sodium. % RDI: 25% calcium, 23% iron, 12% vit A, 32% vit C, 19% folate.

Economical ingredients, such as potatoes, spinach and ham, really stretch to make the ultimate one-dish meal. This casserole looks and tastes spectacular, so it's ideal for casual entertaining.

Scalloped Potato, Mushroom and Ham Casserole

In saucepan of boiling salted water, cover and cook potatoes until tender when pierced with tip of knife, about 10 minutes. Drain and let cool.

Meanwhile, rinse spinach; shake off excess water. In large saucepan, cover and cook spinach over medium heat, with just the water clinging to leaves, stirring once, until wilted, about 3 minutes. Transfer to sieve; press out moisture.

Meanwhile, in large nonstick skillet, heat oil over medium-high heat; sauté mushrooms, onion, garlic, thyme, salt and pepper until golden and liquid is evaporated, about 8 minutes.

Sprinkle flour into skillet; cook, stirring, for 1 minute. Add broth, evaporated milk and mustard; cook over medium heat, stirring, until thickened, about 10 minutes.

Cut potatoes into ⅛-inch (3 mm) thick slices. Arrange one-third of the potatoes in greased 11- x 7-inch (2 L) baking dish; top with half of the spinach. Repeat layers. Spread remaining potatoes over top. Sprinkle with ham. Pour sauce evenly over top. Sprinkle with cheese and bread crumbs. (*Make-ahead: Cover loosely and refrigerate for up to 4 hours; add 10 minutes to baking time.*)

Bake on rimmed baking sheet in 350°F (180°C) oven until filling is bubbly and top is golden and crisp, about 1 hour. Let stand for 10 minutes before serving.

Makes 8 servings. PER SERVING: about 323 cal, 26 g pro, 11 g total fat (5 g sat. fat), 31 g carb, 3 g fibre, 50 mg chol, 1,330 mg sodium. % RDI: 29% calcium, 21% iron, 35% vit A, 25% vit C, 35% folate.

6 **Yukon Gold potatoes**
(2 lb/900 g), peeled

1 pkg (10 oz/284 g) **fresh spinach**

1 tbsp **vegetable oil**

3 cups thinly sliced **mushrooms**

1 **onion,** chopped

2 cloves **garlic,** minced

½ tsp **dried thyme**

¼ tsp each **salt** and **pepper**

3 tbsp **all-purpose flour**

1 cup **chicken broth**

1 can (385 mL) **2% evaporated milk**

1 tbsp **Dijon mustard**

1 lb (450 g) **Black Forest ham,**
cut in ¾-inch (2 cm) cubes

1 cup shredded **Cheddar cheese**

½ cup **fresh bread crumbs**

This braised version of the classic southern barbecue dish uses quite a few ingredients but doesn't require a lot of hands-on cooking. The fennel biscuits cooked on top are a tasty partner, but you can omit the fennel seeds if you prefer plain biscuits.

Pulled Pork With Fennel Biscuits

In large bowl, combine half of the brown sugar, the cumin, oregano, half of the salt, and the pepper; rub all over pork. Let stand for 30 minutes.

In large Dutch oven, heat oil over medium-high heat; brown pork. Transfer to plate. Add onion, red pepper, fennel bulb, carrot, celery and garlic to pan; cook over medium heat, stirring occasionally, until softened, 5 to 8 minutes. Add tomatoes, ½ cup water, vinegar, orange zest and remaining brown sugar and salt; bring to boil.

Return pork and any accumulated juices to pan; return to boil. Cover and braise in 300°F (150°C) oven, turning once, until pork is tender, about 3 hours. Transfer pork to cutting board; tent with foil and let stand for 10 minutes. With 2 forks, shred or "pull" pork.

Meanwhile, skim fat from sauce; discard orange zest. Simmer over medium heat until reduced to 4 cups, about 15 minutes. Stir pork back into pan. Transfer to 8-cup (2 L) ovenproof baking dish.

BISCUITS: In large bowl, whisk together flour, baking powder, fennel seeds and salt. Using pastry blender, cut in butter until crumbly. Pour buttermilk over top, stirring to form soft ragged dough. Gently knead just until dough comes together, adding up to 1 tbsp more buttermilk if needed.

Spoon dough onto pork mixture to make 12 biscuits. Bake in 375°F (190°C) oven until biscuits are golden on top and no longer doughy underneath, 40 to 45 minutes.

Makes 4 to 6 servings. PER EACH OF 6 SERVINGS: about 824 cal, 37 g pro, 49 g total fat (20 g sat. fat), 56 g carb, 4 g fibre, 165 mg chol, 1,231 mg sodium, 946 mg potassium. % RDI: 21% calcium, 54% iron, 43% vit A, 67% vit C, 50% folate.

¼ cup packed **brown sugar**

2 tsp **ground cumin**

1½ tsp **dried oregano**

1¼ tsp **salt**

1 tsp **pepper**

3 lb (1.35 kg) **pork shoulder blade roast**

2 tbsp **vegetable oil**

1 **onion,** finely diced

1 **sweet red pepper,** finely diced

1 small **fennel bulb,** finely diced

1 **carrot,** finely diced

1 rib **celery,** finely diced

3 cloves **garlic,** crushed

1 bottle (680 mL) **strained tomatoes** (passata)

⅓ cup **red wine vinegar**

3 strips **orange zest**

BISCUITS:

2 cups **all-purpose flour**

1 tbsp **baking powder**

1 tsp **fennel seeds,** crushed

¼ tsp **salt**

½ cup cold **butter,** cubed

¾ cup cold **buttermilk** (approx)

Colourful layers of spinach, smoked salmon and potatoes make this an attractive main course, especially for a brunch or buffet. The best part is that you can make it a day ahead for fuss-free entertaining.

Salmon and Potato Napoleon Casserole

8 **Yukon Gold potatoes** (about 2½ lb/1.125 kg), scrubbed

2 pkg (each 10 oz/284 g) **fresh spinach,** trimmed

½ tsp each **salt** and **pepper**

¼ cup **butter**

1 small **onion,** diced

⅓ cup **all-purpose flour**

4 cups **milk**

4 oz (115 g) **herbed cream cheese**

¼ cup chopped **fresh dill** or parsley

1 tbsp grated **lemon zest**

2 **green onions,** chopped

12 oz (340 g) thinly sliced **smoked salmon**

In large pot of boiling salted water, cover and cook potatoes for 10 minutes. Using slotted spoon, remove and let cool slightly. Add spinach to pot; cook until wilted, about 2 minutes. Drain, pressing out liquid; let cool.

Cut potatoes into ¼-inch (5 mm) thick slices; gently toss with half each of the salt and pepper. Set aside.

In large saucepan, melt butter over medium heat; cook onion, stirring occasionally, until softened, about 5 minutes. Add flour; cook, stirring, for 1 minute. Slowly whisk in milk; cook, stirring, until thickened, about 8 minutes. Stir in cream cheese, dill, lemon zest and remaining salt and pepper.

Pour 1 cup of the sauce into 13- x 9-inch (3 L) baking dish. Arrange one-third of the potatoes over sauce; layer spinach, green onions, half of the remaining potatoes then the smoked salmon over top. Top with remaining potatoes. Pour remaining sauce over top. *(Make-ahead: Cover and refrigerate for up to 24 hours.)*

Cover with foil; bake in 375°F (190°C) oven for 45 minutes. Uncover and bake until bubbly, about 30 minutes. Broil until golden, about 3 minutes. Let stand for 10 minutes before serving.

Makes 8 servings. PER SERVING: about 352 cal, 18 g pro, 15 g total fat (8 g sat. fat), 38 g carb, 4 g fibre, 51 mg chol, 1,001 mg sodium. % RDI: 24% calcium, 29% iron, 67% vit A, 38% vit C, 54% folate.

Chicken chili is a crowd-pleaser, especially with a zesty, cheesy cornmeal topping.
We've cut the salt in this dish by using sodium-reduced canned beans and broth.
If you want even less sodium, decrease the amount of salt in the meat mixture.

Corn-Topped White Chili Casserole

In Dutch oven, melt 1 tbsp of the butter over medium heat; cook onion, green pepper, jalapeño pepper, garlic, cumin, coriander, oregano, salt, hot pepper flakes and pepper, stirring occasionally, until softened, about 6 minutes. Transfer to bowl. Add 1 tbsp of the remaining butter to pan and heat over medium-high heat; brown chicken, in batches. Add to onion mixture.

Melt remaining butter in pan; sprinkle with flour and cook, stirring, for 2 minutes. Stir in chicken mixture and beans. Gradually pour in milk and broth, stirring constantly; bring to boil. Reduce heat and simmer, stirring occasionally, until thickened, about 20 minutes. Scrape into 13- x 9-inch (3 L) baking dish; refrigerate until cool and slightly thickened, about 1 hour.

CORNMEAL TOPPING: Meanwhile, in large saucepan, bring 3½ cups water, butter and salt to boil; reduce heat to low. Gradually whisk in cornmeal; cook, stirring often, for 8 minutes. Remove from heat. Stir in Gouda cheese and corn; spread over chili.

Bake in 400°F (200°C) oven until knife inserted in centre comes out hot and top is golden, about 25 minutes.

Makes 8 to 10 servings. PER EACH OF 10 SERVINGS: about 472 cal, 38 g pro, 22 g total fat (11 g sat. fat), 30 g carb, 4 g fibre, 161 mg chol, 638 mg sodium, 653 mg potassium. % RDI: 23% calcium, 24% iron, 15% vit A, 25% vit C, 24% folate.

TO FREEZE: Follow first 3 paragraphs. Let cool. Cover with plastic wrap; overwrap in heavy-duty foil and freeze for up to 2 months. Thaw in refrigerator for 24 hours. Remove plastic wrap; re-cover with foil. Bake in 400°F (200°C) oven until knife inserted in centre comes out hot, about 40 minutes. Uncover; bake in 425°F (220°C) oven until top is golden, about 20 minutes.

⅓ cup **unsalted butter**

1 **sweet onion,** chopped

1 **sweet green pepper,** chopped

1 or 2 **jalapeño peppers,** seeded and diced

3 cloves **garlic,** minced

2 tsp each **ground cumin, ground coriander** and **dried oregano**

½ tsp **salt**

¼ tsp each **hot pepper flakes** and **pepper**

3 lb (1.35 kg) **boneless skinless chicken thighs,** cubed

3 tbsp **all-purpose flour**

1 can (19 oz/540 mL) **no-salt-added white kidney beans,** drained and rinsed

1⅓ cups **milk**

1 cup **sodium-reduced chicken broth**

CORNMEAL TOPPING:

1 tbsp **butter**

½ tsp **salt**

1 cup **cornmeal**

2 cups shredded **Gouda cheese**

1 cup **frozen corn kernels**

This casserole is so-named for the vessel that it cooks in: Dutch ovens are commonly called casseroles in England. But no matter what you call it, this family-friendly dinner is smoky, juicy and delightfully comforting on a cool evening.

Chicken and Kielbasa Rice Casserole

8 **boneless skinless chicken thighs**

½ tsp each **salt** and **pepper**

1 tbsp **vegetable oil**

1 **onion**

1 **sweet red pepper** or sweet green pepper

¾ cup cubed **kielbasa** or ham (about 4 oz/115 g)

1 tsp **dried thyme**

¾ cup **long-grain rice**

1½ cups **sodium-reduced chicken broth**

1 cup **frozen peas**

2 **green onions,** sliced

Season chicken thighs with half each of the salt and pepper. In Dutch oven, heat oil over medium-high heat; brown chicken, about 4 minutes. Transfer to plate; set aside. Drain fat from pan.

Meanwhile, cut onion and red pepper lengthwise into ¼-inch (5 mm) wide slices. In same pan, fry kielbasa, onion, red pepper, thyme and remaining salt and pepper over medium heat, stirring occasionally, until onion is softened, about 5 minutes.

Add rice; fry, stirring, for 1 minute to coat. Add chicken broth. Arrange chicken on rice and bring to boil. Reduce heat to low; cover and simmer until almost no liquid remains and juices run clear when chicken is pierced, about 15 minutes.

Stir in peas and heat through, about 2 minutes. Sprinkle with sliced green onions.

Makes 4 servings. PER SERVING: about 413 cal, 32 g pro, 14 g total fat (3 g sat. fat), 38 g carb, 3 g fibre, 113 mg chol, 887 mg sodium. % RDI: 6% calcium, 21% iron, 15% vit A, 98% vit C, 20% folate.

While Cubanelle peppers, zucchini and whole wheat tortillas are not traditional Tex-Mex ingredients, they boost the nutrient quotient in this cheesy, well-spiced casserole. Quesadillas are a fun way to use up any leftover cheese and tortillas.

Tex-Mex Casserole With Monterey Jack

Reserving juices, drain tomatoes. Chop tomatoes and set aside.

In large saucepan, heat oil over medium heat; cook onions and peppers, stirring occasionally, until softened, about 7 minutes.

Push mixture to side of pan. Add beef to other side; brown over medium-high heat, breaking up with spoon, about 4 minutes.

Stir in garlic, chili powder, cumin seeds, salt, pepper and hot pepper flakes. Stir in tomato paste; cook for 1 minute. Stir in tomatoes with juices, zucchini and broth; simmer, stirring occasionally, for 20 minutes. Let cool.

Spread 1 cup of the beef mixture in 13- x 9-inch (3 L) baking dish. Top with 2 tortillas, then generous 2 cups of the beef mixture; sprinkle with one-third of the cheese. Starting with tortillas, repeat layers twice. Cover with foil.

Bake in 400°F (200°C) oven until knife inserted in centre comes out hot, about 25 minutes. Uncover and broil until cheese is browned, about 4 minutes. Let stand for 10 minutes before serving.

Makes 8 to 10 servings. PER EACH OF 10 SERVINGS: about 453 cal, 34 g pro, 24 g total fat (11 g sat. fat), 26 g carb, 4 g fibre, 85 mg chol, 828 mg sodium, 651 mg potassium. % RDI: 33% calcium, 32% iron, 17% vit A, 35% vit C, 18% folate.

TO FREEZE: Follow first 4 paragraphs. Cover with plastic wrap and overwrap in heavy-duty foil; freeze for up to 2 months. Thaw in refrigerator for 24 hours; remove plastic wrap, re-cover with foil and bake in 400°F (200°C) oven until knife inserted in centre comes out hot, about 30 minutes. Uncover and bake until tortilla edges are browned, about 15 minutes. Broil until cheese is browned, about 4 minutes. Let stand for 10 minutes before serving.

1 can (28 oz/796 mL) **whole tomatoes**

1 tbsp **extra-virgin olive oil**

2 **onions,** chopped

2 **Cubanelle peppers,** chopped

2 lb (900 g) **lean ground beef**

2 cloves **garlic,** minced

2 tbsp **chili powder**

1 tbsp **cumin seeds,** crushed

½ tsp each **salt** and **pepper**

¼ tsp **hot pepper flakes**

3 tbsp **tomato paste**

2 cups chopped **zucchini**

⅔ cup **sodium-reduced beef broth**

6 large (10-inch/25 cm) **whole wheat tortillas**

3½ cups shredded **Monterey Jack cheese** (9 oz/255 g)

Roasting a chicken on the weekend means having lots of tasty leftovers for other dishes during the week. Make the filling for this pie on Sunday, then just add the topping later in the week while the oven heats. Serve with a simple green salad.

Biscuit-Topped Chicken Pot Pie

1 tbsp **vegetable oil**

3 **carrots,** sliced

2 cups quartered **mushrooms**

1 small **onion,** chopped

½ tsp **dried tarragon**

½ tsp each **salt** and **pepper**

⅓ cup **all-purpose flour**

1¾ cups **milk**

1¾ cups **sodium-reduced chicken broth**

2 cups cut **green beans** (2-inch/5 cm pieces)

3 cups shredded **cooked chicken**

1 tsp **Dijon mustard**

BISCUIT TOPPING:

1½ cups **all-purpose flour**

2 tsp **baking powder**

½ tsp **salt**

⅓ cup cold **butter,** cubed

⅔ cup **milk**

In large saucepan, heat oil over medium-high heat; sauté carrots, mushrooms, onion, tarragon, salt and pepper until onion is softened, about 8 minutes.

Add flour; cook, stirring, for 1 minute. Gradually whisk in milk and broth; bring to boil, stirring. Add green beans. Reduce heat and simmer, stirring often, until thick enough to coat back of spoon, about 6 minutes. Stir in chicken and mustard. Spoon into round 8-cup (2 L) baking dish; set aside. (*Make-ahead: Let cool for 30 minutes; refrigerate, uncovered, until cold. Cover and refrigerate for up to 2 days; rewarm in microwave to continue.*)

BISCUIT TOPPING: In food processor, pulse together flour, baking powder and salt; pulse in butter until crumbly. Drizzle in milk, pulsing just until soft sticky dough forms. Turn out onto floured surface; knead 10 times or until smooth. Pat out dough to fit inside rim of baking dish. Cut into 8 wedges; arrange over chicken mixture.

Bake on rimmed baking sheet in 400°F (200°C) oven until biscuits are golden and no longer doughy underneath, about 40 minutes.

Makes 4 servings. PER SERVING: about 716 cal, 45 g pro, 31 g total fat (14 g sat. fat), 65 g carb, 6 g fibre, 154 mg chol, 1,344 mg sodium. % RDI: 29% calcium, 39% iron, 163% vit A, 15% vit C, 52% folate.

These savoury pies, with their golden potato topping, freeze beautifully.
You might want to make a double batch to keep in the freezer for nights when
you don't have time to cook but want something warm and homemade.

Potato-Topped Chicken Pot Pies

TOPPING: Peel potatoes and cut into ½-inch (1 cm) chunks. In large saucepan of boiling salted water, cover and cook potatoes until tender, about 15 minutes; drain and return to pot. Mash in milk, cream cheese, butter, salt and pepper until smooth. Set aside.

Meanwhile, cut chicken into ½-inch (1 cm) chunks. In separate large saucepan, bring broth to boil. Add chicken, mushrooms, onion, carrots, garlic, bay leaves, salt, pepper and nutmeg; reduce heat, cover and simmer until chicken is no longer pink inside, about 6 minutes. Stir in peas, mustard and lemon juice.

Whisk flour with ⅓ cup cold water; whisk into broth mixture and bring to boil. Reduce heat and cook, stirring often, until thick enough to coat back of spoon, about 5 minutes. Discard bay leaves.

Spoon chicken mixture into four 2-cup (500 mL) ovenproof or foil dishes; spoon or pipe potato mixture over top.

Cover and bake in 400°F (200°C) oven until hot, about 20 minutes. Uncover and broil until golden, about 3 minutes.

Makes 4 servings. PER SERVING: about 582 cal, 40 g pro, 20 g total fat (11 g sat. fat), 62 g carb, 7 g fibre, 118 mg chol, 1,122 mg sodium. % RDI: 11% calcium, 29% iron, 112% vit A, 35% vit C, 37% folate.

TO FREEZE: Follow first 4 paragraphs. Let pies cool for 30 minutes. Refrigerate until cold. Cover with foil and overwrap in heavy-duty foil; freeze for up to 1 month. Thaw in refrigerator; remove heavy-duty foil. Bake on rimmed baking sheet in 400°F (200°C) oven or toaster oven until knife inserted in centre for 5 seconds comes out hot, 25 minutes. Uncover and broil until golden, 3 minutes.

1 lb (450 g) **boneless skinless chicken breasts** or thighs

2 cups **chicken broth**

2 cups **button mushrooms,** quartered

1 **onion,** chopped

2 **carrots,** chopped

2 cloves **garlic,** minced

2 **bay leaves**

¼ tsp each **salt** and **pepper**

Pinch **nutmeg**

1 cup **frozen peas**

1 tsp **Dijon mustard**

½ tsp **lemon juice**

½ cup **all-purpose flour**

TOPPING:

6 **Yukon Gold potatoes** (2 lb/900 g)

½ cup **milk**

½ cup **cream cheese**

2 tbsp **butter**

½ tsp each **salt** and **pepper**

Don't let the long ingredient list daunt you. This recipe yields two pies – one for dinner tonight and one to freeze for a busy day ahead. Sweet potatoes add a touch of colour and a nutrient boost to the dish.

Sweet Potato Shepherd's Pies

2 lb (900 g) **extra-lean ground beef**

3 cloves **garlic,** minced

¼ cup **tomato paste**

3 ribs **celery,** finely chopped

2 **onions,** finely chopped

2 **carrots,** peeled and diced

1 **turnip** (about 8 oz/225 g), diced

1 **sweet green pepper,** diced

2 **bay leaves**

1¼ tsp **salt**

1 tsp **dried thyme**

½ tsp **pepper**

¼ tsp **nutmeg**

2 tbsp **all-purpose flour**

½ cup **sodium-reduced beef broth**

1½ tsp **Worcestershire sauce**

4 lb (1.8 kg) **sweet potatoes** (about 3), peeled and coarsely chopped

⅓ cup **milk**

2 tbsp **butter**

In Dutch oven, cook beef and garlic over medium heat, breaking up with spoon, until beef is no longer pink, about 10 minutes. Stir in tomato paste; cook, stirring, for 1 minute.

Stir in celery, onions, carrots, turnip, green pepper, bay leaves, ¾ tsp of the salt, the thyme, pepper and nutmeg. Cook, stirring occasionally, until vegetables are tender, about 15 minutes.

Stir in flour; cook, stirring, for 1 minute. Stir in broth, ¼ cup water and Worcestershire sauce; simmer for 3 minutes. Discard bay leaves. Divide between two 8-inch (2 L) square baking dishes.

Meanwhile, in large pot of boiling salted water, cook sweet potatoes until tender, about 12 minutes. Drain and return to pot over medium heat; cook, stirring, until dry, about 1 minute. Stir in milk, butter and remaining salt; mash until smooth. Spread evenly over beef mixture in each dish.

Bake 1 of the pies in 350°F (180°C) oven until bubbly, about 35 minutes. (*Make-ahead: Cover remaining pie with plastic wrap and overwrap in heavy-duty foil; freeze for up to 1 month. Uncover and bake frozen in 350°F/180°C oven for 50 to 60 minutes.*)

Makes 2 pies, 4 to 6 servings each. PER EACH OF 6 SERVINGS: about 311 cal, 18 g pro, 13 g total fat (6 g sat. fat), 31 g carb, 5 g fibre, 51 mg chol, 717 mg sodium, 715 mg potassium. % RDI: 7% calcium, 21% iron, 234% vit A, 48% vit C, 12% folate.

This twist on shepherd's pie features spicy chorizo and flavourful Oka cheese. A frozen casserole this large will take several days to thaw in the fridge, so don't worry if it's still a bit firm after thawing for a day. The partial thawing lets it reheat more evenly.

Pork Pie With Oka Mash

In large saucepan, heat oil over medium heat; cook leeks and garlic, stirring occasionally, until softened, about 6 minutes. Transfer to bowl.

In same pan, brown pork and chorizo over medium-high heat, breaking up pork with spoon, about 5 minutes. Add ¼ cup of the broth; cook, scraping up brown bits from bottom of pan, until no liquid remains. Stir in flour; cook, stirring, for 2 minutes.

Gradually stir in remaining broth; bring to boil. Stir in leek mixture, sweet potato, paprika, salt, pepper and cinnamon; bring to boil. Reduce heat and simmer, stirring often, until slightly thickened, about 15 minutes. Stir in peas; scrape into 13- x 9-inch (3 L) baking dish.

TOPPING: Meanwhile, in large saucepan of boiling salted water, cook potatoes and garlic until tender, about 20 minutes. Drain and return to pan; mash in milk, cheese and butter until smooth. Spread over pork mixture.

Bake in 400°F (200°C) oven until filling is bubbly and topping is golden, about 25 minutes.

Makes 8 to 10 servings. PER EACH OF 10 SERVINGS: about 523 cal, 30 g pro, 29 g total fat (13 g sat. fat), 34 g carb, 3 g fibre, 105 mg chol, 549 mg sodium, 841 mg potassium. % RDI: 20% calcium, 17% iron, 47% vit A, 23% vit C, 19% folate.

TO FREEZE: Follow first 4 paragraphs. Let cool. Cover with plastic wrap and overwrap in heavy-duty foil; freeze for up to 2 months. Thaw in refrigerator for 24 hours; remove plastic wrap, re-cover with foil and bake in 400°F (200°C) oven for 35 minutes. Increase heat to 425°F (220°C); bake, uncovered, until topping is golden, about 10 minutes.

1 tbsp **olive oil**

2 **leeks** (white and light green parts only), thinly sliced

3 cloves **garlic,** minced

2 lb (900 g) **lean ground pork**

4 oz (115 g) **dry-cured chorizo sausage** (see Tip, page 11), cubed

2 cups **sodium-reduced beef broth**

⅓ cup **all-purpose flour**

1 **sweet potato,** peeled and finely chopped

1 tsp **smoked paprika**

¼ tsp each **salt** and **pepper**

Pinch **cinnamon**

1 cup **frozen peas**

TOPPING:
3 lb (1.35 kg) **potatoes,** peeled and quartered

2 cloves **garlic**

1 cup **milk**

8 oz (225 g) shredded **Oka cheese**

2 tbsp **butter**

Technically, shepherd's pie is made with lamb or mutton. Cottage pie is the correct name for the beef version of this dish. But no matter which name you use, this meat-and-potatoes one-pot meal is a comfort food favourite.

Cheddar Cottage Pie

CHEDDAR MASHED POTATOES: In large saucepan of boiling salted water, cook potatoes until tender, about 10 minutes. Drain and set aside.

In same saucepan, heat milk until small bubbles form around edge; remove from heat. Add potatoes; mash with potato masher. Using electric beater, beat until smooth. Stir in cheese.

Meanwhile, in large skillet, heat oil over medium heat; cook onion, carrots and garlic, stirring occasionally, until softened, about 5 minutes. Add beef, thyme, salt and pepper; cook, stirring, until beef is no longer pink. Stir in tomato paste.

Stir in broth and Worcestershire sauce; bring to boil. Cover, reduce heat and simmer for 15 minutes.

Pour meat mixture into 6-cup (1.5 L) casserole dish. Spread mashed potatoes evenly over top. Bake in 400°F (200°C) oven until bubbly and browned, about 20 minutes.

Makes 4 to 6 servings. PER EACH OF 6 SERVINGS: about 407 cal, 24 g pro, 20 g total fat (9 g sat. fat), 33 g carb, 3 g fibre, 68 mg chol, 470 mg sodium, 864 mg potassium. % RDI: 21% calcium, 18% iron, 61% vit A, 20% vit C, 13% folate.

1 tbsp **vegetable oil**

1 **onion,** diced

2 large **carrots,** diced

2 cloves **garlic,** minced

1 lb (450 g) **lean ground beef**

½ tsp **dried thyme**

¼ tsp each **salt** and **pepper**

2 tbsp **tomato paste**

1⅓ cups **sodium-reduced beef broth**

1 tbsp **Worcestershire sauce**

CHEDDAR MASHED
POTATOES:

2 lb (900 g) **boiling potatoes,** peeled

1 cup **milk**

1 cup shredded **extra-old Cheddar cheese**

Vegetarians and nonvegetarians alike will enjoy the taco-style flavours in this meatless shepherd's pie. Instead of beans or soy-based substitutes, bulgur (cracked wheat) stands in for the traditional meat, adding body and a nutty taste to the filling.

Vegetarian Tex-Mex Shepherd's Pie

6 **Yukon Gold potatoes**
   (2 lb/900 g)

¼ cup **milk**

2 tbsp chopped **fresh parsley**

2 tbsp **butter**

¾ tsp each **salt** and **pepper**

1 tbsp **vegetable oil**

2 **carrots,** diced

1 **onion,** chopped

1 **sweet red pepper,** chopped

1 tbsp **chili powder**

½ tsp **ground cumin**

Pinch **cayenne pepper**

¾ cup **bulgur**

2 tbsp **all-purpose flour**

1½ cups **vegetable broth**

1 cup **corn kernels**

Peel and cut potatoes into 2-inch (5 cm) chunks. In saucepan of boiling water, cover and cook potatoes until tender, about 20 minutes; drain and mash. Mash in milk, parsley, butter and ½ tsp each of the salt and pepper.

Meanwhile, in large skillet, heat oil over medium heat; cook carrots, onion, red pepper, chili powder, cumin and cayenne pepper, stirring occasionally, until onion is softened, about 5 minutes.

Add bulgur and flour; cook, stirring, for 1 minute. Gradually stir in broth; cover and cook over low heat until liquid is absorbed, about 10 minutes.

Add corn and remaining salt and pepper. Spread in 8-inch (2 L) square baking dish; spread potatoes over top. Broil until golden, about 2 minutes. (*Make-ahead: Let cool for 30 minutes; refrigerate until cold. Cover and refrigerate for up to 24 hours; reheat, covered, in 350°F/180°C oven until filling is bubbly, about 30 minutes.*)

Makes 4 to 6 servings. PER EACH OF 6 SERVINGS: about 277 cal, 7 g pro, 7 g total fat (3 g sat. fat), 50 g carb, 6 g fibre, 11 mg chol, 529 mg sodium. % RDI: 5% calcium, 14% iron, 78% vit A, 73% vit C, 19% folate.

Around the holidays, you need a recipe that makes delicious use of turkey leftovers.
Well, look no further. The pastry recipe on page 167 is terrific, but feel free to use your
favourite family recipe or, in a pinch, a sheet of store-bought butter puff pastry.

Turkey Pot Pie

In Dutch oven, heat oil over medium heat; cook onion, leeks, celery
and carrot, stirring occasionally, until softened, about 5 minutes.
Add mushrooms and garlic; cook, stirring occasionally, until
softened, about 8 minutes.

Add flour, salt, thyme, pepper and savory; cook, stirring, for
1 minute. Slowly pour in stock, stirring and scraping up browned
bits; bring to boil. Reduce heat and simmer for 10 minutes. Stir in
turkey and peas. Pour into 6- to 8-cup (1.5 to 2 L) casserole dish.

On floured surface, roll out pastry to fit top of dish. Press over dish;
trim to leave ¾-inch (2 cm) overhang. Fold overhang under pastry
rim; flute to seal. Brush top with water; cut steam vents. Bake in
400°F (200°C) oven for 15 minutes. Reduce heat to 350°F (180°C);
bake until pastry is golden and filling is bubbly, about 20 minutes.

Makes 4 servings. PER SERVING: about 620 cal, 56 g pro, 25 g total fat
(10 g sat. fat), 40 g carb, 5 g fibre, 130 mg chol, 546 mg sodium, 1,241 mg
potassium. % RDI: 10% calcium, 44% iron, 62% vit A, 12% vit C, 57% folate.

Homemade Turkey Stock

In large stockpot, combine 12 cups cold water; 1 turkey carcass,
broken into 3 or 4 pieces; 2 each ribs celery with leaves, carrots and
onions (unpeeled), coarsely chopped; 1 bay leaf; 1 tbsp black
peppercorns; and 6 stems fresh parsley or cilantro. Bring to boil.
Skim off any foam. Reduce heat and simmer for 4 hours. Strain
through cheesecloth-lined sieve set over large bowl; let cool.
Refrigerate until fat solidifies on surface, about 8 hours. Discard
fat. Refrigerate stock in airtight container for up to 3 days or freeze
for up to 4 months.

Makes 6 cups.

1 tbsp **vegetable oil**

Half **onion,** diced

1 cup chopped **leeks** (white and
light green parts only)

1 cup each chopped **celery**
and **carrot**

8 oz (225 g) **cremini mushrooms,**
quartered

1 clove **garlic,** minced

⅓ cup **all-purpose flour**

½ tsp each **salt** and **dried thyme**

¼ tsp each **pepper** and
dried savory

3 cups **Homemade Turkey
Stock** (recipe, below left)

4 cups chopped **cooked turkey**

1 cup **frozen peas**

Half **Really Flaky Pastry** (recipe,
page 167)

Many tourtières have a medley of meats, often including game. Our version contains pork, chicken and veal, giving it a milder flavour that's still rich and delicious. A simple green salad makes a nice side dish.

Rustic Tourtière

12 oz (340 g) **boneless pork shoulder**

12 oz (340 g) **boneless skinless chicken thighs**

12 oz (340 g) **boneless veal shoulder**

½ cup **all-purpose flour**

½ tsp each **salt** and **pepper**

2 tbsp **vegetable oil**

1 **onion,** chopped

3 cloves **garlic,** minced

1 cup each chopped **carrots** and **celery**

½ tsp **dried savory**

¼ tsp each crumbled **dried rosemary** and **nutmeg**

Pinch **cinnamon**

1 **bay leaf**

2 cups **chicken broth**

2 cups **pearl onions**

Really Flaky Pastry (recipe, opposite)

1 **egg yolk**

Cut pork, chicken and veal into ¾-inch (2 cm) cubes. Toss together meat cubes, flour, salt and pepper.

In large saucepan, heat 1 tbsp of the oil over medium-high heat; reserving remaining flour mixture, brown meat mixture, in batches and adding remaining oil as necessary. Transfer to plate.

Drain fat from pan; fry onion, garlic, carrots, celery, savory, rosemary, nutmeg, cinnamon and bay leaf over medium heat, stirring occasionally, until onion is softened, about 5 minutes.

Sprinkle with reserved flour mixture; cook, stirring, for 1 minute. Add broth and bring to boil, stirring and scraping up brown bits from bottom of pan. Return meat mixture and any accumulated juices to pan; reduce heat, cover and simmer for 45 minutes.

Add pearl onions; cover and simmer until tender, about 30 minutes. Discard bay leaf; let cool.

On lightly floured surface, roll out 1 of the pastry discs to scant ¼-inch (5 mm) thickness. Fit into deep 9-inch (23 cm) pie plate. Spoon in filling. Roll out remaining pastry. Brush pie rim with water; cover with top pastry and press edge to seal. Trim and flute.

If desired, roll out scraps; cut out decorative shapes. (*Make-ahead:
Wrap tourtière and shapes separately; refrigerate for up to 24 hours.
Or overwrap in heavy-duty foil and freeze for up to 2 weeks; thaw in
refrigerator. Uncover and bake, adding 20 to 30 minutes to baking
time and covering with foil after 45 minutes; remove foil for last
10 minutes.*)

Mix egg yolk with 2 tsp water; brush three-quarters over top.
Arrange shapes on top; brush with remaining egg wash. Cut steam
vents in top.

Bake in bottom third of 400°F (200°C) oven until hot and golden
brown, about 1 hour.

Makes 8 servings. PER SERVING: about 675 cal, 34 g pro, 37 g total fat
(16 g sat. fat), 48 g carb, 3 g fibre, 194 mg chol, 876 mg sodium. % RDI:
6% calcium, 33% iron, 48% vit A, 8% vit C, 43% folate.

Really Flaky Pastry

In bowl, whisk 3 cups all-purpose flour with 1 tsp salt. Using pastry
blender or 2 knives, cut in ½ cup each cold butter and lard, cubed,
until in coarse crumbs with a few larger pieces. In liquid measure,
beat 1 egg with 2 tsp white vinegar; add enough ice water to make
⅔ cup. Drizzle over flour mixture, tossing with fork until ragged
dough forms. Press into 2 discs. Wrap and refrigerate until chilled,
about 30 minutes. (*Make-ahead: Refrigerate for up to 3 days.*)

Makes enough pastry for 1 double-crust 9-inch (23 cm) pie.

Saffron adds a subtle accent to this deep-dish pie filled with a luxurious mix of seafood. Expect raves! You can replace the lobster with 12 oz (340 g) bay scallops; just simmer in cooking liquid until opaque, about 3 minutes.

Seafood Pie

1½ lb (675 g) **firm fish fillets** (such as tilapia, monkfish or salmon)

¾ cup **white wine** or water

1 lb (450 g) **raw large shrimp,** peeled and deveined

Pinch **saffron**

2 tbsp **butter**

1 **onion,** chopped

3 cloves **garlic,** minced

1 rib **celery,** sliced

1 tsp **dried thyme**

½ tsp each **salt** and **pepper**

⅓ cup **all-purpose flour**

¾ cup **whipping cream** or 10% cream

¼ cup chopped **fresh parsley**

1 can (11.3 oz/320 g) **frozen lobster,** thawed

1½ cups cubed (1 inch/2.5 cm) peeled **potatoes**

Half **Really Flaky Pastry** (recipe, page 167)

1 **egg yolk**

Cut fish into 1-inch (2.5 cm) pieces. In large saucepan, bring wine and ½ cup water to boil; simmer fish until fish flakes easily when tested, about 5 minutes. Using slotted spoon, transfer to strainer set over bowl. Add shrimp to pan; simmer until pink but still translucent, about 3 minutes. Add to strainer. Strain cooking liquid through fine sieve into glass measure to make 1½ cups, adding water if necessary. Stir in saffron. Cover and set aside.

In saucepan, melt butter over medium heat; fry onion, garlic, celery, thyme, salt and pepper, stirring occasionally, until onion is softened, 5 minutes. Sprinkle with flour; cook, stirring, for 1 minute. Whisk in reserved cooking liquid and cream; bring to boil and boil gently until thick enough to coat spoon, 5 minutes. Add parsley. Set aside.

Drain lobster in sieve; press out moisture. Remove cartilage from claw meat. Cut lobster into bite-size pieces; place in shallow 10-cup (2.5 L) casserole dish. Add fish mixture and potatoes. Pour in sauce and stir gently. Let cool.

On lightly floured surface, roll out pastry to scant ¼-inch (5 mm) thickness. Brush rim of dish with water; cover with pastry and trim to leave 1-inch (2.5 cm) overhang. Press overhang around outside of dish, fluting edge if desired. *(Make-ahead: Cover and refrigerate for up to 24 hours; add 15 minutes to baking time.)*

Mix egg yolk with 2 tsp water; brush about three-quarters over pastry. If desired, roll out pastry scraps; cut out decorative shapes. Arrange on top. Brush pastry with remaining egg mixture; cut steam vents in top. Bake in bottom third of 375°F (190°C) oven until filling is hot and pastry is golden, about 40 minutes.

Makes 8 to 10 servings. PER EACH OF 10 SERVINGS: about 559 cal, 28 g pro, 32 g total fat (16 g sat. fat), 39 g carb, 2 g fibre, 202 mg chol, 625 mg sodium. % RDI: 7% calcium, 26% iron, 22% vit A, 8% vit C, 33% folate.

Rustic skillet pies are beautiful for casual entertaining. They come to the table looking so inviting, just waiting for you to cut into them and reveal the treasures inside. In this one, it's a rich combination of earthy greens and salty cheese.

Greens and Feta Pie

In large bowl, whisk together flour, salt and baking powder. Whisk together oil, milk and egg; pour over dry ingredients. Using wooden spoon, stir to form fairly smooth dough. Turn out onto lightly floured surface; knead until smooth, about 2 minutes. Press into disc; wrap in plastic wrap and refrigerate for 30 minutes. (Dough will seem oily when removed from refrigerator.)

FILLING: Meanwhile, in skillet, heat oil over medium heat; cook onion and leek, stirring occasionally, until softened, about 5 minutes. Transfer to large bowl.

Wash spinach and beet greens in several changes of water; drain. In large pot, in batches, cover and cook spinach and greens over medium-high heat, with just water clinging to leaves, stirring once, until wilted, about 3 minutes. Let cool.

Transfer to sieve; squeeze out moisture. Add to onion mixture along with feta and mozzarella cheeses, eggs, dill, salt and pepper; mix well. Set aside.

On floured surface, roll out dough to 16-inch (40 cm) circle. Loosely roll around rolling pin; unroll onto 9-inch (23 cm) cast-iron skillet or metal baking dish, letting dough hang over edge. Mound filling in centre; lift pastry up over filling, letting pastry fall naturally into folds and leaving 5-inch (12 cm) opening in centre.

Bake in bottom third of 375°F (190°C) oven until pastry is golden and filling is steaming, about 45 minutes. Let cool for 30 minutes. Refrigerate until cold. Cover and refrigerate for up to 24 hours. Cut into wedges.

Makes 8 servings. PER SERVING: about 387 cal, 15 g pro, 24 g total fat (8 g sat. fat), 31 g carb, 4 g fibre, 106 mg chol, 1,248 mg sodium, 674 mg potassium. % RDI: 34% calcium, 35% iron, 94% vit A, 25% vit C, 82% folate.

1¾ cups **all-purpose flour**

1 tsp **salt**

1 tsp **baking powder**

⅓ cup **extra-virgin olive oil**

⅓ cup **milk**

1 **egg**

FILLING:

2 tbsp **extra-virgin olive oil**

1 small **sweet onion,** diced

1 **leek** (white and light green parts only), diced

2 bunches or bags (each 10 oz/284 g) **fresh spinach,** trimmed and coarsely chopped

1 lb (450 g) **beet greens** or Swiss chard leaves (about 1 bunch), stems removed and coarsely shredded

1½ cups crumbled **feta cheese**

¾ cup shredded **mozzarella cheese**

2 **eggs**

1 cup loosely packed chopped **fresh dill**

1½ tsp each **salt** and **pepper**

Although the recipe looks long, this pie is easy to make and will be the star of any occasion. The pie is a heartier version of the famous Greek spinach-and-cheese pie called spanakopita.

Spinach and Rice Phyllo Pie

¾ cup **parboiled whole grain brown rice**

½ tsp **salt**

1½ pkg (each 10 oz/284 g) **fresh spinach,** trimmed

¼ cup **pine nuts**

1 cup **ricotta cheese** or cottage cheese

1 cup shredded **old Cheddar cheese**

1 **egg**

1 tbsp finely chopped **fresh dill** (or 1 tsp dried dillweed)

1 tsp grated **lemon zest**

1 tbsp **lemon juice**

¼ tsp **pepper**

Pinch **nutmeg**

6 sheets **phyllo pastry**

¼ cup **butter,** melted, or vegetable oil

2 cups **tomato pasta sauce**

In saucepan, bring 1½ cups water, rice and salt to boil; cover and cook over low heat until tender and water is absorbed, 20 minutes. Let stand for 5 minutes; transfer to large bowl. Let cool.

Meanwhile, rinse spinach; shake off excess water. In large saucepan, cover and cook spinach over medium-high heat, with just water clinging to leaves, until wilted, about 3 minutes. Drain and squeeze dry; chop coarsely and add to cooled rice.

In small skillet, toast pine nuts over medium-low heat, stirring often, until golden, about 5 minutes. Add to rice along with ricotta and Cheddar cheeses, egg, dill, lemon zest and juice, pepper and nutmeg; mix well.

Lay 1 sheet of phyllo on work surface, covering remainder with damp cloth. Brush with some of the butter; lay in greased 9-inch (23 cm) pie plate, leaving overhang. Repeat with 4 more sheets of phyllo, alternating direction of each. Spoon in rice mixture.

Brush remaining sheet of phyllo with butter. Fold in half and lay over rice mixture; tuck in around edge. Bring overhang over top and crumple slightly. Brush top with remaining butter.

Bake in bottom third of 350°F (180°C) oven until golden and crisp, about 45 minutes. Let stand for 5 minutes before slicing.

Meanwhile, in small saucepan, heat pasta sauce over medium heat; spoon onto each of 6 plates. Top each with slice of pie.

Makes 6 servings. PER SERVING: about 494 cal, 19 g pro, 28 g total fat (14 g sat. fat), 44 g carb, 5 g fibre, 96 mg chol, 949 mg sodium. % RDI: 31% calcium, 36% iron, 73% vit A, 23% vit C, 61% folate.

Available in the health food section of grocery stores and in natural food stores, mildly flavoured millet is a perfect backdrop for stronger seasonings. Here, it's an interesting alternative to regular rice stuffing.

Millet and Sausage– Stuffed Peppers

1⅓ cups **vegetable broth**

⅔ cup **hulled millet**

3 **mild Italian sausages,** casings removed

1 tbsp **vegetable oil**

⅓ cup **pine nuts**

1 small **onion,** diced

2 cloves **garlic,** minced

¼ cup drained **oil-packed sun-dried tomatoes,** chopped

¼ tsp each **salt** and **pepper**

Pinch **cinnamon**

¼ cup chopped **fresh basil** or parsley

4 **sweet red peppers** or sweet yellow peppers

In saucepan, bring broth to boil; stir in millet. Reduce heat, cover and simmer until no liquid remains, about 25 minutes.

Meanwhile, in skillet, sauté sausage over medium-high heat, breaking up with spoon, until no longer pink, about 8 minutes. Transfer to paper towel–lined plate.

Drain fat from pan; add oil. Toast pine nuts over medium heat, stirring, until light golden, about 2 minutes. Stir in onion, garlic, sun-dried tomatoes, salt, pepper and cinnamon; fry, stirring, until onions are softened, about 5 minutes.

Combine millet, sausage, onion mixture and basil; set aside.

Cut peppers in half lengthwise; with spoon, remove seeds and ribs. Fill peppers with millet mixture; place in roasting pan just large enough to hold peppers snugly.

Pour in ⅔ cup water; cover with lightly greased foil. Bake in 400°F (200°C) oven until peppers are tender, about 55 minutes.

Makes 4 servings. PER SERVING: about 436 cal, 18 g pro, 24 g total fat (5 g sat. fat), 40 g carb, 6 g fibre, 32 mg chol, 824 mg sodium. % RDI: 4% calcium, 21% iron, 47% vit A, 342% vit C, 22% folate.

Chili con queso is typically served as a dip with tortilla chips or vegetables. Here, this creamy cheese-and-chili combo becomes the sauce for an enchilada-style dish. The sauce may seem too generous at first, but it will thicken up nicely as it cooks.

Turkey con Queso Bake

In saucepan, melt butter over medium heat; fry onion and garlic, stirring occasionally, until softened, about 2 minutes.

Add flour; cook, stirring, for 2 minutes. Whisk in stock and milk and bring to boil, stirring; reduce heat and simmer until thickened, about 5 minutes. Remove from heat. Add 2½ cups of the cheese, salt and pepper; set aside.

FILLING: In large bowl, combine turkey, tomatoes, olives, onions, cilantro and jalapeño pepper; stir in ½ cup of the cheese sauce. Spoon ¾ cup filling into greased 13- x 9-inch (3 L) baking dish.

Divide remaining filling evenly among centres of tortillas; roll up loosely. Place, seam side down, on sauce. Spoon remaining sauce over top; sprinkle with remaining cheese. (*Make-ahead: Cover and refrigerate for up to 8 hours; let stand at room temperature for 30 minutes.*)

Bake in 350°F (180°C) oven until golden and bubbly, 35 to 40 minutes. Let stand for 15 minutes before serving.

Makes 8 servings. PER SERVING: about 463 cal, 28 g pro, 25 g total fat (13 g sat. fat), 32 g carb, 2 g fibre, 87 mg chol, 813 mg sodium. % RDI: 35% calcium, 21% iron, 22% vit A, 13% vit C, 35% folate.

3 tbsp **butter**

1 **onion,** chopped

2 cloves **garlic,** minced

¼ cup **all-purpose flour**

1½ cups **Homemade Turkey Stock** (recipe, page 165) or chicken broth

1 cup **milk**

3 cups shredded **old Cheddar cheese**

½ tsp each **salt** and **pepper**

8 **tortillas** (7 inches/18 cm)

FILLING:

2 cups diced **cooked turkey**

2 **tomatoes,** seeded and diced

¼ cup chopped **green olives**

3 **green onions,** chopped

2 tbsp chopped **fresh cilantro**

1 **jalapeño pepper,** seeded and chopped

This rich puff looks gorgeous on a brunch buffet table – and it tastes even better. Packed with layers of buttery croissants, eggs, cheese and smoked salmon, it's an indulgent meal you'll want to serve again and again.

Smoked Salmon and Goat Cheese Strata

10 cups cubed **croissants** (6 or 7)

5 oz (140 g) thinly sliced **smoked salmon,** torn or cut in pieces

4 oz (115 g) **soft goat cheese,** crumbled

⅓ cup thinly sliced **shallots** or red onion

2 tbsp chopped **fresh dill**

4 tsp **capers,** drained and rinsed

10 **eggs**

4 cups **milk**

1 tbsp **Dijon mustard**

¼ tsp each **salt** and **pepper**

In greased 13- x 9-inch (3 L) baking dish, toss together croissant cubes, salmon, goat cheese, shallots, dill and capers.

Whisk together eggs, milk, Dijon mustard, salt and pepper; pour over croissant mixture, pressing to soak. Let stand for 10 minutes.

Bake in 350°F (180°C) oven until puffed, golden and set enough that strata doesn't jiggle in centre when gently shaken, about 1 hour. Let cool for 5 minutes before cutting.

Makes 8 to 10 servings. PER EACH OF 10 SERVINGS: about 313 cal, 17 g pro, 17 g total fat (8 g sat. fat), 22 g carb, 1 g fibre, 225 mg chol, 620 mg sodium, 298 mg potassium. % RDI: 16% calcium, 13% iron, 22% vit A, 24% folate.

Strata is simply a savoury take on bread pudding, with layers of cubed bread and tasty tidbits of meat and/or vegetables bathed in an eggy custard. The best part is that this strata can be made a day ahead, giving you time to relax and enjoy your meal.

Spinach, Ham and Cheese Strata

In skillet, heat oil over medium-high heat; sauté spinach, garlic, salt and pepper until spinach is wilted and no liquid remains, 5 to 7 minutes.

Stir together spinach mixture, bread, onions, Swiss cheese and ham. Spread in greased 8-cup (2 L) casserole dish or 8-inch (2 L) square baking dish.

Whisk together eggs, milk and mustard; pour over bread mixture and let stand for 20 minutes. *(Make-ahead: Cover and refrigerate for up to 24 hours.)*

Bake in 375°F (190°C) oven until puffed and golden, about 45 minutes.

Makes 4 servings. PER SERVING: about 411 cal, 26 g pro, 18 g total fat (7 g sat. fat), 36 g carb, 4 g fibre, 220 mg chol, 899 mg sodium, 661 mg potassium. % RDI: 38% calcium, 34% iron, 87% vit A, 13% vit C, 78% folate.

1 tbsp **olive oil**

1 bunch (10 oz/280 g) **fresh spinach,** chopped

1 clove **garlic,** minced

¼ tsp each **salt** and **pepper**

6 cups cubed (1 inch/2.5 cm) **sourdough bread**

3 **green onions,** thinly sliced

¾ cup shredded **Swiss cheese**

½ cup chopped sliced **ham**

4 **eggs**

1¼ cups **milk**

1½ tsp **Dijon mustard**

Looking for a hearty, crowd-pleasing vegetarian recipe to bring to a potluck or party? This rich-tasting ragout is just the thing. It's crowned with a feta-infused topping that adds just the right amount of crunch to each bite.

Eggplant and Potato Ragout With Feta Topping

1 **eggplant** (1½ lb/675 g), cut in ¾-inch (2 cm) cubes

2 tsp **salt**

⅓ cup **extra-virgin olive oil**

4 **Yukon Gold potatoes** (2 lb/900 g), unpeeled and cut in ¾-inch (2 cm) cubes

4 cups sliced **mushrooms** (about 12 oz/340 g)

1 large **onion,** chopped

6 cloves **garlic,** minced

1 tbsp **dried oregano**

½ tsp **dried basil**

½ tsp **pepper**

1 each **sweet red** and **green pepper,** chopped

2 cans (each 19 oz/540 mL) **stewed tomatoes**

1 cup **vegetable broth**

¼ cup **tomato paste**

FETA TOPPING:

2½ cups **fresh bread crumbs**

1¾ cups crumbled **feta cheese**

¼ cup chopped **oil-cured black olives**

¼ cup chopped **fresh parsley**

1 tsp **dried oregano**

In colander, sprinkle eggplant with 1 tsp of the salt; set aside.

Meanwhile, in large deep Dutch oven, heat 3 tbsp of the oil over medium-high heat; brown potatoes. Transfer potatoes to plate.

Rinse eggplant; pat dry. Add half of the remaining oil to pan; brown eggplant, in 2 batches and adding remaining oil as necessary. Add to potatoes.

In same skillet over medium-high heat, sauté mushrooms, onion, garlic, oregano, basil, pepper and remaining salt until no liquid remains, about 8 minutes. Add red and green peppers; sauté until beginning to brown, about 5 minutes.

Add eggplant mixture, tomatoes, broth and tomato paste; bring to boil. Reduce heat and simmer until potatoes are tender, about 40 minutes. (*Make-ahead: Let cool for 30 minutes. Refrigerate, uncovered, in airtight container until cold. Cover and refrigerate for up to 24 hours. Reheat.*) Pour into 13- x 9-inch (3 L) baking dish.

FETA TOPPING: Meanwhile, combine bread crumbs, feta cheese, olives, parsley and oregano. (*Make-ahead: Cover and refrigerate for up to 24 hours.*)

Spread topping over eggplant mixture; bake in 375°F (190°C) oven until bubbly and golden, about 25 minutes.

Makes 8 servings. PER SERVING: about 360 cal, 9 g pro, 16 g total fat (5 g sat. fat), 49 g carb, 8 g fibre, 17 mg chol, 1,162 mg sodium. % RDI: 18% calcium, 28% iron, 20% vit A, 120% vit C, 26% folate.

Keep this recipe handy for times when you need a satisfying homemade dinner but don't have time to cook. Tomatoes and peppers contain lots of vitamins, but you can add a simple green salad alongside if you want some extra vegetables.

Italian Sausage Bean Bake

In large heatproof skillet, heat oil over medium-high heat; brown sausages, turning once, about 5 minutes. Transfer to plate; cut into ¾-inch (2 cm) thick slices.

Drain any fat from pan; fry onion and red pepper over medium heat until onion is softened, about 4 minutes. Return sausages to pan. Stir in beans and pasta sauce; bring to boil.

Meanwhile, in food processor, whirl bread into fine crumbs. Add parsley and butter; pulse to moisten. Sprinkle over bean mixture.

Bake in 450°F (230°C) oven until filling is bubbly and topping is golden, about 10 minutes.

Makes 4 servings. PER SERVING: about 641 cal, 37 g pro, 25 g total fat (8 g sat. fat), 69 g carb, 7 g fibre, 57 mg chol, 2,332 mg sodium. % RDI: 14% calcium, 45% iron, 15% vit A, 70% vit C, 63% folate.

1 tsp **vegetable oil**

4 **lean Italian sausages** (about 1 lb/450 g)

1 **onion,** sliced

Half **sweet red pepper,** chopped

2 cans (each 19 oz/540 mL) **navy beans,** drained and rinsed

1 jar (675 mL) **pasta sauce**

1 slice **whole grain bread**

1 tbsp chopped **fresh parsley**

1 tbsp **butter,** melted

This casserole is like an upside-down shepherd's pie, with polenta instead of potatoes. You can, of course, use mashed potatoes or even noodles as a base. The beef and vegetable topping will taste just as good on them.

Beef and Polenta Bake

1 lb (450 g) **lean ground beef**

1 **onion,** chopped

3 cloves **garlic,** minced

3 **carrots,** finely chopped

2 ribs **celery,** chopped

2 cups chopped **mushrooms**

1 tbsp **dried Italian herb seasoning**

½ tsp each **salt** and **pepper**

½ cup **red wine** or beef broth

¼ cup **tomato paste**

1 can (28 oz/796 mL) **whole tomatoes**

2 tbsp minced **fresh parsley**

½ cup shredded **provolone cheese** or mozzarella cheese

POLENTA:

5 cups **water**

½ tsp **salt**

1 cup **cornmeal**

¼ cup grated **Parmesan cheese**

POLENTA: In large saucepan, bring water and salt to boil over high heat; reduce heat to low. Gradually whisk in cornmeal; cook, stirring often with wooden spoon, until thick enough to mound on spoon, about 10 minutes. Stir in Parmesan cheese. Spoon into greased 13- x 9-inch (3 L) baking dish. Set aside.

In large Dutch oven, sauté beef over medium-high heat, breaking up with spoon, until no longer pink, 5 minutes. Drain off any fat.

Add onion, garlic, carrots, celery, mushrooms, Italian herb seasoning, salt and pepper; cook over medium heat until onion is softened, about 4 minutes. Stir in wine, tomato paste and tomatoes, breaking up tomatoes with potato masher. Bring to boil; reduce heat and simmer until thickened enough to mound on spoon, about 20 minutes. Stir in parsley.

Spoon over polenta. Sprinkle with provolone cheese. (*Make-ahead: Let cool for 30 minutes; refrigerate until cold. Cover and refrigerate for up to 24 hours; uncover.*)

Bake in 375°F (190°C) oven until cheese is melted and golden, about 15 minutes.

Makes 8 servings. PER SERVING: about 276 cal, 18 g pro, 11 g total fat (5 g sat. fat), 26 g carb, 3 g fibre, 41 mg chol, 630 mg sodium. % RDI: 15% calcium, 21% iron, 80% vit A, 35% vit C, 13% folate.

The potatoes at the bottom of this dish crisp up nicely as the tomato-topped fish cooks to succulent tenderness. A quick tossed salad and crusty rolls are delicious side dishes if you want a little something extra.

Tomato-Topped Fish and Potato Bake

¼ cup **extra-virgin olive oil**

4 **potatoes** (1½ lb/675 g), peeled and thinly sliced

Half **onion,** thinly sliced

½ tsp each **salt** and **pepper**

2 **tomatoes,** seeded and finely chopped

2 cloves **garlic,** minced

2 tbsp chopped **fresh parsley**

1½ lb (675 g) **white fish fillets,** such as halibut, cod or haddock

½ tsp **fennel seeds,** lightly crushed, or dried oregano

Spread 2 tbsp of the oil in large cast-iron or ovenproof skillet. Layer potatoes, onion and half each of the salt and pepper in pan; sprinkle with 1 tbsp of the remaining oil. Heat over high heat until sizzling, about 2 minutes. Reduce heat to medium; cover and cook for 12 minutes.

Meanwhile, mix together tomatoes, garlic, parsley and remaining oil, salt and pepper; set aside.

Remove pan from heat. Arrange fish over potatoes; top with tomato mixture. Sprinkle with fennel seeds. Bake in 450°F (230°C) oven until fish flakes easily when tested, about 12 minutes.

Makes 4 servings. PER SERVING: about 408 cal, 38 g pro, 18 g total fat (2 g sat. fat), 24 g carb, 3 g fibre, 54 mg chol, 389 mg sodium. % RDI: 9% calcium, 17% iron, 14% vit A, 37% vit C, 13% folate.

You can wrap the salmon package early in the day, then drizzle with the wine mixture just before baking. To tempt your guests with a wave of herbal aromas, open the package at the table, averting your face and fingers from the very hot escaping steam.

Salmon en Papillote With Root Vegetables

Peel and cut carrots, parsnips and rutabaga into 2- x ¼- x ¼-inch (5 cm x 5 mm x 5 mm) sticks. Cut celery into similar-size sticks.

In large pot of boiling water, blanch vegetables until tender-crisp, about 2 minutes. Drain and chill under cold water; drain and pat dry.

Centre 30-inch (75 cm) long piece of parchment paper crosswise on large rimmed baking sheet; arrange vegetables in line down centre, same length as salmon. Sprinkle with parsley and thyme.

Cut salmon crosswise into 8 pieces; arrange over vegetables as though still whole. (*Make-ahead: Wrap paper loosely over salmon, cover with plastic wrap and refrigerate for up to 6 hours; increase cooking time by 5 minutes.*)

Arrange lemon on salmon. Whisk together wine, oil, garlic, salt and pepper; drizzle over salmon. Fold short ends of paper over salmon; bring long edges together and fold tightly to form package. Secure with toothpicks if necessary.

Bake in 425°F (220°C) oven until vegetables are tender and fish flakes easily when tested, about 20 minutes.

Makes 8 servings. PER SERVING: about 358 cal, 31 g pro, 18 g total fat (3 g sat. fat), 16 g carb, 3 g fibre, 84 mg chol, 267 mg sodium. % RDI: 7% calcium, 9% iron, 62% vit A, 40% vit C, 38% folate.

2 large **carrots**

2 large **parsnips** or kohlrabi

Half **rutabaga**

2 ribs **celery**

1 tbsp chopped **fresh parsley**

1 tbsp chopped **fresh thyme**

3 lb (1.35 kg) **salmon fillet**

8 thin slices **lemon**

¼ cup **white wine** or lemon juice

1 tbsp **vegetable oil**

1 clove **garlic,** minced

½ tsp each **salt** and **pepper**

Stuffed cabbage leaves are a favourite comforting fall dish. There are endless variations from across eastern Europe – our version is inspired by Polish, Czech, Slovakian and Hungarian recipes.

Cabbage Rolls

Core cabbage. In large pot of boiling water, blanch cabbage, covered, until leaves are softened, 10 to 15 minutes. Working from core end, carefully pull pliable outer leaves off with tongs; return cabbage to boiling water for 2 to 3 minutes when leaves become difficult to remove. Remove 14 to 20 leaves total; drain on tea towels.

In skillet over medium heat, fry bacon until crisp; drain on paper towel–lined plate. Set aside 1 tbsp bacon fat; drain off all but 2 tbsp of the remaining fat from pan. Chop bacon; place in large bowl.

Add onions and carrots to pan; fry until onions are golden, about 15 minutes. Stir into bowl along with beef, pork, ½ cup of the strained tomatoes, egg, parsley, garlic, 1½ tsp of the salt, marjoram and pepper.

Pat each cabbage leaf dry; cut off any tough ribs. For each roll, spoon 2 to 3 tbsp filling onto leaf; tuck in sides and roll up. Place, seam side down, in greased 13- x 9-inch (3 L) or larger baking dish. If desired, shred a few of the leftover cabbage leaves; scatter thin layer over top.

In bowl or large glass measure, whisk together tomato paste, reserved bacon fat and ¼ cup warm water; whisk in remaining strained tomatoes, sugar, lemon juice, vinegar and remaining salt. Spread over cabbage rolls. Cover with foil; bake on rimmed baking sheet in 350°F (180°C) oven for 1¼ hours. Uncover; bake until cabbage is soft and translucent and filling is firm, about 45 minutes. Serve with sour cream.

Makes 7 to 10 servings. PER EACH OF 10 SERVINGS: about 280 cal, 17 g pro, 17 g total fat (6 g sat. fat), 14 g carb, 2 g fibre, 71 mg chol, 817 mg sodium, 560 mg potassium. % RDI: 5% calcium, 22% iron, 25% vit A, 33% vit C, 15% folate.

1 large head **cabbage**

8 oz (225 g) **bacon**

2 **onions,** finely chopped

1 cup finely diced **carrots**

1 lb (450 g) **lean ground beef**

8 oz (225 g) **ground pork** or ground beef

1 bottle (680 mL) **strained tomatoes** (passata)

1 **egg,** beaten

½ cup finely chopped **fresh parsley**

2 cloves **garlic,** pressed or minced

2 tsp **salt**

1½ tsp **dried marjoram**

1¼ tsp **pepper**

3 tbsp **tomato paste**

2 tbsp **granulated sugar**

2 tbsp **lemon juice**

2 tsp **cider vinegar**

Sour cream

**Creamy Meatballs and
Noodles, page 205**

Skillets, Simmers & Stir-Fries

Serve this strata for breakfast, brunch or dinner. It's great with juice and coffee in the morning, or with a glass of wine and a tossed salad for dinner.

Skillet Bacon and Cheese Strata

Beat together eggs, milk, 1 cup of the Gruyère cheese, parsley and pepper; set aside.

In 10-inch (25 cm) cast-iron or ovenproof nonstick skillet, cook bacon over medium-high heat until lightly browned, 2 to 3 minutes. Add onion; cook, stirring, until softened and golden, 2 to 3 minutes.

Using rubber spatula, gently fold in bread to coat with bacon mixture. Cook over medium heat, turning often, until lightly toasted, 5 to 6 minutes. Remove from heat.

Stir egg mixture and pour over bread, folding to coat evenly. Bake in 425°F (220°C) oven until puffed and edge comes away from side of pan, 12 to 15 minutes.

Sprinkle with remaining Gruyère cheese; bake until cheese is melted, 1 to 2 minutes. Let stand for 5 minutes before serving.

Makes 6 servings. PER SERVING: about 394 cal, 23 g pro, 25 g total fat (11 g sat. fat), 19 g carb, 2 g fibre, 236 mg chol, 489 mg sodium, 287 mg potassium. % RDI: 36% calcium, 14% iron, 20% vit A, 5% vit C, 20% folate.

6 **eggs**

1½ cups **milk**

1½ cups shredded **Gruyère cheese** (about 4 oz/115 g)

¼ cup chopped **fresh parsley**

¼ tsp **pepper**

7 slices **sodium-reduced bacon** (about 7 oz/200 g), chopped

1 **onion,** finely chopped

5 slices **whole wheat sandwich bread,** cut in 1-inch (2.5 cm) cubes (about 5 cups)

This stove-top cobbler tastes just like a chicken pot pie, but it's easier and faster to make. If your nonstick skillet has a plastic or wooden handle, wrap it in a double layer of foil to make it ovenproof.

Skillet Chicken Cobbler

1 tbsp **vegetable oil**

1 tbsp **unsalted butter**

1 **onion,** chopped

8 oz (225 g) **button mushrooms,** quartered

1 lb (450 g) **boneless skinless chicken thighs,** cut in bite-size pieces

1 clove **garlic,** minced

¼ tsp each **salt** and **pepper**

2 tbsp **all-purpose flour**

1 cup **sodium-reduced chicken broth**

2 ribs **celery,** chopped

2 **carrots,** thinly sliced

1 **bay leaf**

1 sprig **fresh thyme**

1 cup **frozen peas**

TOPPING:

1⅛ cups **all-purpose flour**

1 tsp **baking powder**

¼ tsp **salt**

3 tbsp cold **unsalted butter,** cubed

½ cup **buttermilk** (approx)

In 10-inch (25 cm) cast-iron or ovenproof nonstick skillet, heat oil and butter over medium-high heat; cook onion and mushrooms, stirring often, until mushrooms are lightly browned, 5 to 6 minutes.

Add chicken, garlic, salt and pepper; cook, stirring, until chicken is browned, 2 to 3 minutes. Stir in flour; cook, stirring, for 1 minute. Add broth and bring to boil, stirring.

Stir in celery, carrots, bay leaf and thyme; reduce heat, cover and simmer until thickened and vegetables are tender-crisp, 3 to 5 minutes. Stir in peas. Discard bay leaf and thyme. Remove from heat and set aside.

TOPPING: In bowl, whisk together flour, baking powder and salt. Using pastry blender or 2 knives, cut in butter until crumbly. Drizzle in ½ cup buttermilk, stirring just until soft sticky dough forms. Turn out onto floured surface; knead 6 times or just until smooth. Roll out into 6-inch (15 cm) square; brush with 2 tsp more buttermilk. Cut into 6 biscuits. Arrange over chicken mixture.

Bake in 375°F (190°C) oven until biscuits are golden and no longer doughy underneath, and filling is bubbly, 30 to 35 minutes. Let stand for 5 minutes before serving.

Makes 6 servings. PER SERVING: about 337 cal, 21 g pro, 15 g total fat (6 g sat. fat), 30 g carb, 3 g fibre, 85 mg chol, 466 mg sodium, 481 mg potassium. % RDI: 8% calcium, 21% iron, 56% vit A, 12% vit C, 39% folate.

Simmering the potatoes right along with the chicken makes for an easy one-pot supper.
Sweet potatoes are nutritional powerhouses: They are high in fibre, and very high in
beta-carotene and a good source of vitamin C, both of which are antioxidants.

Skillet Chicken and
Sweet Potatoes

8 **bone-in skinless chicken
thighs** (2 lb/900 g)

½ tsp each **salt** and **pepper**

2 tsp **canola oil**

2 **onions,** sliced

2 cloves **garlic,** minced

½ tsp **dried thyme**

1 tbsp **all-purpose flour**

1 cup **apple cider** or juice

2 **sweet potatoes** (about
1½ lb/675 g total)

1 tbsp chopped **fresh parsley**

Trim any fat from chicken thighs; sprinkle with salt and pepper.
In large cast-iron or nonstick skillet, heat oil over medium-high
heat; brown chicken. Transfer to plate.

Drain any fat from pan; cook onions, garlic and thyme over medium
heat, stirring occasionally, until softened, about 5 minutes.

Sprinkle with flour; cook, stirring, for 1 minute. Add cider; bring to
boil, scraping up any brown bits from bottom of pan. Return
chicken, fleshier side down, and any accumulated juices to pan.
Reduce heat to medium-low; cover and simmer for 10 minutes.

Meanwhile, peel and cut potatoes into 1-inch (2.5 cm) cubes;
add to pan. Turn chicken over; simmer, covered, until juices run
clear when chicken is pierced and potatoes are tender, about
30 minutes. Sprinkle with parsley.

Makes 4 servings. PER SERVING: about 450 cal, 35 g pro, 11 g total fat
(2 g sat. fat), 52 g carb, 5 g fibre, 138 mg chol, 453 mg sodium. % RDI:
6% calcium, 24% iron, 258% vit A, 57% vit C, 17% folate.

Just like *pastel de choclo,* a popular dish from Chile, this pie is loaded with raisins, olives and hard-cooked eggs. Its double-corn topping is made with both puréed corn and cornmeal. Serve with fresh tomato salsa or a squeeze of lime.

Skillet Beef and Corn Pie

In deep 10-inch (25 cm) cast-iron or ovenproof nonstick skillet, heat oil over medium-high heat; brown beef, breaking up with spoon, about 2 minutes.

Add onions; cook, stirring often, until softened, about 6 minutes. Add garlic, chili powder, cumin, salt and pepper; cook, stirring, for 3 minutes.

Reduce heat to medium. Mix in flour until absorbed. Stir in broth, scraping up brown bits from bottom of pan; cook, stirring occasionally, until thickened, 3 to 5 minutes. Stir in corn, raisins and olives. Remove from heat. Nestle eggs in beef mixture. Set aside.

CORN TOPPING: In food processor, purée corn until almost smooth, about 1 minute. Blend in buttermilk, egg and butter. Whisk together cornmeal, flour, baking powder, baking soda and salt; stir into corn mixture just until combined. Spoon evenly over beef, leaving ½-inch (1 cm) border around edge for steam to escape.

Bake in 400°F (200°C) oven until topping is golden, 20 to 25 minutes. Let stand for 5 minutes before serving.

Makes 6 servings. PER SERVING: about 549 cal, 34 g pro, 23 g total fat (9 g sat. fat), 53 g carb, 4 g fibre, 182 mg chol, 777 mg sodium, 748 mg potassium. % RDI: 11% calcium, 33% iron, 15% vit A, 7% vit C, 45% folate.

1 tbsp **vegetable oil**

1½ lb (675 g) **extra-lean ground beef**

2 **onions,** chopped

2 cloves **garlic,** minced

1 tbsp **chili powder**

1 tsp **ground cumin**

¼ tsp each **salt** and **pepper**

3 tbsp **all-purpose flour**

1½ cups **sodium-reduced beef broth**

1 cup **frozen corn kernels**

½ cup **dark raisins**

⅓ cup **Kalamata olives,** halved

2 **hard-cooked eggs,** quartered

CORN TOPPING:

1 cup **frozen corn kernels**

½ cup **buttermilk**

1 **egg**

3 tbsp **unsalted butter,** melted

⅓ cup each **cornmeal** and **all-purpose flour**

1½ tsp **baking powder**

½ tsp **baking soda**

¼ tsp **salt**

Consider this dish a sort of Greek paella: Greek because of the classic shrimp, feta and dill combination; paella because all the ingredients are cooked with the rice and served right out of the pan at the table.

Skillet Rice With Shrimp and Feta

2 tbsp **extra-virgin olive oil**

1 **onion,** chopped

1 **sweet yellow pepper,** diced

1 cup diced **fennel bulb**

2 cloves **garlic,** minced

¼ tsp each **salt** and **pepper**

1½ cups **long-grain rice,** rinsed and drained well

½ cup **white wine**

2½ cups **sodium-reduced chicken broth**

1 lb (450 g) **raw large shrimp,** peeled and deveined

2 **tomatoes,** seeded and chopped

¼ cup chopped **fresh dill**

6 oz (170 g) **feta cheese,** crumbled (about 1¼ cups)

1 **lemon,** cut in 6 to 8 wedges

In 12-inch (30 cm) nonstick skillet, heat oil over medium-high heat; sauté onion, yellow pepper, fennel, garlic, salt and pepper until tender-crisp, 4 to 5 minutes.

Add rice; cook, stirring, until becoming translucent, about 1 minute. Stir in wine until absorbed. Stir in broth and ¼ cup water; bring to boil. Cover and reduce heat to medium-low; simmer until rice is tender but still firm, about 12 minutes.

Stir in shrimp, tomatoes and 2 tbsp of the dill; cook, covered, until shrimp are pink, 8 to 10 minutes.

Remove from heat; let stand for 2 minutes. Sprinkle with feta cheese and remaining dill. Serve with lemon wedges.

Makes 6 servings. PER SERVING: about 383 cal, 22 g pro, 12 g total fat (5 g sat. fat), 45 g carb, 2 g fibre, 112 mg chol, 756 mg sodium, 419 mg potassium. % RDI: 19% calcium, 16% iron, 10% vit A, 67% vit C, 15% folate.

If you're gluten-sensitive, check packaged food labels, including sriracha, fish sauce and ketchup (Heinz is gluten-free). Homemade broth and home-roasted peanuts are safest. In dry skillet over medium heat, toast nuts, shaking often, until golden, about 4 minutes.

Gluten-Free Pad Thai

In large bowl, soak noodles in warm water for 15 minutes; drain and set aside.

Meanwhile, whisk together ketchup, chicken broth, fish sauce, lime juice, sugar and chili sauce; set aside.

In wok or large skillet, heat 1 tbsp of the oil over medium-high heat; cook eggs, stirring occasionally, until scrambled and set, about 30 seconds. Transfer to separate bowl.

Wipe out wok. Add 1 tbsp of the remaining oil and heat over high heat; stir-fry shrimp until pink, about 1 minute. Transfer to plate.

Heat 1 tbsp of the remaining oil in wok over high heat; stir-fry chicken until browned and no longer pink inside, about 1 minute. Add to shrimp.

Heat remaining oil in wok over high heat; cook shallots, garlic, red pepper and ginger until softened, about 2 minutes.

Stir in ketchup mixture and noodles. Return shrimp mixture to pan; cook, stirring to coat, until noodles are tender, about 3 minutes.

Return scrambled eggs to pan along with tofu, bean sprouts and green onions; heat through just until sprouts begin to wilt, about 1 minute. Serve garnished with cilantro, peanuts and lime wedges.

Makes 6 to 8 servings. PER EACH OF 8 SERVINGS: about 340 cal, 21 g pro, 13 g total fat (2 g sat. fat), 35 g carb, 2 g fibre, 100 mg chol, 931 mg sodium, 416 mg potassium. % RDI: 8% calcium, 15% iron, 12% vit A, 55% vit C, 23% folate.

Half pkg (454 g pkg) **wide rice sticks**

⅓ cup **ketchup**

⅓ cup **sodium-reduced chicken broth**

¼ cup **fish sauce**

3 tbsp **lime juice**

2 tsp **granulated sugar**

1 tsp **Asian chili sauce** (sriracha) or hot pepper sauce

¼ cup **vegetable oil** or peanut oil

2 **eggs,** lightly beaten

8 oz (225 g) **frozen raw large shrimp,** thawed, peeled and deveined

10 oz (280 g) **boneless skinless chicken breasts,** thinly sliced

4 **shallots** or 1 onion, thinly sliced

4 cloves **garlic,** minced

1 **sweet red pepper,** thinly sliced

2 tsp minced **fresh ginger**

6 oz (170 g) **medium tofu,** cubed

3 cups **bean sprouts**

3 **green onions,** sliced

½ cup **fresh cilantro leaves**

¼ cup chopped toasted **unsalted peanuts**

Lime wedges

Lively Southeast Asian flavours marry with a touch of Indian-style spice in this vegetable-packed dinner. Rice stick vermicelli is readily available in many supermarkets. Look for it alongside the Asian spices and sauces.

Vegetarian Singapore Noodles

In large bowl, soak vermicelli in warm water until softened and separate, about 5 minutes. Drain and set aside.

Meanwhile, whisk together soy sauce, sugar and ¾ cup water; set aside.

In wok, heat oil over medium-high heat; stir-fry cabbage, tofu, red pepper, snow peas, green onions and garlic for 2 minutes. Add curry powder, cumin, coriander, salt and pepper; stir-fry for 1 minute.

Stir in soy sauce mixture; bring to boil. Stir in noodles, tossing to combine; stir-fry until tender, about 7 minutes. Sprinkle with peanuts (if using).

Makes 4 servings. PER SERVING: about 444 cal, 18 g pro, 15 g total fat (2 g sat. fat), 61 g carb, 5 g fibre, 0 mg chol, 658 mg sodium, 478 mg potassium. % RDI: 20% calcium, 31% iron, 16% vit A, 117% vit C, 32% folate.

8 oz (225 g) **rice stick vermicelli**

3 tbsp **sodium-reduced soy sauce**

2 tsp **granulated sugar**

2 tbsp **vegetable oil**

2 cups shredded **napa cabbage**

1½ cups cubed drained **firm tofu**

1 **sweet red pepper**, julienned

4 oz (115 g) **snow peas**, julienned

4 **green onions**, thinly sliced

2 cloves **garlic**, minced

4 tsp **curry powder**

1½ tsp **ground cumin**

1½ tsp **ground coriander**

¼ tsp each **salt** and **pepper**

¼ cup chopped **unsalted peanuts** (optional)

To make this tasty dish for two, you'll need cooked thick yellow miki noodles, which come in 400 g packages and are ready to use. If you can't find miki noodles, use Shanghai-style noodles instead (see Tip, below) – you just need to cook them first.

Shanghai Noodles

4 **boneless skinless chicken thighs**

1 tbsp **sodium-reduced soy sauce**

1 tbsp **Chinese rice wine** or dry sherry (optional)

1½ tsp **cornstarch**

2 **green onions**

1 **sweet green pepper**

2 tbsp **vegetable oil**

1 clove **garlic,** minced

1 cup shredded **cabbage**

Pinch **granulated sugar**

Pinch **salt**

1 pkg (400 g) **precooked miki noodles**

2 tbsp **hoisin sauce**

1½ tsp **sesame oil**

Cut chicken into 1-inch (2.5 cm) cubes; place in bowl. Add soy sauce, rice wine (if using) and cornstarch; toss to coat. Marinate for 30 minutes.

Meanwhile, cut white parts of green onions into 1-inch (2.5 cm) lengths; thinly slice green parts. Set aside separately. Cut green pepper into quarters; thinly slice on diagonal. Set aside.

In wok or large skillet, heat half of the oil over medium-high heat; stir-fry garlic and white parts of green onions until fragrant, about 1 minute. Add chicken mixture; stir-fry until juices run clear when chicken is pierced, about 3 minutes. Scrape into bowl.

Add remaining oil to wok; stir-fry cabbage, green pepper, sugar and salt for 1 minute. Add ¼ cup water; cover and steam until no liquid remains and cabbage is tender, about 3 minutes.

Add noodles, hoisin sauce and sesame oil, tossing to coat. Return chicken mixture to pan along with green parts of green onions; cook until heated through.

Makes 2 servings. PER SERVING: about 757 cal, 36 g pro, 32 g total fat (4 g sat. fat), 85 g carb, 4 g fibre, 96 mg chol, 1,005 mg sodium. % RDI: 5% calcium, 45% iron, 5% vit A, 92% vit C, 16% folate.

Tip: Shanghai-style noodles are uncooked white wheat noodles found in many Asian grocery stores. They must be cooked and rinsed before using. Half a 454 g pkg will be enough for this recipe.

Dried Chinese wheat noodles are flat, thin noodles available in Chinese grocery stores and some supermarkets. However, you can easily replace them with linguine or fettuccine, cooking them for 8 to 10 minutes.

Chicken Lo Mein

In bowl, cover mushrooms with 1 cup warm water; let stand until softened, about 15 minutes. Reserving ½ cup soaking liquid, drain mushrooms. Cut off stems and discard; slice caps. Set aside.

Meanwhile, in large pot of boiling salted water, cook noodles until tender but firm, about 2 minutes; drain and set aside.

Meanwhile, cut chicken into thin slices. In wok or large deep skillet, heat half of the oil over high heat; stir-fry chicken, in batches, until no longer pink inside, about 2 minutes. With slotted spoon, transfer to bowl.

Add remaining oil to wok; reduce heat to medium-high. Add snow peas, red pepper, green onions, garlic and ginger; stir-fry until tender-crisp, about 3 minutes.

Whisk together chicken broth, oyster sauce, soy sauce and cornstarch. Add to wok along with chicken and any accumulated juices, corn, noodles, mushrooms and reserved soaking liquid; cook, stirring, until sauce is thickened and glossy, 2 to 3 minutes.

Makes 4 to 6 servings. PER EACH OF 6 SERVINGS: about 369 cal, 26 g pro, 8 g total fat (1 g sat. fat), 50 g carb, 2 g fibre, 44 mg chol, 1,475 mg sodium. % RDI: 4% calcium, 15% iron, 8% vit A, 85% vit C, 10% folate.

10 **dried shiitake mushrooms**

12 oz (340 g) **Chinese wheat noodles**

1 lb (450 g) **boneless skinless chicken breasts**

2 tbsp **vegetable oil**

2 cups **snow peas,** trimmed

1 **sweet red pepper,** thinly sliced

2 **green onions,** chopped

3 cloves **garlic,** minced

2 tsp minced **fresh ginger**

½ cup **chicken broth**

2 tbsp **oyster sauce**

2 tbsp **soy sauce**

2 tsp **cornstarch**

1 can (14 oz/398 mL) **whole baby corn,** drained

Simple pantry staples and familiar ingredients get a little Asian flair in this weeknight stir-fry. For a change of pace and a fibre boost, try whole wheat or multigrain linguine in place of the regular and cook according to package directions until al dente.

Steak Stir-Fry With Noodles

3 carrots

1 sweet green pepper

1 lb (450 g) top sirloin grilling steak, thinly sliced

¼ tsp each salt and pepper

2 tbsp vegetable oil

1 onion, sliced

2 cloves garlic, minced

¾ cup beef broth

1 tsp grated orange zest

¼ cup orange juice

1 tbsp cornstarch

¾ tsp hot pepper sauce

¼ cup chopped fresh parsley

8 oz (225 g) linguine

Thinly slice carrots and green pepper; set aside. Season steak with salt and pepper. In wok or large skillet, heat half of the oil over high heat; stir-fry steak, in batches, until browned but still pink inside, about 2 minutes. Transfer to plate.

Heat remaining oil in wok over medium heat; cook onion and garlic for 2 minutes. Add carrots and green pepper; cook until slightly softened, about 4 minutes.

Whisk together broth, orange zest and juice, cornstarch and hot pepper sauce; add to wok and bring to boil. Return steak and any accumulated juices to wok along with parsley.

Meanwhile, in large pot of boiling salted water, cook linguine until tender but firm, 6 to 8 minutes; drain and add to wok. Toss to coat.

Makes 4 servings. PER SERVING: about 478 cal, 33 g pro, 12 g total fat (2 g sat. fat), 57 g carb, 5 g fibre, 54 mg chol, 555 mg sodium. % RDI: 6% calcium, 34% iron, 140% vit A, 55% vit C, 50% folate.

Fried rice is an easy and delicious way to make over leftovers. Substitute whatever cooked meat you have on hand for the steak, such as cubed chicken or pork. Or go vegetarian and use tofu in place of meat.

Steak Fried Rice

3 tbsp **vegetable oil**

1 **tomato,** diced

3 **green onions,** thinly sliced (white and green parts separated)

3 cloves **garlic,** minced

1 tbsp minced **fresh ginger**

4 **mushrooms,** sliced

1 **carrot,** diced

1 rib **celery,** diced

Half **sweet red pepper,** diced

5 cups **cooked rice**

2 cups cubed **cooked beef** (steak or roast)

½ cup **frozen peas**

2 tbsp **sodium-reduced soy sauce**

1 tbsp **oyster sauce**

1 tsp **sesame oil**

In wok, heat vegetable oil over high heat; stir-fry tomato, white parts of green onions, garlic and ginger for 1 minute.

Add mushrooms, carrot, celery and red pepper; stir-fry until vegetables are tender-crisp, about 4 minutes.

Stir in rice, beef, peas, soy sauce and oyster sauce; stir-fry for 3 minutes. Remove from heat. Stir in green parts of green onions and sesame oil.

Makes 4 servings. PER SERVING: about 531 cal, 28 g pro, 16 g total fat (3 g sat. fat), 66 g carb, 4 g fibre, 51 mg chol, 500 mg sodium, 601 mg potassium. % RDI: 5% calcium, 25% iron, 45% vit A, 55% vit C, 18% folate.

Tip: For best results, ensure the cooked rice is cold before stir-frying. Either cook and refrigerate it in the morning or make extra for dinner the night before.

If you're a fan of Swedish meatballs, you'll enjoy this dinner-size serving of meatballs, peas and noodles in a creamy sauce. If you have time, chill the meatballs in the refrigerator for 10 minutes before frying: They'll hold their shape a little better.

Creamy Meatballs and Noodles

In large bowl, stir together bread crumbs, onion, egg, salt, pepper and allspice; mix in beef. Shape into 20 balls.

In large nonstick skillet, heat oil over medium-high heat; cook meatballs until digital thermometer inserted into centre of several registers 160°F (71°C), about 10 minutes. Transfer to plate.

Drain all but 2 tbsp fat from pan. Whisk in flour; cook over medium heat, whisking constantly, for 1 minute. Whisk in broth and ½ cup water; bring to boil. Reduce heat and simmer for 3 minutes.

Stir in meatballs; cook until thickened, about 3 minutes. Add peas and cream; simmer for 1 minute.

Meanwhile, in large pot of boiling salted water, cook egg noodles according to package directions; drain. Serve with meatball mixture.

Makes 4 servings. PER SERVING: about 540 cal, 33 g pro, 26 g total fat (10 g sat. fat), 41 g carb, 4 g fibre, 134 mg chol, 765 mg sodium, 409 mg potassium. % RDI: 5% calcium, 30% iron, 10% vit A, 3% vit C, 57% folate.

½ cup **fresh bread crumbs**

1 **onion,** grated

1 **egg**

½ tsp each **salt** and **pepper**

¼ tsp **ground allspice**

1 lb (450 g) **lean ground beef** or medium ground beef

1 tbsp **vegetable oil**

3 tbsp **all-purpose flour**

1½ cups **sodium-reduced beef broth**

½ cup **frozen peas**

¼ cup **whipping cream** or 10% cream

4 cups **no-yolk egg noodles**

If your family likes spicy foods, add more chipotle chilies to taste. And if you're looking for ways to reduce your sodium intake, replace the sodium-reduced chicken broth with water and look for no-salt-added canned beans.

Chipotle Chicken With Rice and Beans

Toss chicken with half each of the chili powder, salt and pepper. In large Dutch oven, heat half of the oil over medium-high heat; brown chicken. Transfer to bowl.

Add remaining oil to pan and heat over medium heat; cook onion, garlic and remaining chili powder, salt and pepper, stirring occasionally and scraping up brown bits from bottom of pan, until softened, about 5 minutes.

Stir in rice and chipotle chili; cook, stirring, for 2 minutes. Stir in broth and 1 cup water; bring to boil. Reduce heat, cover and simmer for 10 minutes.

Add chicken and black beans; cook, covered, until rice is tender and juices run clear when chicken is pierced, about 10 minutes. Stir in cilantro.

Makes 4 servings. PER SERVING: about 491 cal, 33 g pro, 14 g total fat (2 g sat. fat), 58 g carb, 9 g fibre, 94 mg chol, 738 mg sodium, 659 mg potassium. % RDI: 7% calcium, 25% iron, 6% vit A, 13% vit C, 33% folate.

1 lb (450 g) **boneless skinless chicken thighs,** cubed

1 tsp **chili powder**

¼ tsp each **salt** and **pepper**

2 tbsp **vegetable oil**

1 **onion,** diced

3 cloves **garlic,** minced

1 cup **long-grain rice**

1 **chipotle chili in adobo sauce,** seeded and chopped

¾ cup **sodium-reduced chicken broth**

1 can (19 oz/540 mL) **black beans,** drained and rinsed

¼ cup chopped **fresh cilantro**

Mustard and capers give this simple chicken-and-rice dish a tangy edge. Green beans add a nice hit of fresh vegetable flavour and some fibre, making this a well-rounded meal-in-a-bowl.

One-Pot Mustard Chicken and Rice

1½ lb (675 g) **boneless skinless chicken thighs,** cubed

¾ tsp each **salt** and **pepper**

2 tbsp **vegetable oil**

1 large **sweet onion,** diced

3 ribs **celery,** sliced

1½ tsp **dried dillweed**

1½ cups **basmati rice**

2 tbsp rinsed drained **capers,** chopped

1 cup **sodium-reduced chicken broth**

3 tbsp **Dijon mustard**

2 cups **green beans,** cut in 1-inch (2.5 cm) lengths

⅓ cup chopped **fresh parsley**

2 **green onions** (green parts only), thinly sliced

Sprinkle chicken with ¼ tsp each of the salt and pepper. In large Dutch oven, heat oil over medium-high heat; brown chicken, in batches. Using slotted spoon, transfer to plate.

Add onion, celery, dillweed and remaining salt and pepper to pan; cook over medium heat until onion is light golden, about 8 minutes.

Stir in rice; cook, stirring, for 2 minutes. Stir in chicken and capers.

Whisk together broth, mustard and enough water to make 1¾ cups. Add to rice mixture and bring to boil; reduce heat, cover and simmer for 10 minutes.

Add green beans; simmer, covered, for 5 minutes. Turn off heat; let stand on burner for 10 minutes. Stir in parsley and green onions.

Makes 4 to 6 servings. PER EACH OF 6 SERVINGS: about 404 cal, 28 g pro, 11 g total fat (2 g sat. fat), 47 g carb, 3 g fibre, 94 mg chol, 697 mg sodium, 545 mg potassium. % RDI: 8% calcium, 19% iron, 8% vit A, 25% vit C, 21% folate.

A traditional New Orleans staple, this melange of shrimp, sausage and spiced rice is flavourful and filling. This version is not ultraspicy, but you can increase the amount of cayenne if you prefer a little more burn in each bite.

Jambalaya

In large shallow Dutch oven, heat half of the oil over medium-low heat; brown sausage. Transfer to paper towel–lined bowl. Add chicken to pan; brown well. Add to sausage.

Drain fat from pan; add remaining oil. Cook onion and garlic over medium-low heat until softened and light golden, about 8 minutes.

Stir in celery, green pepper, thyme, oregano, paprika, cumin, basil, salt, pepper, cayenne and bay leaves; cook until softened, about 4 minutes.

Stir in tomatoes and chicken broth, scraping up brown bits. Stir in sausage mixture; bring to boil. Stir in rice; reduce heat, cover and simmer until rice is almost tender, about 15 minutes.

Stir in shrimp; cover and cook until shrimp are pink, about 5 minutes. Discard bay leaves; stir in green onions. *(Make-ahead: Let cool for 30 minutes; refrigerate, uncovered, in airtight container until cold. Cover and refrigerate for up to 24 hours. Reheat in 375°F/190°C oven for 30 minutes.)*

Makes 12 servings. PER SERVING: about 296 cal, 19 g pro, 10 g total fat (3 g sat. fat), 32 g carb, 2 g fibre, 92 mg chol, 598 mg sodium. % RDI: 7% calcium, 19% iron, 5% vit A, 32% vit C, 9% folate.

2 tbsp **vegetable oil**

12 oz (340 g) **smoked sausage,** sliced

6 **boneless skinless chicken thighs,** cubed

1 **onion,** chopped

4 cloves **garlic,** minced

4 ribs **celery,** chopped

1 **sweet green pepper,** chopped

1 tsp each **dried thyme, dried oregano** and **sweet paprika**

½ tsp each **dried cumin** and **basil**

¼ tsp each **salt** and **pepper**

¼ tsp **cayenne pepper**

2 **bay leaves**

1 can (28 oz/796 mL) **diced tomatoes**

1½ cups **sodium-reduced chicken broth**

2 cups **parboiled long-grain rice**

1 lb (450 g) **raw large shrimp,** peeled and deveined

3 **green onions,** sliced

Spanish chorizo, called *chouriço* in Portuguese, is a mild or spicy dry-cured paprika sausage available in the deli section of the supermarket. It's not the same as uncooked Mexican or South American chorizo; if Spanish is unavailable, substitute another smoked sausage.

Spanish Chicken and Rice With Chorizo

Sprinkle chicken with ¼ tsp of the salt. In large shallow Dutch oven, heat oil over medium-high heat; brown chicken. Transfer to plate.

Add chorizo, onion, garlic, pepper, turmeric and remaining salt to pan; cook over medium heat, stirring occasionally, until onion is softened, about 4 minutes.

Stir in tomatoes and broth, scraping up brown bits from bottom of pan. Return chicken and any accumulated juices to pan; bring to boil. Reduce heat, cover and simmer for 15 minutes.

Stir in rice; cook, covered, for 20 minutes. Stir in yellow pepper, peas and parsley; cook, covered, until rice is tender and juices run clear when chicken is pierced, about 5 minutes.

Makes 6 to 8 servings. PER EACH OF 8 SERVINGS: about 506 cal, 35 g pro, 19 g total fat (6 g sat. fat), 45 g carb, 2 g fibre, 118 mg chol, 1,151 mg sodium. % RDI: 6% calcium, 22% iron, 10% vit A, 57% vit C, 15% folate.

2½ lb (1.125 kg) **skinless chicken thighs** or pieces

1 tsp **salt**

1 tbsp **olive oil**

8 oz (225 g) **dry-cured chorizo sausage,** cut in 1-inch (2.5 cm) pieces

1 **onion,** chopped

3 cloves **garlic,** minced

¾ tsp **pepper**

¾ tsp **turmeric**

1 can (28 oz/796 mL) **diced tomatoes,** drained

3 cups **chicken broth**

2 cups **long-grain rice**

1 **sweet yellow pepper,** chopped

1 cup **frozen peas**

2 tbsp chopped **fresh parsley**

Traditional Spanish paella can be quite a production to make. This simplified meat-focused paella has many of the dish's typical flavours – saffron, sweet peppers and sausage – but doesn't require hours of chopping, prepping and cooking.

Kielbasa Sausage and Saffron Paella

3 cups **chicken broth** or vegetable broth

¼ tsp **saffron threads**

1 tbsp **vegetable oil**

1 **onion,** chopped

2 cloves **garlic,** minced

1 each small **sweet green** and **red pepper,** chopped

1 **zucchini,** chopped

¼ tsp each **salt** and **pepper**

10 oz (280 g) **kielbasa sausage** or smoked sausage, chopped

1½ cups **arborio rice** or long-grain rice

In saucepan, bring broth to boil; add saffron and set aside.

In Dutch oven or deep wide skillet, heat oil over medium heat; fry onion, garlic, green and red peppers, zucchini, salt and pepper until onion is softened, about 4 minutes.

Stir in kielbasa, rice and broth mixture; bring to boil. Cover and simmer over low heat until broth is absorbed and rice is tender, about 20 minutes.

Makes 6 to 8 servings. PER EACH OF 8 SERVINGS: about 257 cal, 11 g pro, 8 g total fat (2 g sat. fat), 35 g carb, 1 g fibre, 24 mg chol, 715 mg sodium. % RDI: 3% calcium, 8% iron, 4% vit A, 40% vit C, 6% folate.

Looking for a quick weeknight dinner? This combination of spiced pork, rice, corn and peas is ready in about 30 minutes. Using bone-in chops gives the dish a little meatier taste, as meat cooked on the bone is usually more flavourful.

One-Pot Rice and Pork Chops

In bowl, mix together half of the parsley, the garlic, cumin, salt, pepper and cayenne; rub all over chops.

In Dutch oven, heat oil over medium-high heat; brown chops, turning once, about 4 minutes. Transfer to plate.

Drain fat from pan. Add broth and 1 cup water; bring to boil, stirring. Add rice, corn and peas; reduce heat, cover and simmer for 10 minutes. Stir in remaining parsley.

Add pork and any accumulated juices, nestling pork into rice; cook until rice is tender, liquid is absorbed and just a hint of pink remains inside pork, about 10 minutes.

Makes 4 servings. PER SERVING: about 492 cal, 29 g pro, 15 g total fat (3 g sat. fat), 60 g carb, 3 g fibre, 58 mg chol, 826 mg sodium, 460 mg potassium. % RDI: 6% calcium, 21% iron, 8% vit A, 10% vit C, 16% folate.

¼ cup chopped **fresh parsley**

2 cloves **garlic,** minced

1 tbsp **ground cumin**

½ tsp each **salt** and **pepper**

¼ tsp **cayenne pepper**

4 **bone-in pork loin chops**

2 tbsp **vegetable oil**

2 cups **chicken broth**

1⅓ cups **long-grain rice**

1 cup **frozen corn kernels**

1 cup **frozen peas**

Kedgeree is a British dish made with a mix of traditional English and Indian ingredients. It's usually made with smoked fish, but this version gives a nod to Canadian culture by putting salmon in the starring role. Look for ghee, or clarified butter, in South Asian stores.

Salmon Kedgeree

8 oz (225 g) **skinless salmon fillet**

1 tsp **vegetable oil**

¾ tsp **salt**

¼ tsp **pepper**

1 tbsp **ghee** or vegetable oil

1 small **onion,** chopped

2 tsp minced **fresh ginger**

2 tsp **curry powder**

¼ tsp **turmeric**

3 **cardamom pods,** broken (optional)

1 **bay leaf**

1 cup **basmati rice**

1½ cups **sodium-reduced chicken broth**

1 cup **frozen peas**

2 tbsp chopped **fresh cilantro** or parsley

4 to 6 **hard-cooked eggs,** quartered

On greased baking sheet, brush salmon with oil; sprinkle with half each of the salt and pepper. Bake in 400°F (200°C) oven until fish flakes easily when tested, about 20 minutes. Flake into about 2-inch (5 cm) chunks; set aside.

Meanwhile, in saucepan, heat ghee over medium heat; cook onion until softened and golden, about 8 minutes.

Stir in ginger, curry powder, turmeric, cardamom pods (if using), bay leaf, and remaining salt and pepper; cook until fragrant, about 30 seconds. Stir in rice; cook, stirring, for 1 minute.

Add broth and bring to boil; reduce heat, cover and simmer until rice is tender and no liquid remains, about 20 minutes. Remove from heat. Stir in peas and cilantro; let stand, covered, for 2 minutes. Discard bay leaf.

Gently stir in salmon. Transfer to platter; arrange eggs on top.

Makes 4 servings. PER SERVING: about 413 cal, 23 g pro, 15 g total fat (5 g sat. fat), 45 g carb, 3 g fibre, 222 mg chol, 765 mg sodium, 369 mg potassium. % RDI: 6% calcium, 14% iron, 18% vit A, 8% vit C, 30% folate.

Greens are packed with healthy vitamins and antioxidants. This 30-minute recipe makes delicious use of them, pairing them with tender rice and meaty shrimp. If you're not a fish fan or have a vegetarian at your table, try the variation with feta cheese instead.

Rice and Greens With Shrimp

1 tbsp **extra-virgin olive oil**

1 **onion,** chopped

4 cloves **garlic,** minced

¼ tsp each **salt** and **pepper**

1⅓ cups **long-grain rice**

2⅔ cups **chicken broth**

1 tsp grated **lemon zest**

1 lb (450 g) **raw large shrimp,** peeled and deveined

3 cups packed **Swiss chard leaves** or fresh spinach, coarsely shredded

1 tbsp chopped **fresh dill**

1 tbsp **lemon juice**

Lemon wedges

In large saucepan, heat oil over medium heat; cook onion, garlic, salt and pepper, stirring occasionally, until softened, about 5 minutes.

Stir in rice. Add broth and lemon zest; bring to boil. Reduce heat, cover and simmer until liquid is almost absorbed, about 15 minutes.

With fork, gently stir in shrimp, Swiss chard, dill and lemon juice; cover and cook until shrimp are pink and greens are wilted, about 5 minutes. Serve with lemon wedges.

Makes 4 servings. PER SERVING: about 394 cal, 27 g pro, 6 g total fat (1 g sat. fat), 55 g carb, 2 g fibre, 129 mg chol, 821 mg sodium. % RDI: 10% calcium, 28% iron, 37% vit A, 15% vit C, 35% folate.

VARIATION
Vegetarian Rice and Greens
Omit shrimp. Replace chicken broth with vegetable broth. Serve sprinkled with ½ cup crumbled feta cheese, if desired.

Mussels are less expensive than many other types of shellfish, plus they're a sustainable seafood choice. Most mussels these days don't have beards, but if you run into one and it's tough to pull, save your fingers and try a pair of needle-nose pliers. Works every time!

Mussel Simmer Supper

Rinse mussels and remove any beards; discard any mussels that do not close when tapped. Set aside.

In Dutch oven or large saucepan, heat oil over medium heat; cook potatoes, onion, garlic, basil, salt and pepper, stirring occasionally, for 4 minutes.

Add broth; simmer for 2 minutes. Add red and yellow peppers; bring to boil. Add mussels and peas; cover and simmer until mussels open, about 5 minutes. Discard any that do not open.

Makes 4 servings. PER SERVING: about 184 cal, 11 g pro, 5 g total fat (1 g sat. fat), 23 g carb, 3 g fibre, 18 mg chol, 591 mg sodium. % RDI: 4% calcium, 28% iron, 21% vit A, 180% vit C, 25% folate.

2 lb (900 g) **mussels**

1 tbsp **vegetable oil**

2 **new potatoes,** cubed (about 10 oz/280 g total)

1 **onion,** sliced

2 cloves **garlic,** sliced

½ tsp **dried basil**

½ tsp each **salt** and **pepper**

½ cup **chicken broth**

1 each **sweet red** and **yellow pepper,** chopped

½ cup **frozen peas**

A stylish vegetarian dish can be a welcome change to your menu, and this one especially will please both vegetarians and meat lovers.

Spaghetti Squash With Mushroom and Pearl Onion Ragout

1 **spaghetti squash** (about 3 lb/1.35 kg)

1 lb (450 g) **pearl onions**

⅓ cup **extra-virgin olive oil**

2 tsp **granulated sugar**

2 ribs **celery,** diced

1 **carrot,** diced

1 **sweet red pepper,** diced

1 tsp each **salt** and **pepper**

¼ tsp each **dried thyme** and **sage**

1 lb (450 g) **mixed mushrooms** (such as oyster, shiitake and cremini), trimmed and thinly sliced

2 cloves **garlic,** minced

1 cup **vegetable broth**

3 tbsp **soy sauce**

2 tbsp **balsamic vinegar**

2 tbsp **tomato paste**

1 tbsp **butter,** softened

1 tbsp **all-purpose flour**

2 tbsp chopped **fresh parsley**

Using fork, pierce squash all over. Roast in roasting pan in 375°F (190°C) oven, turning twice, until tender when pressed, about 1¾ hours.

Meanwhile, in saucepan of boiling water, blanch onions for 1 minute; transfer to bowl of ice water. Peel onions; cut any large ones in half. In large skillet, heat 2 tbsp of the oil over medium heat; cook onions and sugar, stirring often, until onions start to turn golden, about 15 minutes.

Stir in celery, carrot, red pepper, half each of the salt and pepper, the thyme and sage; cook, stirring often, until onions are deep caramel colour, about 10 minutes. Transfer to bowl.

Add 2 tbsp of the remaining oil to pan; cook mushrooms and garlic, stirring often, until no liquid remains and mushrooms start to turn golden, about 10 minutes.

Return onion mixture to pan along with broth, soy sauce, vinegar and tomato paste; cook, stirring, for 5 minutes. Meanwhile, stir butter with flour; add to pan and cook, stirring gently, until sauce is thickened, about 2 minutes.

Cut squash in half lengthwise and scoop out seeds. Using fork, pull apart strands and place in bowl; discard skin. Add remaining oil, salt and pepper; toss to coat. Mound on plates; spoon ragout over top. Garnish with parsley.

Makes 4 servings. PER SERVING: about 378 cal, 8 g pro, 22 g total fat (4 g sat. fat), 43 g carb, 8 g fibre, 9 mg chol, 1,630 mg sodium. % RDI: 10% calcium, 23% iron, 65% vit A, 117% vit C, 31% folate.

Easy enough for a weeknight supper, a frittata also makes a satisfying weekend brunch. For added calcium, mash in the salmon bones – you won't even notice them. Serve with crusty whole wheat bread.

Salmon, Zucchini and Potato Frittata

Brush oil over 9- or 10-inch (23 or 25 cm) ovenproof nonstick skillet; heat over medium heat. Add onion, garlic, potatoes and dill; cover and cook, stirring often, for 10 minutes. Add zucchini; cook until potatoes are almost tender, about 5 minutes.

Meanwhile, drain salmon and coarsely flake. In bowl, whisk together eggs, green onions, ¾ cup of the cheese, milk, salt and pepper; mix in salmon. Pour into pan, stirring gently to combine.

Sprinkle with remaining cheese; cook over medium-low heat until bottom and side are firm yet top is still slightly runny, 10 minutes. Broil until golden and set, 3 to 5 minutes. Cut into wedges.

Makes 4 servings. PER SERVING: about 415 cal, 33 g pro, 21 g total fat (8 g sat. fat), 24 g carb, 2 g fibre, 402 mg chol, 827 mg sodium. % RDI: 23% calcium, 16% iron, 24% vit A, 18% vit C, 34% folate.

2 tsp **canola oil**

1 **onion,** chopped

2 cloves **garlic,** minced

2 large **potatoes,** peeled and cubed

1 tbsp chopped **fresh dill**

1 **zucchini,** chopped

1 can (7½ oz/213 g) **red sockeye salmon**

8 **eggs**

2 **green onions,** chopped

1 cup shredded **light Havarti cheese** or Danbo cheese

¼ cup **milk**

½ tsp **salt**

¼ tsp **pepper**

Omelettes are perfect weeknight suppers because they usually feature everyday staples and the cooking time is minimal. To speed up this dish even more, use 2 cups leftover cooked rice instead of cooking the rice from scratch.

Sesame Rice Omelette

½ tsp **salt**

1 cup **long-grain rice**

2 tbsp **sesame seeds**, toasted

2 tsp **sesame oil**

1 tbsp **vegetable oil**

2 **green onions**, sliced

1 small **zucchini** (about 6 oz/ 170 g), grated

1 **sweet red pepper**, diced

4 **eggs**

2 tbsp **soy sauce**

¼ tsp **pepper**

In saucepan, bring 2 cups water and salt to boil. Add rice; cover and simmer over low heat until tender and no liquid remains, about 20 minutes. Using fork, stir in sesame seeds and sesame oil; set aside.

Meanwhile, in large ovenproof nonstick skillet, heat vegetable oil over medium-high heat; cook green onions, zucchini and red pepper, stirring often, until onions are golden, about 5 minutes. Stir in rice mixture.

Meanwhile, in bowl, beat eggs; whisk in soy sauce and pepper. Pour over rice mixture in pan, stirring with spatula for 30 seconds. Cook over medium heat, uncovered and without stirring, until almost set and bottom is golden, about 10 minutes.

Broil until golden and knife inserted in centre comes out clean, about 5 minutes. Cut into quarters.

Makes 4 servings. PER SERVING: about 338 cal, 12 g pro, 14 g total fat (3 g sat. fat), 42 g carb, 2 g fibre, 870 mg sodium. % RDI: 5% calcium, 13% iron, 20% vit A, 85% vit C, 22% folate.

When tender stalks of asparagus start appearing in your local farmer's market, you know it's really spring. Serve this light, easy-to-cook frittata with toasted slices of sourdough bread for a springtime dinner or brunch.

Asparagus Frittata

1 tbsp **butter**

2 cups chopped trimmed **asparagus**

1 **sweet red pepper,** diced

1 clove **garlic,** minced

2 tsp chopped **fresh thyme** (or 1 tsp dried)

¼ tsp each **salt** and **pepper**

8 **eggs**

¼ cup **milk**

⅓ cup crumbled **feta cheese**

In 9- or 10-inch (23 or 25 cm) ovenproof nonstick skillet, melt butter over medium heat; cook asparagus, red pepper, garlic, thyme, salt and pepper, stirring occasionally, until asparagus is tender-crisp, about 5 minutes.

Whisk eggs with milk. Stir into asparagus mixture; sprinkle with feta cheese. Cover and cook over medium-low heat until bottom and side are firm but top is still slightly runny, about 7 minutes. Broil until golden and set, about 1 minute. Cut into wedges.

Makes 4 servings. PER SERVING: about 230 cal, 16 g pro, 16 g total fat (7 g sat. fat), 7 g carb, 2 g fibre, 391 mg chol, 425 mg sodium. % RDI: 13% calcium, 14% iron, 35% vit A, 93% vit C, 67% folate.

VARIATION
Broccoli Frittata
Replace asparagus with chopped broccoli florets and peeled stems.

Spanish tortillas are usually cooked on the stove top, then flipped in the pan to finish cooking. Some cooks find this daunting, so this one is finished in the oven – no need to flip. Just cut and serve from the skillet, paired with fresh bread and perhaps a salad.

Chorizo Spanish Tortilla

In 12-inch (30 cm) ovenproof nonstick skillet, heat oil over medium-high heat; cook potatoes, onions, ¼ tsp of the salt and pepper for 2 minutes, turning to coat.

Add garlic; cover and cook over medium heat, turning potatoes occasionally, until golden and tender, 12 to 15 minutes. Using slotted spoon, transfer potato mixture to bowl; drain and reserve oil from pan.

Add red pepper and chorizo to pan; cook, stirring often, until pepper is tender-crisp, 3 to 5 minutes. Add to potato mixture.

In large bowl, beat together eggs, green onions and remaining salt; stir in potato mixture.

Wipe out skillet. Add 1 tbsp of the reserved oil and heat over medium-high heat. Pour in egg mixture and cook until edge starts to set, 1 to 2 minutes.

Transfer skillet to 350°F (180°C) oven. Bake until knife inserted in centre comes out clean, 20 to 25 minutes. Let stand for 5 minutes before cutting.

Makes 6 servings. PER SERVING: about 358 cal, 15 g pro, 23 g total fat (7 g sat. fat), 23 g carb, 2 g fibre, 211 mg chol, 608 mg sodium, 593 mg potassium. % RDI: 4% calcium, 11% iron, 12% vit A, 53% vit C, 20% folate.

¼ cup **extra-virgin olive oil**

1½ lb (675 g) **Yukon Gold potatoes,** peeled, halved and sliced ⅛ inch (3 mm) thick

2 **onions,** finely chopped

½ tsp **salt**

¼ tsp **pepper**

2 cloves **garlic,** minced

1 small **sweet red pepper,** diced

6 oz (170 g) **hot dry-cured chorizo sausages,** thinly sliced (see Tip, page 11)

6 **eggs**

2 **green onions,** thinly sliced

Tip: If you prefer a less-spicy tortilla, substitute the mild variety of Spanish dry-cured chorizo.

Macaroni and Cheese With
Ham and Broccoli, page 237

Pasta & Risotto

Lasagna is the go-to meal that feeds a crowd and leaves everyone asking for seconds. We have many different lasagnas in our repertoire, but this one is a classic meat-based recipe that's elegant in its simplicity.

Classic Lasagna

12 **lasagna noodles**

1 tub (475 g) **extra-smooth ricotta cheese**

2 **eggs**

Pinch **pepper**

3 cups shredded **mozzarella cheese**

1 cup grated **Parmesan cheese**

TOMATO MEAT SAUCE:
2 tbsp **olive oil**

2 **onions,** diced

1 rib **celery,** diced

1 **carrot,** diced

4 cloves **garlic,** minced

1½ lb (675 g) **lean ground beef**

⅓ cup **tomato paste**

2 cans (each 28 oz/796 mL) **diced tomatoes**

1 cup **red wine** or white wine

2 **bay leaves**

1 tsp **dried oregano**

½ tsp **pepper**

2 tbsp chopped **fresh basil**

TOMATO MEAT SAUCE: In Dutch oven, heat oil over medium heat; cook onions, celery, carrot and garlic, stirring occasionally, until softened, about 5 minutes. Add beef; cook, breaking up with spoon, until browned and liquid is evaporated, about 6 minutes. Stir in tomato paste. Add tomatoes, wine, bay leaves, oregano and pepper; simmer, stirring occasionally, until slightly thickened, 40 minutes. Stir in basil. Discard bay leaves. (*Make-ahead: Let cool for 30 minutes; refrigerate in airtight container for up to 3 days.*)

Meanwhile, in large pot of boiling salted water, cook noodles for 2 minutes less than package directions for al dente. Drain and arrange noodles, keeping separate, on towels.

Stir together ricotta cheese, eggs and pepper until combined.

In 13- by 9-inch (3 L) baking dish, spread 1½ cups of the meat sauce; arrange 3 noodles over top. Sprinkle with half of the mozzarella cheese. Top with 2½ cups of the meat sauce, 3 noodles, ricotta mixture, 3 noodles, 2½ cups of the meat sauce, 3 noodles, then remaining meat sauce and mozzarella cheese. Sprinkle with Parmesan cheese. (*Make-ahead: Cover with plastic wrap and refrigerate for up to 3 days; remove plastic wrap.*)

Cover with foil. Bake in 375°F (190°C) oven for 45 minutes. Uncover and bake until cheese is golden, about 15 minutes. Loosely cover with foil and let stand for 30 minutes before serving.

Makes 12 servings. PER SERVING: about 474 cal, 31 g pro, 25 g total fat (12 g sat. fat), 31 g carb, 3 g fibre, 113 mg chol, 585 mg sodium, 669 mg potassium. % RDI: 38% calcium, 25% iron, 26% vit A, 35% vit C, 15% folate.

Short ribs add richness to this sauce, and their meat turns meltingly tender with long cooking. A short tubular pasta, such as penne rigate or ziti, catches all the delicious sauce inside and out.

Beef Ragout With Penne Rigate

1 lb (450 g) **beef simmering short ribs**

½ tsp each **salt** and **pepper**

2 tbsp **vegetable oil**

1 **onion,** finely diced

1 **carrot,** finely diced

1 rib **celery,** finely diced

2 cloves **garlic,** minced

1 tsp **dried thyme**

2 **bay leaves**

2 cups **sodium-reduced beef broth**

⅔ cup **red wine**

3 **plum tomatoes** (fresh or canned), coarsely chopped

¼ cup chopped **fresh parsley**

4 cups **penne rigate pasta** or ziti pasta

Sprinkle ribs with half each of the salt and pepper. In shallow Dutch oven, heat half of the oil over medium-high heat; brown ribs. Transfer to plate.

Drain fat from pan. Add remaining oil and heat over medium heat; fry onion, carrot, celery, garlic, thyme, bay leaves and remaining salt and pepper, stirring occasionally, until vegetables are softened, about 6 minutes. Stir in broth, wine and tomatoes; bring to boil. Return ribs to pan; reduce heat, cover and simmer until tender, 2 to 2½ hours.

Transfer ribs to plate. Bring sauce to boil; boil until reduced to about 2½ cups, about 12 minutes.

Meanwhile, discarding bones, remove meat from ribs; dice and return to pan. *(Make-ahead: Let cool for 30 minutes. Refrigerate, uncovered, in airtight container until cold. Cover and refrigerate for up to 2 days or freeze for up to 1 month. Reheat.)*

Stir in parsley; simmer until heated through, about 3 minutes. Discard bay leaves.

Meanwhile in large pot of boiling salted water, cook pasta until al dente, about 8 minutes. Drain; return to pot or transfer to serving bowl. Spoon sauce over top.

Makes 4 servings. PER SERVING: about 585 cal, 30 g pro, 14 g total fat (4 g sat. fat), 83 g carb, 7 g fibre, 39 mg chol, 922 mg sodium. % RDI: 7% calcium, 45% iron, 39% vit A, 20% vit C, 102% folate.

VARIATION
Gluten-Free Beef Ragout With Penne Rigate
Use brown rice penne, or wild rice penne or radiatore, instead of the white pasta.

No need to buy overly salty packaged dinner mixes when you can create your own quick one-pot suppers using pantry staples and budget-friendly ground beef. For a change of pace, you can substitute pork, turkey, chicken or veal.

One-Pot Macaroni With Beef and Tomatoes

In Dutch oven or large deep saucepan, cook beef over medium-high heat, breaking up with spoon, until no longer pink, about 8 minutes.

Drain fat from pan; add onion, garlic, green pepper, carrots, oregano, basil, salt and pepper. Cook over medium heat, stirring occasionally, until onion is softened, about 5 minutes.

Add tomatoes and 3 cups water; bring to boil. Stir in macaroni; reduce heat, cover and simmer, stirring occasionally, until pasta is al dente, about 20 minutes. Sprinkle with cheese and parsley.

Makes 4 servings. PER SERVING: about 554 cal, 35 g pro, 18 g total fat (8 g sat. fat), 64 g carb, 8 g fibre, 71 mg chol, 491 mg sodium. % RDI: 16% calcium, 49% iron, 110% vit A, 80% vit C, 52% folate.

1 lb (450 g) **lean ground beef**

1 **onion,** chopped

3 cloves **garlic,** minced

1 **sweet green pepper,** chopped

2 **carrots,** thinly sliced

1 tsp **dried oregano**

1 tsp **dried basil**

½ tsp each **salt** and **pepper**

1 can (28 oz/796 mL) **crushed tomatoes**

2 cups **macaroni** or Scoobi doo pasta

¼ cup shredded **Cheddar cheese**

¼ cup minced **fresh parsley**

Cannelloni is a bit labour-intensive, but this recipe makes two pans – one to eat tonight and another that freezes well for later. The rich combination of veal and spinach makes this a perfect dish for company.

Veal and Spinach Cannelloni

1 tbsp **olive oil**

½ cup chopped **onion**

1 clove **garlic,** minced

1 lb (450 g) **ground veal**

½ cup each **dry white wine** and **milk**

3 tbsp **tomato paste**

¼ tsp each **salt** and **pepper**

1 fresh **bay leaf**

8 cups packed chopped trimmed **fresh spinach**

¼ cup chopped **fresh parsley**

2 cups shredded **mozzarella cheese**

6 sheets (9 x 7 inches/ 23 x 18 cm) **fresh lasagna noodles**

¼ cup grated **Parmesan cheese**

PURÉED TOMATO SAUCE:
2 tbsp **olive oil**

¼ cup chopped **onion**

1 clove **garlic,** minced

1 can (28 oz/796 mL) **whole tomatoes**

1 can (5½ oz/156 mL) **tomato paste**

1 sprig **fresh basil** and/or **parsley**

1 fresh **bay leaf**

½ tsp **salt**

PURÉED TOMATO SAUCE: In saucepan, heat oil over medium-high heat; sauté onion and garlic until softened, 3 minutes. Stir in tomatoes, breaking up with spoon. Stir in tomato paste, 1 cup water, basil, parsley, bay leaf and salt; bring to boil. Reduce heat, cover and simmer, stirring often, for 30 minutes. In food processor or blender, in batches, purée sauce until smooth. Press through fine sieve.

In Dutch oven, heat oil over medium-high heat; sauté onion and garlic until softened, 3 minutes. Add veal; cook, breaking up with spoon, until no longer pink but still moist. Stir in wine, milk, tomato paste, salt, pepper and bay leaf; bring to boil. Reduce heat to low; simmer, covered, for 40 minutes, stirring occasionally and adding up to ½ cup water if necessary to moisten. Add spinach and parsley; cook, covered and stirring occasionally, until wilted, 10 minutes. Discard bay leaf. Let cool slightly, 10 minutes. Stir in mozzarella.

Meanwhile, cut each lasagna sheet in half lengthwise, then crosswise in thirds. In pot of boiling salted water, cook pasta, in batches, until pliable but not fully cooked, 3 to 4 minutes. Drain, keeping separate.

Divide about ½ cup of the tomato sauce over bottoms of two 13- x 9-inch (3 L) baking dishes. Spoon rounded 1 tbsp of veal mixture along 1 short edge of each pasta rectangle. Roll up; place, seam side down, on sauce, making 2 rows of 9 in each dish. Divide remaining tomato sauce evenly over rolls, covering pasta well; sprinkle with Parmesan. Bake 1 dish, covered, in 350°F (180°C) oven until bubbly, 30 minutes, uncovering for last 10 minutes. *(Make-ahead: Double-wrap second dish in foil; freeze for up to 1 month. Bake from frozen, as directed, adding 30 minutes to covered baking time.)*

Makes 8 to 12 servings. PER EACH OF 12 SERVINGS: about 449 cal, 20 g pro, 15 g total fat (5 g sat. fat), 34 g carb, 2 g fibre, 78 mg chol, 692 mg sodium, 897 mg potassium. % RDI: 22% calcium, 32% iron, 33% vit A, 48% vit C, 45% folate.

This homestyle Italian favourite is a hit. The recipe makes a double batch of sausage-and-tomato sauce, so freeze the extra to heat and toss with your favourite pasta another night.

Baked Sausage and Pepper Pasta With Mozzarella and Provolone

In large Dutch oven, heat oil over medium heat; cook onions, red and yellow peppers, garlic, bay leaves and hot pepper flakes, stirring occasionally, until vegetables are softened, about 8 minutes.

Add sausage; cook over medium-high heat, breaking up with wooden spoon, until no longer pink, about 6 minutes. Stir in strained tomatoes and basil; reduce heat and simmer until thickened, about 20 minutes. Discard bay leaves.

Let cool for 30 minutes; divide sauce in half, reserving 1 half for another use. (*Make-ahead: Refrigerate in airtight containers for up to 2 days.*)

Meanwhile, in large pot of boiling salted water, cook pasta until slightly undercooked, about 3 minutes less than package directions. Drain and return to pot. Add remaining meat sauce; toss to combine. Spread in 13- x 9-inch (3 L) baking dish.

Sprinkle with mozzarella and provolone cheeses; cover with foil. Bake in 375°F (190°C) oven until bubbly and cheese is melted, 25 to 30 minutes.

Makes 6 servings. PER SERVING: about 753 cal, 35 g pro, 37 g total fat (15 g sat. fat), 69 g carb, 6 g fibre, 86 mg chol, 1,191 mg sodium, 651 mg potassium. % RDI: 39% calcium, 36% iron, 27% vit A, 122% vit C, 82% folate.

TO FREEZE: Follow first 3 paragraphs. Divide sauce between 2 airtight containers and freeze for up to 2 months. Thaw 1 container in refrigerator or microwave oven, then warm in saucepan over medium heat, 8 to 10 minutes. Continue with recipe.

3 tbsp **olive oil**

2 **onions,** thinly sliced

2 each **sweet red** and **yellow peppers,** thinly sliced

3 cloves **garlic,** minced

2 **bay leaves**

¼ tsp **hot pepper flakes**

2 lb (900 g) **Italian sausages,** casings removed

4 cups **bottled strained tomatoes** (passata)

10 sprigs **fresh basil**

1 pkg (454 g) **rigatoni pasta**

2 cups shredded **mozzarella cheese**

1 cup shredded **provolone cheese**

Cabbage isn't an ingredient you usually see in pasta dishes. But here, the combination of the sweet cooked cabbage with smoky bacon will ensure that everyone asks for seconds. Shred the whole head of cabbage while you're at it and use the leftovers in salads.

Smoky Bacon and Cabbage Pasta

4 slices **bacon,** chopped

1 small **red onion,** chopped

2 cloves **garlic,** minced

Pinch **hot pepper flakes**

¼ cup **dry white wine** or chicken broth

¼ tsp each **salt** and **pepper**

4 cups shredded **cabbage**

5 cups **rotini pasta** (1 lb/450 g)

2 tbsp grated **Parmesan cheese**

2 tbsp chopped **fresh parsley**

In skillet, cook bacon over medium-high heat until crisp; drain fat from pan. Add onion, garlic and hot pepper flakes; cook, stirring often, until golden, about 3 minutes.

Add wine, salt and pepper; bring to boil. Add cabbage; cover and cook until tender, about 6 minutes.

Meanwhile, in large pot of boiling salted water, cook pasta until al dente, about 8 minutes. Reserving ½ cup of the cooking liquid, drain pasta; return to pot. Add cabbage mixture and reserved cooking liquid; toss to combine.

Serve sprinkled with Parmesan cheese and parsley.

Makes 4 servings. PER SERVING: about 368 cal, 13 g pro, 8 g total fat (3 g sat. fat), 58 g carb, 5 g fibre, 10 mg chol, 486 mg sodium. % RDI: 9% calcium, 15% iron, 2% vit A, 37% vit C, 52% folate.

The simple, rustic pairing of sausage and eggplant creates a rich sauce that's especially nice with just a touch of heat from hot pepper flakes. If you can't find bucatini, substitute another long pasta, such as spaghetti or linguine.

Bucatini With Sausage and Eggplant Sauce

2 large **eggplants**

2 tsp **salt**

1 tbsp **extra-virgin olive oil**

2 **mild Italian sausages,** casings removed

1 can (28 oz/796 mL) **whole tomatoes**

¼ cup **red wine** (optional)

¼ tsp **dried Italian herb seasoning** or dried basil

Pinch **salt**

Pinch **granulated sugar**

1 lb (450 g) **bucatini pasta** or spaghetti

Shaved **Parmesan cheese**

Hot pepper flakes

Peel eggplants; cut into 1-inch (2.5 cm) cubes. Place in colander; toss with salt. Let stand for 10 to 30 minutes to release bitter juices. Squeeze and pat dry.

In Dutch oven, heat oil over medium-high heat; fry sausage, breaking up with spoon, just until starting to brown. Add eggplant; cook, stirring, until softened and sausage is no longer pink.

Add tomatoes, breaking up with spoon; add wine (if using), herb seasoning, salt and sugar. Bring to boil; reduce heat, cover and simmer, stirring occasionally, for 20 minutes.

Meanwhile, cook pasta until al dente, 8 to 10 minutes; drain and serve with sauce. Sprinkle with cheese and hot pepper flakes.

Makes 4 servings. PER SERVING: about 697 cal, 25 g pro, 18 g total fat (5 g sat. fat), 112 g carb, 12 g fibre, 26 mg chol, 1,466 mg sodium, 863 mg potassium. % RDI: 10% calcium, 52% iron, 3% vit A, 52% vit C, 124% folate.

Rigatoni is a sturdy pasta that holds its own against the sausage and artichoke in this homey pasta entrée. A green salad makes a nice side if you have extra time and energy to prepare it.

Rigatoni With Sausage and Artichoke

In large pot of boiling salted water, cook pasta until al dente, 8 to 10 minutes; drain and return to pot.

Meanwhile, in skillet, heat oil over medium heat; cook sausages, onion, garlic, salt, pepper and hot pepper flakes, stirring often, until sausage is no longer pink, about 5 minutes.

Drain any fat from pan. Add tomatoes, wine, Italian herb seasoning and sugar; bring to boil, scraping up any brown bits from bottom of pan. Reduce heat and simmer for 15 minutes.

Add artichokes; simmer for 10 minutes. Stir in parsley. Add to pasta and toss to coat.

Makes 4 to 6 servings. PER EACH OF 6 SERVINGS: about 452 cal, 19 g pro, 18 g total fat (4 g sat. fat), 53 g carb, 5 g fibre, 28 mg chol, 821 mg sodium, 316 mg potassium. % RDI: 5% calcium, 34% iron, 3% vit A, 15% vit C, 65% folate.

12 oz (340 g) **rigatoni pasta**

2 tbsp **extra-virgin olive oil**

4 mild or hot **Italian sausages,** casings removed

1 **onion,** chopped

2 cloves **garlic,** minced

¼ tsp each **salt** and **pepper**

¼ tsp **hot pepper flakes**

1½ cups **bottled strained tomatoes** (passata)

¼ cup **dry red wine**

¼ tsp **dried Italian herb seasoning**

Pinch **granulated sugar**

2 jars (each 6 oz/170 mL) **marinated artichoke hearts,** drained and rinsed

¼ cup chopped **fresh parsley**

Based on Italian pasta carbonara, this dish uses ham instead of the usual bacon, which reduces the fat to 10 g per serving. The spinach adds colour and lots of nutrients to make this a well-rounded meal.

Ham and Egg Pasta

1 tsp **vegetable oil**

1¾ cups diced **ham** (about 8 oz/225 g)

1 **onion,** chopped

4 cloves **garlic,** minced

3 **eggs**

½ tsp **salt**

1 lb (450 g) **spaghetti**

2 cups packed trimmed **fresh spinach**

½ cup grated **Parmesan cheese**

2 tbsp chopped **fresh parsley**

Brush nonstick skillet with oil and heat over medium-high heat; fry ham, stirring occasionally, until golden, about 5 minutes. Add onion and garlic; cook over medium heat until softened, about 5 minutes. Set aside.

In small bowl, lightly beat eggs with salt; set aside.

Meanwhile, in large pot of boiling salted water, cook spaghetti until al dente, 8 to 10 minutes. Add spinach. Reserving ½ cup of the cooking liquid, drain pasta mixture; return to pot over medium heat.

Immediately stir in Parmesan cheese, parsley, ham mixture and reserved cooking liquid. Stir in eggs; toss until sauce is opaque and pasta is coated, about 30 seconds.

Makes 4 to 6 servings. PER EACH OF 6 SERVINGS: about 443 cal, 26 g pro, 10 g total fat (4 g sat. fat), 60 g carb, 4 g fibre, 123 mg chol, 1,227 mg sodium. % RDI: 16% calcium, 2% iron, 20% vit A, 8% vit C, 68% folate.

Whether you're young or old, macaroni and cheese is probably on your list of favourites.

Here, it has a crunchy bread crumb topping to complement the creamy sauce and noodles.

No need for a side dish – healthy broccoli is baked right in!

Macaroni and Cheese With Ham and Broccoli

In saucepan, melt butter over medium heat; cook onion and ham until onion is softened, about 5 minutes.

Add flour; cook, stirring, for 1 minute. Gradually whisk in milk; cook, whisking, until thick enough to coat back of spoon, about 8 minutes.

Add mustard, salt, pepper and cayenne. Stir in Cheddar cheese just until melted.

Meanwhile, in large pot of boiling salted water, cook macaroni for 5 minutes. Add broccoli; cook until pasta is al dente, 3 minutes more. Drain and return to pot. Add sauce and stir to combine. Pour into 8-inch (2 L) square baking dish.

In small bowl, combine bread crumbs with Parmesan cheese; sprinkle over macaroni mixture. Broil until browned, about 3 minutes.

Makes 4 to 6 servings. PER EACH OF 6 SERVINGS: about 590 cal, 31 g pro, 26 g total fat (15 g sat. fat), 57 g carb, 4 g fibre, 86 mg chol, 1,120 mg sodium, 503 mg potassium. % RDI: 51% calcium, 24% iron, 28% vit A, 40% vit C, 81% folate.

2 tbsp **butter**

1 small **onion,** chopped

1 cup diced **cooked ham**

⅓ cup **all-purpose flour**

3 cups **milk**

1 tsp **dry mustard**

½ tsp each **salt** and **pepper**

Pinch **cayenne pepper**

2½ cups shredded **old Cheddar cheese** (10 oz/280 g)

3 cups **macaroni**

2½ cups **chopped broccoli**

½ cup **fresh bread crumbs**

¼ cup grated **Parmesan cheese**

The word *gemelli* means "twins," which describes the double-helix shape of this pasta. It picks up chunky sauces nicely, but you can substitute another short pasta with ridges or grooves if you prefer.

Mushrooms, Bacon and Swiss Chard With Gemelli

2 tsp **extra-virgin olive oil**

4 slices **thick-cut bacon,** diced

1 **onion,** finely chopped

2 sprigs **fresh thyme**

1 pkg (340 g) **mixed fresh mushrooms,** sliced

½ tsp each **salt** and **pepper**

½ cup **white wine**

½ cup **sodium-reduced chicken broth**

1 bunch **Swiss chard,** stemmed and leaves cut in thirds

¾ cup **whipping cream**

4 cups **gemelli pasta** or other short ridged pasta

1 cup grated **Parmesan cheese**

In Dutch oven, heat oil over medium-high heat; cook bacon until crisp, about 4 minutes. Drain all but 1 tbsp fat from pan. Add onion and thyme; cook until onion is softened, about 3 minutes.

Stir in mushrooms and half each of the salt and pepper; cook until mushrooms are browned and no liquid remains, about 5 minutes.

Stir in wine, scraping up brown bits from bottom of pan. Add chicken broth and Swiss chard; cook until tender-crisp, about 4 minutes. Stir in cream and remaining salt and pepper. Discard thyme sprigs.

Meanwhile, in large pot of boiling salted water, cook pasta until al dente, 8 to 10 minutes. Reserving ½ cup of the cooking liquid, drain pasta; add to mushroom mixture. Toss in half of the Parmesan cheese and enough of the cooking liquid to coat. Top with remaining cheese.

Makes 6 to 8 servings. PER EACH OF 8 SERVINGS: about 397 cal, 15 g pro, 17 g total fat (9 g sat. fat), 45 g carb, 4 g fibre, 45 mg chol, 688 mg sodium, 449 mg potassium. % RDI: 17% calcium, 23% iron, 17% vit A, 8% vit C, 54% folate.

Frozen peas are an excellent staple to keep on hand for quick-cooking dishes like this. But during the summer, small fresh sweet peas from the farmer's market (or your garden) are a divine substitution.

Pasta With Peas and Bacon

In large skillet, fry bacon over medium heat until crisp, about 8 minutes. Drain on paper towel–lined plate; chop and set aside.

Drain fat from pan; add oil and heat over medium heat. Fry onion, garlic, pepper and salt, stirring occasionally, until onion is softened, about 3 minutes. Stir in peas, lemon zest and juice, and bacon; cook, stirring, until heated through, about 3 minutes.

Meanwhile, in large pot of boiling salted water, cook pasta until al dente, about 10 minutes. Reserving ½ cup of the cooking liquid, drain pasta; return to pot.

Add pea mixture, parsley and reserved cooking liquid; toss to coat. Sprinkle with Parmesan cheese.

Makes 4 servings. PER SERVING: about 513 cal, 19 g pro, 16 g total fat (4 g sat. fat), 74 g carb, 7 g fibre, 13 mg chol, 677 mg sodium. % RDI: 12% calcium, 32% iron, 6% vit A, 25% vit C, 96% folate.

4 slices **bacon**

2 tbsp **extra-virgin olive oil**

1 **onion,** finely diced

1 clove **garlic,** minced

½ tsp **pepper**

¼ tsp **salt**

1½ cups **frozen small peas**

1 tsp grated **lemon zest**

2 tbsp **lemon juice**

4 cups **small shell pasta** (12 oz/340 g)

¼ cup chopped **fresh parsley**

¼ cup grated **Parmesan cheese**

Tip: Using whole grain pasta instead of white will boost your fibre intake by up to 4 g per serving.

Peas and prosciutto are a classic Italian combination made even better by this creamy garlic and rosemary sauce. Orecchiette, or "little ears," is a good match for this dish because it holds the peas so snugly. Of course, any similar-size pasta can be substituted.

Orecchiette With Prosciutto and Peas

1 tbsp **vegetable oil**

3 cloves **garlic,** minced

4 tsp minced **fresh rosemary**
   (or 1 tsp dried, crumbled)

¼ tsp each **salt** and **pepper**

½ cup **white wine** or
   vegetable broth

1 cup **10% cream**

1 cup grated **Parmesan cheese**

1½ cups **fresh peas** or
   frozen peas

4 thin slices **prosciutto** (about
   2 oz/55 g), cut in strips

4 cups **orecchiette pasta**
   (about 12 oz/340 g)

In saucepan, heat oil over medium heat; fry garlic, rosemary, salt and pepper until fragrant and garlic is light golden, 1 to 2 minutes. Add wine; simmer until reduced by half, about 1 minute.

Add cream; simmer until reduced by one-third, about 5 minutes. Add ¾ cup of the Parmesan cheese, the peas and prosciutto; simmer until slightly thickened, 2 to 3 minutes.

Meanwhile, in large pot of boiling salted water, cook pasta until al dente, about 10 minutes.

Reserving ½ cup of the cooking liquid, drain pasta; return to pot. Stir reserved cooking liquid into sauce; return to boil. Pour over pasta; toss well. Serve with remaining Parmesan cheese.

Makes 4 to 6 servings. PER EACH OF 6 SERVINGS: about 411 cal, 19 g pro, 13 g total fat (6 g sat. fat), 51 g carb, 5 g fibre, 31 mg chol, 726 mg sodium. % RDI: 27% calcium, 16% iron, 8% vit A, 10% vit C, 47% folate.

The crunch of walnuts is a pleasant surprise in this simple, elegant pasta. For the best flavour, use fresh walnuts from California. Once you get all the ingredients prepped, the dish only takes about 15 minutes to cook.

Ziti With Chicken, Spinach and Walnuts

In dry large nonstick skillet, toast walnuts over medium heat, shaking pan occasionally, until fragrant, about 5 minutes. Remove from pan; set aside.

Slice chicken thinly across the grain; sprinkle with half each of the salt and pepper. In same pan, heat oil over medium-high heat; sauté chicken, in 2 batches, until golden and no longer pink inside, about 4 minutes. Using slotted spoon, transfer chicken to bowl.

Add garlic, spinach and remaining salt and pepper to pan; cover and cook over medium heat just until spinach begins to wilt, about 1 minute. Return chicken and any accumulated juices to pan. Stir in broth and vinegar; bring to simmer.

Meanwhile, in large pot of boiling salted water, cook pasta until al dente, 8 to 10 minutes. Drain; return to pot. Add chicken mixture and walnuts; toss to coat. Serve sprinkled with Parmesan cheese.

Makes 4 to 6 servings. PER EACH OF 6 SERVINGS: about 596 cal, 35 g pro, 23 g total fat (4 g sat. fat), 62 g carb, 6 g fibre, 50 mg chol, 682 mg sodium. % RDI: 20% calcium, 31% iron, 36% vit A, 10% vit C, 86% folate.

1 cup chopped **walnuts**

1 lb (450 g) **boneless skinless chicken breasts**

½ tsp each **salt** and **pepper**

2 tbsp **extra-virgin olive oil**

4 cloves **garlic,** minced

1 bag (10 oz/284 g) **fresh spinach,** trimmed

½ cup **chicken broth**

2 tbsp **wine vinegar**

5 cups **ziti pasta** (about 1 lb/450 g)

½ cup grated **Parmesan cheese**

This pasta is packed with nutrients: potassium from the spinach and calcium from the evaporated milk, which has 80 per cent more calcium than regular milk. Serve with a lightly dressed green salad.

Creamy Chicken and Spinach Pasta

1 tsp **vegetable oil**

12 oz (340 g) **boneless skinless chicken breasts,** cubed

1 **onion,** chopped

2 cloves **garlic,** minced

½ tsp **pepper**

2 tbsp **all-purpose flour**

1 can (385 mL) **evaporated fat-free milk**

5 cups **whole wheat penne pasta** (12 oz/340 g)

Half bag (10 oz/284 g bag) **fresh spinach,** trimmed

¾ cup diced **sweet red pepper**

⅓ cup shredded **fresh basil**

3 tbsp **lemon juice**

2 **green onions,** chopped

In large nonstick skillet, heat oil over medium-high heat; brown chicken. Transfer to bowl.

Drain any fat from pan; fry onion, garlic and pepper over medium heat until softened, about 5 minutes. Sprinkle with flour; cook, stirring, for 1 minute.

Return chicken and any accumulated juices to pan. Add evaporated milk; cook, stirring and without boiling, until thick enough to coat back of spoon, about 5 minutes.

Meanwhile, in pot of boiling salted water, cook pasta until al dente, about 12 minutes. Add spinach; drain and return to pot. Add chicken mixture, red pepper, basil, lemon juice and green onions; toss to coat.

Makes 4 servings. PER SERVING: about 590 cal, 45 g pro, 5 g total fat (1 g sat. fat), 98 g carb, 11 g fibre, 53 mg chol, 744 mg sodium, 980 mg potassium. % RDI: 38% calcium, 39% iron, 41% vit A, 55% vit C, 39% folate.

Tip: If you don't have fresh basil, use 1½ tsp dried basil and fry it with the onions. Add ⅓ cup chopped fresh parsley and toss in just before serving.

The pasta in this kid-friendly dinner cooks right in the sauce, saving you valuable cleanup time on a busy weeknight. For variety, use any vegetable or short pasta shape that your children like instead of the zucchini and wagon wheels.

One-Pot Chicken Pesto Pasta

1 lb (450 g) **boneless skinless chicken breasts**

1 tbsp **vegetable oil**

1 **onion,** chopped

3 cloves **garlic,** minced

2 **zucchini,** sliced (about 12 oz/340 g total)

½ tsp **dried oregano**

¼ tsp each **salt** and **pepper**

1 jar (700 mL) **tomato basil pasta sauce**

3 cups **wagon wheel pasta**

¼ cup **prepared pesto**

1 cup shredded **mozzarella cheese**

2 tbsp grated **Parmesan cheese**

2 tbsp chopped **fresh parsley**

Cut chicken into 1-inch (2.5 cm) chunks. In Dutch oven, heat oil over medium-high heat; fry chicken, in batches, until golden and no longer pink inside, about 4 minutes. Transfer to bowl.

Add onion, garlic, zucchini, oregano, salt and pepper to pan; cook over medium heat, stirring occasionally, until onion is softened, about 4 minutes.

Add pasta sauce, 2½ cups water and pasta to pan; bring to boil, scraping up brown bits from bottom of pan. Reduce heat, cover and simmer, stirring occasionally, for 8 minutes. Uncover and simmer, stirring occasionally, until pasta is tender and sauce is thickened, about 5 minutes.

Return chicken and any accumulated juices to pan. Add pesto; stir until heated through. Sprinkle each serving with mozzarella and Parmesan cheeses and parsley.

Makes 4 servings. PER SERVING: about 684 cal, 46 g pro, 24 g total fat (8 g sat. fat), 69 g carb, 8 g fibre, 99 mg chol, 1,298 mg sodium. % RDI: 30% calcium, 29% iron, 21% vit A, 38% vit C, 57% folate.

Mussels are an excellent choice for a quick supper because they steam in about five minutes. You can often buy them – scrubbed clean with the beards mostly removed – in 2-lb (900 g) bags in the fish section of the supermarket.

Linguine With Tomato Mussel Sauce

In large shallow Dutch oven, heat oil over medium heat; cook garlic, salt, hot pepper flakes and pepper until fragrant, about 30 seconds. Add tomatoes and wine, breaking up tomatoes with spoon; bring to boil. Reduce heat and simmer until spoon scraped across bottom of pan leaves gap that fills in slowly, about 20 minutes.

Meanwhile, rinse mussels and remove any beards; discard any mussels that do not close when tapped. Add mussels to pan; cover and cook, shaking pan occasionally, until mussels open, about 5 minutes. Discard any mussels that do not open.

Meanwhile, in large pot of boiling salted water, cook pasta until al dente, 8 to 10 minutes. Drain and return to pot. Add sauce and parsley; toss to coat.

Makes 4 to 6 servings. PER EACH OF 6 SERVINGS: about 371 cal, 16 g pro, 5 g total fat (1 g sat. fat), 65 g carb, 4 g fibre, 12 mg chol, 716 mg sodium. % RDI: 7% calcium, 31% iron, 11% vit A, 40% vit C, 59% folate.

1 tbsp **extra-virgin olive oil**

3 cloves **garlic,** minced

½ tsp **salt**

¼ tsp **hot pepper flakes**

¼ tsp **pepper**

1 can (28 oz/796 mL) **whole tomatoes**

¾ cup **dry white wine** or vegetable broth

2 lb (900 g) **fresh mussels**

1 lb (450 g) **linguine**

¼ cup chopped **fresh parsley**

Fresh lasagna sheets cut into strips taste luxurious in this dish. Add the natural sweetness of tomatoes, the gentle bitterness of rapini and the meaty taste of shrimp, and you have one fantastic dish that's fancy enough for casual entertaining.

Rapini and Shrimp Pasta

In Dutch oven, heat oil over medium-high heat. Prick hot pepper 4 times with fork; add to oil. Add garlic, anchovies and capers; cook for 2 minutes. Stir in ¼ cup water, scraping up brown bits from bottom of pan and stirring until dissolved.

Add tomatoes and bring to boil; reduce heat and simmer until reduced by half, about 7 minutes.

Sprinkle shrimp with salt and pepper; add to pan and simmer for 3 minutes.

Meanwhile, trim ½ inch (1 cm) off base of rapini stems; cut rapini into thirds. In large pot of boiling salted water, cook rapini until tender, about 4 minutes. With slotted spoon, remove rapini and drain; stir into sauce.

Cut lasagna sheets into thick strips; add to boiling salted water and cook until al dente, about 4 minutes. Drain and add to sauce; toss to coat.

Makes 4 to 6 servings. PER EACH OF 6 SERVINGS: about 332 cal, 21 g pro, 10 g total fat (1 g sat. fat), 39 g carb, 3 g fibre, 133 mg chol, 761 mg sodium, 279 mg potassium. % RDI: 11% calcium, 40% iron, 19% vit A, 23% vit C, 57% folate.

3 tbsp **extra-virgin olive oil**

1 **red hot pepper**

3 cloves **garlic,** thinly sliced

5 **anchovy fillets,** chopped

3 tbsp drained rinsed **capers**

1¾ cups **bottled strained tomatoes** (passata)

1 lb (450 g) **frozen raw large shrimp,** thawed, peeled and deveined

Pinch each **salt** and **pepper**

1 bunch (12 oz/340 g) **rapini**

1 pkg (360 g) **fresh lasagna sheets**

The word *arrabbiata* means "angry" and is used for pasta dishes that feature fiery hot pepper flakes. But, despite its name, this dish – packed with briny-sweet scallops and a hint of meaty pancetta – will make you happy. A green salad is a nice accompaniment.

Spaghettini With Scallop Arrabbiata

16 **sea scallops** (about 14 oz/ 400 g)

½ tsp **salt**

2 tbsp **extra-virgin olive oil**

2 oz (55 g) **pancetta,** coarsely chopped

1 small **onion,** chopped

2 cloves **garlic,** minced

½ tsp **hot pepper flakes**

¼ tsp **pepper**

1 can (19 oz/540 mL) **whole tomatoes**

12 oz (340 g) **spaghettini**

2 tbsp chopped **fresh parsley**

Remove tough muscle from each scallop; sprinkle scallops with ¼ tsp of the salt. In skillet, heat 1 tbsp of the oil over medium-high heat; cook scallops, in batches, until golden, about 2 minutes. Transfer to plate; set aside.

Wipe out skillet; heat remaining oil over medium heat. Cook pancetta until crisp, about 5 minutes. Add onion, garlic, hot pepper flakes, pepper and remaining salt; cook, stirring occasionally, until onion is softened, about 5 minutes.

Mash tomatoes and add to pan; cook, stirring occasionally, until thickened, about 10 minutes.

Meanwhile, in large pot of boiling salted water, cook pasta until al dente, 8 to 10 minutes; drain and return to pot.

Add parsley and scallops to sauce; cook until scallops are opaque, about 1 minute. Toss with pasta.

Makes 4 to 6 servings. PER EACH OF 6 SERVINGS: about 372 cal, 20 g pro, 10 g total fat (3 g sat. fat), 49 g carb, 3 g fibre, 28 mg chol, 810 mg sodium, 465 mg potassium. % RDI: 6% calcium, 26% iron, 4% vit A, 23% vit C, 58% folate.

Smoked fish is a scrumptious addition to pasta. Look for small whole smoked trout at your favourite fishmonger or the fish counter at the supermarket. If you use salmon, choose larger hot-smoked fillets for a more substantial texture.

Penne With Smoked Trout and Asparagus

1 lb (450 g) **asparagus**

4 cups **penne pasta** (about 12 oz/340 g)

1 cup **frozen peas**

1 cup chopped **smoked trout** or smoked salmon (8 oz/ 225 g)

¼ cup minced **fresh dill** or parsley

2 tbsp **extra-virgin olive oil**

2 tbsp **prepared horseradish**

¼ cup **light sour cream** or ricotta cheese

Snap woody ends off asparagus; cut stalks into 1-inch (2.5 cm) pieces. Set aside.

In large pot of boiling salted water, cook pasta for 7 minutes. Add asparagus and frozen peas; cook until pasta is al dente, about 2 minutes. Reserving 1 cup of the cooking liquid, drain pasta mixture. Return to pot.

Add reserved cooking liquid, trout, dill, oil and horseradish; toss to combine. Garnish each serving with sour cream.

Makes 4 servings. PER SERVING: about 544 cal, 31 g pro, 13 g total fat (3 g sat. fat), 74 g carb, 6 g fibre, 47 mg chol, 1,772 mg sodium. % RDI: 7% calcium, 24% iron, 14% vit A, 23% vit C, 120% folate.

Keeping budget-smart pantry items, such as pasta, canned fish and frozen vegetables, on hand means you can make a quick dinner instead of calling for takeout. Salmon bones are soft and contain a lot of calcium, so blend them in with the fish for a nutritional boost.

Creamy Salmon Pasta With Vegetables

In large pot of boiling salted water, cook pasta until al dente, about 10 minutes. Reserving 1 cup of the cooking liquid, drain pasta. Return to pot.

Meanwhile, in skillet, heat oil over medium-high heat; sauté onion and garlic until softened, about 4 minutes. Add to pasta.

Meanwhile, in food processor or blender, pulse 1 can of the salmon. Add broth, mayonnaise, half of the parsley, the lemon zest and juice, mustard, salt and pepper; pulse until smooth. Scrape over pasta mixture.

Add remaining can of salmon, frozen vegetables and reserved cooking liquid to pasta mixture; heat through, gently tossing to combine. Sprinkle with remaining parsley.

Makes 4 servings. PER SERVING: about 577 cal, 31 g pro, 15 g total fat (2 g sat. fat), 78 g carb, 7 g fibre, 29 mg chol, 1,092 mg sodium. % RDI: 26% calcium, 27% iron, 39% vit A, 18% vit C, 69% folate.

4 cups **fusilli pasta** (about 12 oz/340 g)

1 tbsp **vegetable oil**

1 **onion,** chopped

2 cloves **garlic,** minced

2 cans (each 7½ oz/213 g) **salmon,** drained

½ cup **chicken broth**

¼ cup **light mayonnaise**

¼ cup minced **fresh parsley**

1 tsp grated **lemon zest**

1 tbsp **lemon juice**

1 tbsp **Dijon mustard**

¼ tsp each **salt** and **pepper**

2 cups **frozen mixed vegetables**

There's always a can or two of tuna lurking in the cupboard, so why not turn it into a feast? This sauce tastes quite a bit like puttanesca sauce, but it substitutes tuna for the anchovies – a plus if you don't have anchovy lovers at the table.

Mediterranean Tuna Pasta

In large skillet, heat oil over medium heat; cook onion, garlic, Italian herb seasoning and hot pepper flakes, stirring occasionally, until onion is softened, about 5 minutes.

Squeeze spinach dry; add to pan along with tomatoes, breaking up tomatoes with spoon. Add olives and capers; bring to boil. Reduce heat and simmer until thickened, about 10 minutes. Break tuna into chunks; add to sauce.

Meanwhile, in large pot of boiling salted water, cook pasta until al dente, 8 to 10 minutes. Drain and return to pot. Add sauce; toss to coat. Serve sprinkled with cheese (if using).

Makes 4 servings. PER SERVING: about 565 cal, 32 g pro, 12 g total fat (2 g sat. fat), 84 g carb, 8 g fibre, 20 mg chol, 1,367 mg sodium. % RDI: 17% calcium, 39% iron, 52% vit A, 58% vit C, 84% folate.

2 tbsp **olive oil**

1 small **onion,** chopped

4 cloves **garlic,** minced

½ tsp **dried Italian herb seasoning**

¼ tsp **hot pepper flakes**

1 pkg (10 oz/300 g) **frozen chopped spinach,** thawed

1 can (28 oz/796 mL) **stewed tomatoes**

¼ cup **oil-cured olives,** chopped

2 tbsp drained rinsed **capers**

2 cans (each 170 g) **tuna,** drained

4 cups **penne rigate** (12 oz/340 g)

Grated **Parmesan cheese** (optional)

Look for dried green lentils in bulk and specialty food shops. They are smaller than the more common brown lentil and have exceptional flavour and texture. This thick tomato sauce is a great place to use up a Parmesan rind: Add it when adding the tomatoes.

Penne With Tomato Lentil Sauce

2 tbsp **extra-virgin olive oil**

1 **onion,** diced

1 **carrot,** diced

1 rib **celery,** diced

3 cloves **garlic,** minced

¼ cup diced **pancetta** or thick-cut bacon (1 oz/30 g), optional

2 **bay leaves**

¾ tsp **salt**

¼ tsp **pepper**

¼ tsp **dried thyme**

¾ cup **dried green lentils**

1 can (28 oz/796 mL) **whole tomatoes**

¼ cup **dry red wine** or water

2 tbsp chopped **celery leaves** and/or **fresh parsley**

4 cups **penne pasta** or other tube pasta (12 oz/340 g)

In large shallow Dutch oven, heat oil over medium heat; fry onion, carrot, celery, garlic, pancetta (if using), bay leaves, salt, pepper and thyme, stirring occasionally, until softened, about 8 minutes.

Stir in lentils, tomatoes, wine and 1½ cups water; bring to boil. Reduce heat, cover and simmer, stirring occasionally, until thickened and lentils are tender, about 35 minutes. Discard bay leaves. Stir in celery leaves and parsley.

Meanwhile, in large pot of boiling salted water, cook pasta until al dente, about 8 minutes. Drain and return to pot or place in serving bowl. Spoon sauce over top.

Makes 4 servings. PER SERVING: about 558 cal, 22 g pro, 9 g total fat (1 g sat. fat), 98 g carb, 11 g fibre, 0 mg chol, 939 mg sodium. % RDI: 11% calcium, 64% iron, 35% vit A, 52% vit C, 174% folate.

The humble casserole gets a delicious Mediterranean makeover with the addition of feta cheese and fresh spinach. Oregano and nutmeg give the sauce another Greek accent.

Greek-Style Macaroni and Cheese

In large pot, cook spinach with 2 tbsp water over medium-high heat, stirring once, until wilted, about 3 minutes. Transfer to sieve; press out liquid. Chop and set aside.

In saucepan, melt ¼ cup of the butter over medium heat; cook onion, stirring occasionally, until softened, about 5 minutes. Add garlic and oregano; cook for 1 minute. Sprinkle with flour; cook, stirring, for 1 minute. Stir in mustard.

Whisk in milk until smooth; bring to simmer and cook, stirring frequently, until thickened, about 6 minutes. Sprinkle with salt, pepper and nutmeg. Stir in provolone, ¾ cup of the feta and the Romano cheese until smooth.

Meanwhile, in large pot of boiling salted water, cook pasta until still slightly firm in centre, about 6 minutes. Reserving ½ cup of the cooking liquid, drain pasta; return to pot. Stir in milk mixture, reserved cooking liquid and spinach. Transfer to greased 13- x 9-inch (3 L) baking dish.

Combine bread crumbs with remaining butter; sprinkle over pasta. Top with remaining feta cheese. Bake on baking sheet in 375°F (190°C) oven until bubbly and golden, 30 to 35 minutes.

Makes 6 to 8 servings. PER EACH OF 8 SERVINGS: about 548 cal, 27 g pro, 28 g total fat (17 g sat. fat), 49 g carb, 3 g fibre, 84 mg chol, 1,056 mg sodium, 583 mg potassium. % RDI: 65% calcium, 33% iron, 81% vit A, 10% vit C, 89% folate.

2 bags (each 8 oz/225 g) **fresh spinach**

¾ cup **butter,** melted

1 **onion,** finely chopped

2 cloves **garlic,** minced

2 tbsp chopped **fresh oregano** (or 2 tsp dried)

¼ cup **all-purpose flour**

4 tsp **Dijon mustard**

4 cups **milk**

¼ tsp each **salt** and **pepper**

¼ tsp **nutmeg**

2 cups shredded **provolone cheese**

1¼ cups crumbled **feta cheese**

1 cup grated **Romano cheese**

4 cups **Scoobi doo pasta**

1½ cups **fresh bread crumbs**

When it's pepper season in your garden – or local grocery store – whip up a batch of this fresh, homey pasta. Whole wheat penne contains more fibre, but if you're not a fan of it, substitute regular white penne.

Mixed Pepper and Feta Pasta

2 **sweet red peppers**

1 each **sweet orange** and **yellow pepper**

¼ cup **extra-virgin olive oil**

1 **onion,** chopped

1 **tomato,** chopped

½ cup **pimiento-stuffed olives,** halved

3 cloves **garlic,** thinly sliced

1 sprig **fresh rosemary**

¼ tsp each **salt** and **pepper**

⅓ cup chopped **fresh oregano**

4 slices **Genoa salami** or other mild salami, halved and cut crosswise in thin strips

5 cups **whole wheat penne pasta**

½ cup crumbled **feta cheese**

Cut red, orange and yellow peppers into small chunks. In large Dutch oven, heat half of the oil over medium-high heat; cook peppers and onion, stirring occasionally, until softened, 8 minutes.

Stir in tomato, olives, garlic, rosemary, salt and pepper; cover and cook, stirring occasionally, until tender, about 8 minutes.

Add oregano, salami and remaining oil; cook for 4 minutes.

Meanwhile, in large pot of boiling salted water, cook pasta until al dente, about 11 minutes. Reserving ½ cup of the cooking liquid, drain pasta. Stir pasta and enough of the cooking liquid into pepper mixture to coat.

Divide among bowls; top with feta cheese.

Makes 4 to 6 servings. PER EACH OF 6 SERVINGS: about 488 cal, 17 g pro, 16 g total fat (4 g sat. fat), 76 g carb, 11 g fibre, 16 mg chol, 773 mg sodium, 382 mg potassium. % RDI: 13% calcium, 29% iron, 23% vit A, 215% vit C, 18% folate.

Elegantly simple, these shells taste heavenly and look gorgeous on the table. You don't need much ricotta in this recipe, so splurge on the full-fat variety. Its creamy taste is much richer than that of reduced-fat versions.

Zucchini and Ricotta Shells

In saucepan of boiling salted water, cook pasta until al dente, 8 to 10 minutes. Reserving ½ cup of the cooking liquid, drain pasta.

In large bowl, toss together pasta, ricotta, lemon zest, salt, pepper and half of the reserved cooking liquid.

Meanwhile, quarter each zucchini lengthwise. Cut away core; cut diagonally into slices.

In skillet, heat oil over medium-high heat; sauté zucchini until tender, about 5 minutes. Add to pasta along with mint, green onion, lemon juice and enough of the remaining cooking liquid to create desired creaminess; toss to coat.

Makes 4 servings. PER SERVING: about 404 cal, 14 g pro, 9 g total fat (3 g sat. fat), 66 g carb, 5 g fibre, 16 mg chol, 580 mg sodium, 282 mg potassium. % RDI: 9% calcium, 26% iron, 12% vit A, 12% vit C, 84% folate.

4 cups **medium shell pasta** or large shell pasta

½ cup **ricotta**

1 tsp grated **lemon zest**

½ tsp **salt**

¼ tsp **pepper**

2 **zucchini**

1 tbsp **extra-virgin olive oil**

2 tbsp thinly sliced **fresh mint**

2 tbsp thinly sliced **green onion** (green part only)

2 tbsp **lemon juice**

Hazelnuts add crunch to the soft, rich filling in this vegetarian entrée, which is guaranteed to please cheese lovers. Fresh oven-ready lasagna sheets vary in size and number per package, so you may need two packages. Freeze any leftover sheets.

Roasted Squash, Spinach and Three-Cheese Cannelloni

10 sheets (8- x 6-inch/20 x 15 cm) **fresh lasagna noodles**

SQUASH FILLING:

1 **butternut squash** (about 1¼ lb/ 565 g), peeled and cubed

4 cloves **garlic**

Half **onion,** cut in chunks

2 tbsp **extra-virgin olive oil**

1 tsp **lemon juice**

¼ tsp each **salt** and **pepper**

½ cup **ricotta cheese**

⅓ cup grated **Parmesan cheese**

1 tbsp chopped **fresh sage** (or 1 tsp dried)

¾ cup coarsely chopped toasted **hazelnuts**

SPINACH FILLING:

1 bag (1 lb/450 g) **fresh spinach,** trimmed

4 **green onions,** finely chopped

1 tbsp **extra-virgin olive oil**

½ tsp each **salt** and **pepper**

BÉCHAMEL SAUCE:

2 tbsp **butter**

3 tbsp **all-purpose flour**

2¼ cups **milk** (approx)

¼ tsp each **salt** and **pepper**

¼ tsp **nutmeg**

2½ cups shredded **Gruyère cheese**

SQUASH FILLING: In roasting pan, combine squash, garlic, onion, oil, lemon juice, salt and pepper; roast in 425°F (220°C) oven until tender, 40 minutes. Let cool. In food processor, purée squash mixture, ricotta, Parmesan and sage; scrape into bowl. *(Make-ahead: Cover and refrigerate for up to 24 hours.)* Stir in nuts.

SPINACH FILLING: Rinse spinach; shake off excess water. In saucepan, cook spinach, with just the water clinging to leaves, over medium-high heat until wilted, 5 minutes. Drain and let cool. Squeeze dry; chop. In bowl, mix spinach, onions, oil, salt and pepper.

BÉCHAMEL SAUCE: In saucepan, melt butter over medium heat; whisk in flour. Cook, whisking, for 2 minutes. Whisking constantly, slowly add milk; bring to boil. Reduce heat and simmer, whisking often, until bubbly and thickened, 5 minutes. Whisk in salt, pepper and nutmeg. Remove from heat; whisk in 2 cups of the Gruyère cheese until smooth. *(Make-ahead: Transfer to airtight container; place plastic wrap directly on surface. Cover and refrigerate for up to 24 hours. Whisk in up to ¼ cup more milk if too thick to spread, if desired.)* Spread 1 cup in 13- x 9-inch (3 L) baking dish.

Soak noodles in cold water until pliable, 2 minutes; blot dry. Cut each in half crosswise. Spread scant 3 tbsp squash filling along 1 short side of each rectangle, leaving ½ inch (1 cm) uncovered at ends. Top each with scant 2 tbsp spinach filling; roll up. Place snugly, seam side down, in dish. Pour remaining béchamel over top; sprinkle with remaining Gruyère. Cover with foil; bake on rimmed baking sheet in 375°F (190°C) oven for 25 minutes. Uncover; bake until cheese is lightly browned, 20 minutes. Let stand for 5 minutes before serving.

Makes 10 servings. PER SERVING: about 503 cal, 22 g pro, 25 g total fat (10 g sat. fat), 49 g carb, 4 g fibre, 94 mg chol, 446 mg sodium. % RDI: 43% calcium, 26% iron, 96% vit A, 18% vit C, 74% folate.

So much better than frozen from the grocery store, this lasagna has fresh-tasting vegetables that will appeal to vegetarians and meat eaters alike. Cook the vegetables until they're nice and golden so that they develop a slightly caramelized flavour.

Vegetarian Lasagna

2 tbsp **extra-virgin olive oil**

1 **onion,** diced

4 cloves **garlic,** minced

¼ tsp **hot pepper flakes**

2 **zucchini,** diced

2 **sweet red peppers,** diced

1 **eggplant,** diced

1 **bay leaf**

½ tsp each **dried thyme** and **oregano**

½ tsp each **salt** and **pepper**

1 can (28 oz/796 mL) **whole tomatoes**

¼ cup each chopped **fresh basil** and **parsley** (or ¼ cup chopped fresh parsley)

2 **eggs**

¼ tsp **nutmeg**

1 tub (475 g) **ricotta cheese**

3 cups shredded **mozzarella cheese**

1 cup grated **Parmesan cheese**

15 **lasagna noodles** (about 10 oz/280 g)

In large Dutch oven, heat oil over medium heat; cook onion, garlic and hot pepper flakes until softened, about 6 minutes. Add zucchini, red peppers, eggplant, bay leaf, thyme, oregano, salt and pepper; cook, stirring, until edges of eggplant are golden, about 10 minutes.

Stir in tomatoes, breaking up with spoon; bring to boil. Reduce heat, cover and simmer, stirring occasionally, until thickened, about 30 minutes. Discard bay leaf. Stir in basil and parsley.

In bowl, beat eggs with nutmeg; stir in ricotta, 2 cups of the mozzarella and Parmesan cheese. Set aside.

In large pot of boiling salted water, cook noodles until almost tender, about 6 minutes. Drain; chill under cold water. Drain; arrange one-third of the noodles in single layer in greased 13- x 9-inch (3 L) baking dish. Cover with 1 cup of the vegetable sauce.

Top with one-third of the remaining noodles; spread with one-third of the remaining vegetable sauce, then dot with half of the cheese mixture. Starting with noodles, repeat layers once. Top with remaining noodles; spread with remaining sauce. Sprinkle with remaining mozzarella cheese.

Cover loosely with foil; bake in 375°F (190°C) oven for 20 minutes. Uncover and bake until bubbly and heated through, about 25 minutes. Let stand for 10 minutes before serving. *(Make-ahead: Let cool for 30 minutes; refrigerate until cold. Cover and refrigerate for up to 24 hours. Reheat, covered, in 375°F/190°C oven for 30 minutes; uncover and reheat for 15 minutes more.)*

Makes 12 servings. PER SERVING: about 359 cal, 19 g pro, 18 g total fat (10 g sat. fat), 31 g carb, 4 g fibre, 83 mg chol, 537 mg sodium. % RDI: 35% calcium, 18% iron, 26% vit A, 75% vit C, 37% folate.

Kamut pasta, a whole grain product made from an ancient form of wheat, is found in the organic section of many grocery stores. If you can't find it, you can use any pasta for this dish. Whole grain or multigrain varieties taste best.

Spinach, Tomato and Portobello Pasta

In dry small skillet, toast pine nuts over medium-low heat until golden, about 4 minutes. Set aside.

In large skillet, heat oil over medium heat; cook garlic and shallot, stirring occasionally, until light golden, 3 to 4 minutes.

Add portobello mushrooms; cook, stirring, until beginning to soften, about 4 minutes. Add tomatoes; cook over medium-high heat until skins begin to wrinkle, 1 to 2 minutes.

Meanwhile, in large pot of boiling salted water, cook pasta until al dente, 8 to 10 minutes. Reserving ½ cup of the cooking liquid, drain pasta; return to pot.

Stir in mushroom mixture, spinach, vinegar, salt, pepper, pine nuts and ¼ cup of the cooking liquid, adding more liquid as needed to coat. Serve sprinkled with Parmesan cheese.

Makes 4 servings. PER SERVING: about 520 cal, 21 g pro, 20 g total fat (4 g sat. fat), 72 g carb, 9 g fibre, 11 mg chol, 783 mg sodium, 712 mg potassium. % RDI: 23% calcium, 37% iron, 52% vit A, 20% vit C, 41% folate.

3 tbsp **pine nuts**

3 tbsp **olive oil**

3 cloves **garlic,** minced

1 **shallot,** diced

2 large **portobello mushrooms,** stemmed, halved and thinly sliced

2 cups **grape tomatoes,** halved

12 oz (340 g) **kamut penne pasta** or whole wheat penne pasta

6 cups **fresh baby spinach**

2 tbsp **red wine vinegar**

½ tsp each **salt** and **pepper**

½ cup grated **Parmesan cheese**

Pretty individual baking dishes are just the right size for a meal for two. Prepared pesto is a handy fridge staple to have, and it makes cooking this dish a snap. Serve with a salad of mixed baby greens to round out the meal.

Penne Vegetable Bake

1 cup **penne pasta**

2 tsp **extra-virgin olive oil**

1 small **onion,** chopped

1 cup chopped **carrot**

1 cup **cauliflower florets**

¼ tsp each **salt** and **pepper**

3 tbsp **prepared pesto**

1 **egg**

1 tub (250 mL) **2% cottage cheese**

1 **plum tomato,** sliced

2 tbsp grated or shredded **Parmesan cheese**

In pot of boiling salted water, cover and cook pasta until al dente, about 10 minutes; drain and set aside.

In same pot, heat oil over medium heat; fry onion, carrot, cauliflower, salt and pepper, stirring occasionally, until vegetables are tender-crisp, about 5 minutes. Add pasta and pesto; toss to coat.

Whisk egg with cottage cheese; stir into pasta mixture and toss to coat. Divide between two 2-cup (500 mL) baking dishes; press gently. Arrange tomato over top; sprinkle with cheese. Bake in 375°F (190°C) oven until golden and bubbly, about 30 minutes.

Makes 2 servings. PER SERVING: about 512 cal, 31 g pro, 22 g total fat (7 g sat. fat), 49 g carb, 6 g fibre, 117 mg chol, 1,296 mg sodium. % RDI: 26% calcium, 24% iron, 151% vit A, 53% vit C, 68% folate.

Adding greens to your diet boosts your intake of health-enhancing vitamins and minerals. Kale is an especially tasty green, with lots of body and robust flavour. Accents of pancetta and Fontina cheese give this comforting dish a touch of richness.

Gemelli With Kale, Sage and Potatoes

Trim tough stems and ribs off kale. Coarsely chop leaves to make 10 cups. In large pot of boiling salted water, cover and cook kale until tender, about 3 minutes. Drain and chill in cold water. Drain again; squeeze dry. Set aside. *(Make-ahead: Refrigerate in airtight container for up to 24 hours.)*

In nonstick skillet, heat oil over medium-high heat; sauté potatoes until golden, about 15 minutes. Add pancetta, garlic, sage, salt and hot pepper flakes; sauté for 3 minutes.

Meanwhile, in large pot of boiling salted water, cook pasta until al dente, about 8 minutes. Drain; return to pot. Stir in kale, potato mixture, broth, Fontina cheese and lemon juice; heat through, tossing to coat, about 3 minutes.

Makes 6 servings. PER SERVING: about 412 cal, 14 g pro, 17 g total fat (7 g sat. fat), 52 g carb, 4 g fibre, 26 mg chol, 661 mg sodium. % RDI: 15% calcium, 21% iron, 71% vit A, 90% vit C, 52% folate.

VARIATION

Vegetarian Gemelli with Kale, Sage and Potatoes
Omit pancetta. Replace chicken broth with pasta cooking water or vegetable broth. Sprinkle with ¼ cup Parmesan cheese just before serving.

1 bunch **kale** (about 1 lb/450 g)

2 tbsp **extra-virgin olive oil**

2 **Yukon Gold potatoes,** peeled and cut in 1-inch (2.5 cm) cubes

¾ cup chopped **pancetta**

2 cloves **garlic,** minced

4 tsp chopped **fresh sage**

¼ tsp **salt**

¼ tsp **hot pepper flakes**

10 oz (280 g) **gemelli pasta** or fusilli pasta (2½ cups)

1 cup **sodium-reduced chicken broth**

½ cup cubed (¼ inch/5 mm) **Fontina cheese** or grated Parmesan cheese

2 tsp **lemon juice**

Pasta is al dente when it is tender but firm when you bite into it. This dish is filling with or without the ham, but it does add a pleasant smoky note that complements the sweetness of the caramelized vegetables and the creamy sauce.

Roasted Vegetable Rotini and Cheese

Toss together onions, red and yellow peppers, zucchini, 1 tbsp of the oil, half each of the salt and pepper, and the basil. Spread in single layer on large foil- or parchment paper–lined rimmed baking sheet. Roast in 425°F (220°C) oven, stirring once, until golden and tender, about 45 minutes.

Meanwhile, in large pot of boiling salted water, cook pasta until al dente, about 8 minutes. Drain and return to pot. Add roasted vegetables and ham.

Meanwhile, in saucepan, heat remaining oil over medium heat. Add flour; cook, stirring, for 1 minute. Gradually pour in milk, whisking until combined. Cook, stirring, until thick enough to coat back of spoon, about 10 minutes. Stir in Cheddar and Parmesan cheeses and remaining salt and pepper. Pour over pasta mixture; toss to coat. Divide among 4 plates; sprinkle with parsley.

Makes 4 servings. PER SERVING: about 655 cal, 34 g pro, 22 g total fat (8 g sat. fat), 87 g carb, 11 g fibre, 43 mg chol, 1,557 mg sodium. % RDI: 44% calcium, 31% iron, 22% vit A, 173% vit C, 29% folate.

2 **onions,** coarsely chopped

1 each **sweet red** and **yellow pepper,** chopped

3 **zucchini,** sliced

3 tbsp **extra-virgin olive oil**

1 tsp each **salt** and **pepper**

½ tsp **dried basil**

3 cups **whole wheat rotini** or macaroni (12 oz/340 g)

4 oz (115 g) lean **Black Forest ham** or smoked turkey, cubed

2 tbsp **all-purpose flour**

2 cups hot **milk**

1 cup shredded **light old Cheddar-style cheese** or light ricotta cheese

2 tbsp grated **Parmesan cheese**

2 tbsp minced **fresh parsley**

Tip: To make the cheese sauce in the microwave, omit remaining oil. Whisk flour with milk in 8-cup glass measure. Microwave at high, whisking often, until bubbly, smooth and thick, about 5 minutes. Whisk in cheeses and remaining salt and pepper.

Traditional risotto takes quite a bit of tending at the stove. On nights when you don't have a lot of time to stand around stirring, try this recipe. Dinner will be on the table in about half an hour.

Quick Sausage Risotto

8 oz (225 g) hot or mild **Italian sausages,** casings removed

2 cloves **garlic,** minced

1 **onion,** chopped

1 **zucchini,** chopped

½ tsp **dried oregano**

¼ tsp each **salt** and **pepper**

1½ cups **short-grain Italian rice** (see Tip, below)

3½ cups **chicken broth**

1 **tomato,** chopped

¼ cup grated **Parmesan cheese**

2 tbsp chopped **fresh parsley**

In large saucepan, cook sausage over medium-high heat, breaking up with spoon, until browned, about 4 minutes.

Drain fat from pan; add garlic, onion, zucchini, oregano, salt and pepper. Cook over medium heat, stirring often, until vegetables are softened, about 3 minutes. Add rice, stirring to coat.

Add 3 cups of the broth; bring to boil. Reduce heat to medium-low; cover and simmer, stirring once, for 15 minutes.

Add remaining broth; simmer, stirring often, until moist and creamy, about 5 minutes. Stir in tomato, Parmesan cheese and parsley.

Makes 4 servings. PER SERVING: about 485 cal, 21 g pro, 14 g total fat (5 g sat. fat), 67 g carb, 2 g fibre, 32 mg chol, 1,302 mg sodium. % RDI: 12% calcium, 15% iron, 6% vit A, 17% vit C, 11% folate.

Tip: Different Italian short-grain rices create different textures, depending on their starchiness. Arborio yields a very creamy, slightly sticky risotto. Carnaroli breaks down less than arborio, making a fluffier risotto. Vialone Nano retains its hard interior when cooked, creating the very loose Venetian-style *all'onda* (wavy) risotto.

Pancetta is cured – not smoked – bacon. Italian recipes often call for it to add a savoury note. Look for pancetta in the deli section of your supermarket. If it's not available, substitute thick-cut bacon.

Radicchio and Pancetta Risotto

In saucepan, bring water to boil; reduce heat to low and keep warm.

In large deep skillet, heat oil over medium-high heat; fry pancetta until starting to crisp. Add onion; sauté until softened and translucent, about 2 minutes. Add radicchio and rice; sauté until radicchio is wilted and rice is coated, about 2 minutes. Stir in wine (if using) until absorbed.

Add hot water, ½ cup at a time, stirring after each addition until most of the liquid is absorbed before adding more, about 20 minutes total. Taste before adding last ½ cup; rice should be loose, creamy but not mushy, and still slightly firm in centre.

Remove from heat. Stir in Parmesan cheese, butter, balsamic vinegar, salt and pepper.

Makes 4 to 6 servings. PER EACH OF 6 SERVINGS: about 287 cal, 8 g pro, 11 g total fat (6 g sat. fat), 38 g carb, 1 g fibre, 19 mg chol, 591 mg sodium, 142 mg potassium. % RDI: 10% calcium, 4% iron, 3% vit A, 2% vit C, 6% folate.

4½ cups **water** or sodium-reduced chicken broth

1 tbsp **extra-virgin olive oil**

2 oz (55 g) **pancetta** or thick-cut bacon, diced

½ cup finely chopped **onion**

3 cups shredded **radicchio**

1⅓ cups **short-grain Italian rice** (see Tip, opposite)

¼ cup **red wine** (optional)

½ cup grated **Parmesan cheese**

1 tbsp **butter**

1 tbsp **balsamic vinegar**

1 tsp **salt**

¼ tsp **pepper**

Lemon and shellfish are a natural pairing. A scallop has a tough muscle along one side that attaches it to the shell. This piece is unpleasantly chewy, so remove it if it's still attached. Just grab the protruding bit on top and gently pull the muscle down and off the scallop.

Lemon and Seafood Risotto

2 tbsp **extra-virgin olive oil**

½ cup finely chopped **onion**

¼ cup finely chopped **celery**

1¾ cups **short-grain Italian rice** (see Tip, page 272)

½ cup **white wine**

8 oz (225 g) **raw medium shrimp,** peeled and deveined

8 oz (225 g) **raw bay scallops,** muscles removed

2 tsp grated **lemon zest**

3 tbsp **lemon juice**

1 tbsp **butter,** softened

1¼ tsp **salt**

¼ tsp **pepper**

In saucepan, bring 4½ cups water to boil; reduce heat to low and keep warm.

In large deep skillet, heat oil over medium-high heat; sauté onion and celery until softened and translucent, about 5 minutes. Add rice, stirring to coat and toast grains, about 2 minutes. Stir in wine until absorbed, about 2 minutes.

Add ½ cup of hot water, stirring to prevent rice from sticking and scraping bottom and side of pan, until liquid is absorbed, about 3 minutes.

Add two-thirds of the remaining water, ½ cup at a time and stirring after each addition until most of the liquid is absorbed before adding more, about 15 minutes total.

Stir in shrimp, scallops, lemon zest and ½ cup of the remaining water; cook, stirring, until shrimp are pink, about 2 minutes. Continue adding remaining water, tasting before adding last ½ cup; rice should be loose, creamy but not mushy, and still slightly firm in centre.

Remove from heat. Stir in lemon juice, butter, salt and pepper. Let stand for 2 minutes before serving.

Makes 4 to 6 servings. PER EACH OF 6 SERVINGS: about 293 cal, 15 g pro, 7 g total fat (2 g sat. fat), 39 g carb, 1 g fibre, 61 mg chol, 718 mg sodium, 270 mg potassium. % RDI: 4% calcium, 10% iron, 4% vit A, 10% vit C, 5% folate.

Fresh pea shoots are one of the early spring delights from the garden or farmer's market. They make excellent delicate salad greens as well, so don't worry if you buy more than you need for this recipe.

Pea Shoot and Shrimp Risotto

1 lb (450 g) **raw colossal shrimp** (about 8), peeled and deveined

3 tbsp **extra-virgin olive oil**

1 tbsp **lemon juice**

1 clove **garlic,** minced

½ tsp **salt**

¼ tsp **pepper**

1½ cups **sodium-reduced chicken broth**

1 **leek** (white and light green parts only), finely diced

1 cup **arborio rice**

¼ cup **white wine**

4 oz (115 g) **pea shoots** or pea sprouts, coarsely chopped

¾ cup shaved **Parmesan cheese**

In bowl, toss shrimp with 1 tbsp of the oil, lemon juice, garlic, half of the salt and the pepper; let stand for 10 minutes. Place on greased grill over medium-high heat or under broiler; close lid and grill or broil until pink, 6 to 8 minutes. Keep warm.

Meanwhile, in small saucepan, bring broth and 1½ cups water to boil; reduce heat to low and keep warm.

In large saucepan, heat remaining oil over medium heat; cook leek and remaining salt, stirring occasionally, until softened, about 4 minutes. Add rice, stirring to coat and toast grains, about 2 minutes. Add wine; cook, stirring, until no liquid remains, about 2 minutes.

Add 2½ cups of the broth mixture, ½ cup at a time and stirring after each addition until most of the liquid is absorbed before adding more, about 20 minutes total. Rice should be loose, creamy but not mushy, and still slightly firm in centre.

Stir in pea shoots and remaining broth; cook until pea shoots are slightly wilted, 3 minutes. Serve with shrimp and Parmesan cheese.

Makes 4 servings. PER SERVING: about 412 cal, 25 g pro, 14 g total fat (3 g sat. fat), 44 g carb, 2 g fibre, 134 mg chol, 753 mg sodium, 246 mg potassium. % RDI: 13% calcium, 21% iron, 15% vit A, 28% vit C, 14% folate.

This springtime risotto can be made with vegetable broth instead of chicken broth for a delicious one-pot vegetarian meal. If you're pressed for time, try the convenient pressure-cooker option, which requires no stirring.

Risotto Primavera

In saucepan, bring chicken broth and 1 cup water to simmer over medium heat; reduce heat to low and keep warm.

In large shallow Dutch oven, melt butter over medium heat; cook onion, carrot, garlic and pepper, stirring occasionally, until onion is softened, about 5 minutes. Add rice, stirring to coat and toast grains, about 2 minutes.

Stir in ½ cup of the broth mixture; cook, stirring constantly, until liquid is absorbed. Stir in wine; cook, stirring, until wine is absorbed. Add red pepper and green beans.

Add remaining broth mixture, ½ cup at a time and stirring after each addition until most of the liquid is absorbed, about 20 minutes total. Rice should be loose, creamy but not mushy, and still slightly firm in centre.

Stir in cheese; cook, stirring, for 2 minutes. Stir in parsley, green onion and lemon zest.

Makes 6 servings. PER SERVING: about 370 cal, 12 g pro, 8 g total fat (4 g sat. fat), 60 g carb, 2 g fibre, 17 mg chol, 724 mg sodium. % RDI: 14% calcium, 11% iron, 44% vit A, 62% vit C, 10% folate.

VARIATION
Pressure Cooker Risotto Primavera
Follow first paragraph. Using pressure cooker instead of large shallow Dutch oven, follow second paragraph. Add wine; cook, stirring, until absorbed. Add broth mixture, red pepper and green beans. Secure lid and bring to high pressure over high heat. Reduce heat to maintain pressure; cook for 7 minutes. Remove from heat; let pressure release completely, 10 minutes. Stir in cheese, parsley, green onion and lemon zest; cook over medium heat for 2 minutes.

4 cups **chicken broth** or vegetable broth

2 tbsp **butter**

1 **onion,** chopped

1 **carrot,** chopped

3 cloves **garlic,** minced

¼ tsp **pepper**

2 cups **arborio rice** or other short-grain Italian rice (see Tip, page 272)

½ cup **dry white wine** or vegetable broth

1 **sweet red pepper,** chopped

1 cup chopped **green beans** (about 4 oz/115 g)

½ cup grated **Parmesan cheese**

2 tbsp chopped **fresh parsley**

1 **green onion,** finely chopped

½ tsp grated **lemon zest**

Delicate shreds of richly flavoured dried mushrooms dot this creamy, light risotto. Try different mushroom varieties, such as porcini, chanterelle or even shiitake. A mix of gourmet dried mushrooms is another delicious option.

Green Bean and Mushroom Risotto

Soak mushrooms in 2 cups boiling water until softened, about 5 minutes. Remove with slotted spoon; chop and set aside. Strain soaking liquid into measuring cup; add broth and enough water to make 3 cups. Set aside and keep warm.

In large shallow saucepan, melt 1 tbsp of the butter over medium heat; fry mushrooms, onion, garlic, thyme, salt and pepper, stirring occasionally, until onion is softened, about 5 minutes.

Add rice, stirring to coat and toast grains, about 2 minutes. Add wine; cook, stirring constantly, until no liquid remains, about 2 minutes. Add 1½ cups of the broth mixture, ½ cup at a time and stirring after each addition until liquid is absorbed, about 10 minutes total.

Add beans. Add remaining broth mixture, ½ cup at a time, stirring after each addition until most of the liquid is absorbed, 10 minutes total. Rice should be loose, creamy but not mushy, and still slightly firm in centre. Stir in cheese, parsley and remaining butter.

Makes 4 servings. PER SERVING: about 299 cal, 7 g pro, 8 g total fat (5 g sat. fat), 49 g carb, 2 g fibre, 21 mg chol, 528 mg sodium. % RDI: 9% calcium, 9% iron, 11% vit A, 8% vit C, 10% folate.

1 pkg (14 g) **dried mushrooms**

1 cup hot **vegetable broth**

2 tbsp **butter**

1 **onion,** finely chopped

1 clove **garlic,** minced

1 tsp **dried thyme**

¼ tsp each **salt** and **pepper**

1 cup **arborio rice** or other short-grain Italian rice (see Tip, page 272)

¾ cup **dry white wine** or vegetable broth

1 cup cut (1-inch/2.5 cm) **green beans**

¼ cup grated **Parmesan cheese**

2 tbsp chopped **fresh parsley**

Acknowledgments

Like a good lasagna – the ultimate one-dish meal – the team that made this book has many layers. Each person contributed his or her signature skills and flair to make this project a delicious success.

The staff of The Canadian Living Test Kitchen are always at the top of my thank-you list. Their talent, creativity and dedication to excellence are what make the recipes in this book such a pleasure to cook – and eat. Thanks to Test Kitchen manager Adell Shneer for helping pull together the lineup. Special thanks to food director Annabelle Waugh, who helped me comb through piles of recipes to narrow down our selection to the book you see here. Her excellent sense of humour and passion for good food are always the best part of any meeting – no matter how long or involved it may be.

More heartfelt thanks go to art director Chris Bond and creative director Michael Erb, our design team, for creating a visually appealing package. Chris created the warm, inviting interior layouts and worked with our photo team to capture the essence of comfort food in the book's new images. Michael tested a number of different options, finally settling on the tasty chicken pot pie that graces our cover. I am, as always, grateful to editorial assistant Pat Flynn, who cheerfully dug hundreds of photos and text files out of our archives at the beginning of the project. All three of these fellows make it easy – and fun – to work through the long to-do lists that accompany a book project.

No cookbook is complete without gorgeous photography, and a list of the talented photographers and stylists who created the images in this book is on page 288. I'd like to say a special thanks to photographer Jodi Pudge, food stylists Claire Stubbs and David Grenier, and prop stylist Catherine Doherty for the new photos they shot specifically for this book. Their creativity and enjoyment show through in each of the beautiful pictures they shot.

Copy editors always save us from our worst mistakes, and Lisa Fielding did an excellent job catching errors and polishing copy that wasn't quite perfect. Beth Zabloski meticulously wrote and edited the index – with her characteristic enthusiasm – making this time-consuming task look like a breeze.

I'm grateful to work for a trio who are always excited about our newest cookbook adventure: Transcontinental Books publisher Jean Paré, *Canadian Living* editor-in-chief Susan Antonacci and *Canadian Living* publisher Lynn Chambers. Without their support, this book would not exist. Thanks also to the team at Random House Canada, including Janet Joy Wilson, Duncan Shields and Adria Iwasutiak, for getting this book into bookstores across North America.

To these and the other layers of the lasagna who aren't mentioned by name, I offer a hearty helping of thanks.

– *Christina Anson Mine, project editor*

Photography

Michael Alberstat: pages 203 and 245.

Yvonne Duivenvoorden: pages 20, 31, 34, 37, 41, 44, 47, 59, 71, 72, 76, 81, 84, 87, 90, 103, 117, 120, 126, 144, 145, 147, 150, 155, 156, 170, 190, 193, 198, 206, 239, 248, 254, 259, 267, 268, 270 and 278.

Geoff George: page 5.

Jim Norton: pages 139, 178, 215 and 260.

Edward Pond: pages 15, 26, 48, 64, 106, 111, 142 and 251.

Jodi Pudge: pages 6, 8, 9, 10, 23, 56, 57, 67, 75, 100, 101, 112, 125, 129, 132, 136, 162, 169, 173, 177, 183, 188, 189, 210, 221, 224, 225, 227, 233, 263 and 275.

David Scott: pages 53, 97 and 240.

Felix Wedgwood: page 186.

Food Styling

Julie Aldis: pages 72, 254 and 270.

Donna Bartolini: pages 144, 145, 203 and 267.

Carol Dudar: pages 97 and 240.

David Grenier: pages 6 (top centre, bottom centre), 10, 23, 56, 57, 67, 75 and 263.

Adele Hagan: page 227.

Lucie Richard: pages 20, 31, 44, 53, 76, 90, 106, 126, 132, 150, 155, 162, 170, 177, 190, 193, 198, 206, 239, 248, 251, 259, 275 and 278.

Claire Stancer: pages 37, 47, 71, 81, 245 and 268.

Claire Stubbs: pages 6 (top left, centre, bottom left, bottom right), 8, 9, 15, 26, 34, 48, 59, 64, 84, 100, 101, 103, 111, 112, 117, 120, 125, 129, 136, 139, 142, 147, 156, 169, 173, 178, 183, 188, 189, 210, 215, 221, 224, 225, 233 and 260.

Nicole Young: page 186.

Prop Styling

Laura Branson: pages 53, 170, 178 and 227.

Catherine Doherty: pages 6, 8, 9, 10, 23, 26, 44, 48, 56, 57, 59, 64, 67, 75, 84, 90, 100, 101, 106, 111, 112, 125, 126, 129, 132, 136, 169, 173, 177, 183, 188, 189, 190, 193, 206, 210, 221, 224, 225, 233, 251, 263 and 275.

Marc-Philippe Gagné: pages 144 and 145.

Mandy Gyulay: pages 31, 198, 239, 248 and 259.

Madeleine Johari: pages 147 and 156.

Chareen Parsons: page 245.

Oksana Slavutych: pages 15, 20, 34, 37, 41, 47, 71, 72, 76, 81, 87, 97, 103, 117, 120, 142, 155, 203, 240, 254, 267, 268, 270 and 278.

Genevieve Wiseman: pages 139, 150, 162, 186, 215 and 260.

TRANSCONTINENTAL BOOKS
1100 René-Lévesque Boulevard West
24th Floor
Montreal, Que. H3B 4X9
Tel: 514-340-3587
Toll-free: 1-866-800-2500
canadianliving.com

Bibliothèque et Archives nationales du Québec and Library and Archives Canada cataloguing in publication

Main entry under title :
The one dish collection : all-in-one dinners that nourish body and soul
"Canadian living".
Includes index.
ISBN 978-0-9813938-9-6
1. One-dish meals. 2. Comfort food. 3. Casserole cooking. 4. Quick and easy cooking. I. Canadian Living Test Kitchen. II. Title: Canadian living.
TX840.O53O53 2012   641.82   C2011-941962-9

Project editor: Christina Anson Mine
Copy editor: Lisa Fielding
Indexer: Beth Zabloski
Art direction and design: Chris Bond
Front cover design: Michael Erb

Printed in Canada
© Transcontinental Books, 2012
Legal deposit – 1st quarter 2012
National Library of Quebec
National Library of Canada
ISBN 978-0-9813938-9-6

We acknowledge the financial support of our publishing activity by the Government of Canada through the Canada Book Fund.

For information on special rates for corporate libraries and wholesale purchases, please call 1-866-800-2500.